THEMES IN SOCIAL THEORY

Series Editor: Rob Stones

This series explores how cutting-edge research within the social sciences relies on combinations of social theory and empirical evidence. Different books examine how this relationship works in particular subject areas, from technology and health to politics and human rights. Giving the reader a brief overview of the major theoretical approaches used in an area, the books then describe their application in a range of empirical projects. Each text looks at contemporary and classical theories, provides a map of primary research carried out in the subject area and highlights advances in the field. The series is a companion to the *Traditions in Social Theory* series, founded by Ian Craib and edited by Rob Stones.

Published

CRIME AND SOCIAL THEORY
Eammon Carrabine

HEALTH AND SOCIAL THEORY
Fernando De Maio

POLITICS AND SOCIAL THEORY
Will Leggett

TECHNOLOGY AND SOCIAL THEORY
Steve Matthewman

HUMAN RIGHTS AND SOCIAL THEORY
Lydia Morris

INTERNATIONAL MIGRATION AND SOCIAL THEORY
Karen O'Reilly

ENVIRONMENTS, NATURES AND SOCIAL THEORY
Damian F. White, Alan P. Rudy and Brian J. Gareau

Forthcoming

INSTITUTIONAL INTERACTION AND SOCIAL THEORY
Will Gibson and Dirk Vom Lehn

GENDER, WORK AND SOCIAL THEORY
Kate Huppatz

IDENTITY AND SOCIAL THEORY
Stephanie Lawler

TRADITIONS IN SOCIAL THEORY

Founding Editor: Ian Craib
Series Editor: Rob Stones

This series offers a selection of concise introductions to particular traditions in sociological thought. It aims to deepen the reader's knowledge of particular theoretical approaches and at the same time to enhance their wider understanding of sociological theorising. Each book will offer: a history of the chose approach and the debates that have driven it forward; a discussion of the current state of the debates within the approach (or debates with other approaches); an argument for the distinctive contribution of the approach and its likely future value. The series is a companion to the *Themes in Social Theory* series, edited by Rob Stones.

Published

PHILOSOPHY OF SOCIAL SCIENCE (Second Edition)
Ted Benton and Ian Craib

CRITICAL THEORY
Alan How

MARXISM AND SOCIAL THEORY
Jonathon Joseph

MICRO SOCIAL THEORY
Brian Roberts

WEBER AND THE WEBERIANS
Lawrence A. Scaff

STRUCTURATION THEORY
Rob Stones

Forthcoming

POST-STRUCTURALISM AND AFTER
David Howarth

THE SIMMELIAN LEGACY
Olli Pyyhtinen

Crime and Social Theory

Eamonn Carrabine

 macmillan education palgrave

First published 2017 by
PALGRAVE

Palgrave in the UK is an imprint of Macmillan Publishers Limited, registered in England, company number 785998, of 4 Crinan Street, London, N1 9XW.

Palgrave® and Macmillan® are registered trademarks in the United States, the United Kingdom, Europe and other countries.

ISBN 978–0–230–29088–4 hardback
ISBN 978-0-230-29089-1 paperback

This book is printed on paper suitable for recycling and made from fully managed and sustained forest sources. Logging, pulping and manufacturing processes are expected to conform to the environmental regulations of the country of origin.

A catalogue record for this book is available from the British Library.

A catalog record for this book is available from the Library of Congress.

Contents

Series Foreword

The latest books we've had the privilege of publishing in the *Themes in Social Theory* series – Will Leggett's *Politics and Social Theory* and Eamonn Carrabine's *Crime and Social Theory* – reaffirm the simple aim of the series, which is to deepen understanding of the role of social theory in the creation and validation of the most valuable empirical research in the social sciences. The series rests upon a belief that it is important to explore the vast terrain upon which theory and the empirical meet, and it extends an invitation to readers to share in this exploration. Each book takes on a specialized substantive area of research, and the books published so far have covered the fields of health, technology, international migration, human rights, the environment and nature, politics, and crime, with books in preparation focusing on gender and work, identity, and interaction with institutions. The task the books set themselves is to excavate the character of the interplay between social theory and empirical evidence in relation to key themes within their specialized field. I'll say more about this below.

The authors of the volumes in the series write clearly and accessibly even when the material they are dealing with is intrinsically difficult. They have a close knowledge of the relevant field, an enthusiasm for the kind of theoretically informed empirical research that has been produced within it, and possess a flair for theoretical analysis. Within the general rubric of the series each author (or team of authors) has her or his own style and approach, and a distinctive authorial voice. This should translate into a sense of pluralism within the series as a whole, meaning that the investigation of the theory-empirical terrain will take on the broad and varied character required to push forward our understanding in the most open and constructive manner possible.

Each book in the series aims to bring together in one volume some of the most significant theoretically informed empirical work in that subfield. The substantive findings and arguments produced by each of the empirical studies highlighted are valuable and significant in and of themselves, and so will be clearly indicated. It is these fruits that are ultimately at the core of the enterprise. It is hoped that the books in the series will play their part in helping to bridge the harmful gap between theory and the empirical that is still too often present within the social sciences, and that they will not only be used on undergraduate and postgraduate courses to train and sensitize the next generation of social analysts, but will also be helpful more generally to researchers, citizens and activists. The books demonstrate that there is already a large existing literature in each sub-field that has indeed combined theory and the empirical, and they go some way to clarifying the varying levels of descriptive, explanatory and critical power produced by these combinations.

The opening chapters of each book see authors reflecting upon the current state of theory in their field, and there have been a variety of approaches to this task. One of the most striking features of the latest three volumes to be published in the series has been that all the authors have felt the need to draw attention to the shortcomings of dominant current trends in their field, and to argue that a new framework of theoretical guidance is required. Each has offered a constructive way forward, whether in the form of a critically inspired synthesis of current approaches (*Environments, Natures and Social Theory*), a powerful insistence on the renewal of a more holistic, socially embedded, approach that can grasp the interplay between different forces, processes, and scales of activity (*Crime and Social Theory*), or the presentation of a new and imaginative guiding framework explicitly acknowledging the respective powers of social and political paradigms of analysis, and the need to draw from both (*Politics and Social Theory*). One of the previous volumes, *International Migration and Social Theory*, took a similar standpoint, arguing for a major renewal of current theorising in the field focused around a more sophisticated grasp of structure, agency, and the practices resulting from their interplay.

These authors have felt the need to reflect deeply on how theory has framed empirical research in their field. The volumes include fascinating discussions on the tensions and divisions between different theoretical approaches, and on the historical trajectory of such divisions in terms of conflicts, attempted resolutions, and new directions. The implications of all this for the production of particular types of empirical research, and for the emergence of key empirical case studies, is vividly revealed. Authors of these books have typically placed less emphasis on the precise details of how particular theoretical approaches, or hybrids of approaches, have been used in particular empirical studies. There seems to be something about the current state of the relationship between social theory and empirical research that makes the most pressing issue for authors that of theoretical framing itself, and of differences and tensions between framings. It looks like the authors intuitively see this as a necessary first step that must be taken before it is possible to settle into questions around the exact mechanics of application. Some authors also point out that much of the empirical research in their field is not theorized at all, meaning, in effect, that the ideas that organize and make sense of the empirical evidence are *ad hoc*, intuitive, and unsystematic, making the research weak and unlikely to stand up to serious scrutiny. This is what Carrabine is referring to when he criticizes the 'abstracted empiricism' of certain strands within criminology.

This apparently widespread need to rethink the most fundamental bases on which empirical research is carried out in different substantive fields was largely unanticipated. There are many reasons, however, why, on reflection, it isn't surprising. We are living through an age, the age of a globalised radical or late modernity, in which there is a colossal struggle between those for whom it is vital that respect is accorded to the question of the validity and adequacy of knowledge claims and those who believe it is possible to say and claim anything with impunity. There is a frighteningly arbitrary quality to the kinds of knowledge of the social world that are currently allowed to claim authority in the public sphere. Social thinkers are in the strongest position to resist and challenge the validity of weak, reckless knowledge claims. The authors of *Environments, Natures and Social Theory* highlighted the fragmentation of approaches in their field, the chronic over-simplification of approaches to particular issues, and the restrictions imposed on the funding and conduct of research by insufficiently examined ideologies. All of this points to the need to be more reflective about the theoretical paradigms and orientations that guide research. Will Leggett's notion of the 'irreducibly political' dimension of social life in *Politics and Social Theory* draws our attention to – amongst other things – the politics of all knowledge, and the need to scrutinise and assess the theoretical frameworks through which we approach and make sense of empirical evidence. It emphasizes that all social life has a political dimension to it, one in which values, ideas and their contestation inform political agency and strategy. The absorption of series authors in the task of strengthening the theoretical frameworks that guide empirical research – in order that justice can be done to empirical realities – needs to be seen this light.

In the midst of fragmented, contested landscapes it is more important than ever to insist upon what that formidable American sociologist of the mid-twentieth century, Robert K. Merton, called the 'institutionalised vigilance' of intellectual life. By this, Merton meant the examination, appraisal, criticism and verification of knowledge claims by intellectuals and academic peers. Such vigilance needs to be rooted in 'organised scepticism' about theoretical frameworks, their concepts, and the relationship of these to the empirical evidence produced under their aegis. This requires social scientists to invoke doubt in the first instance, and then to find all ways possible to fathom if that doubt is well founded. All this must be done through public scrutiny and criticism, within and by intellectual communities. These communities belong to the realm of what Leggett calls 'the inescapably social', which refers to those areas of social life that have preoccupied sociologists and social theorists: the macro social structures, institutions, norms, relations and practices in which things are made to matter by society, or, more insidiously, made not to matter.

This is the context for Eamonn Carrabine's concern in *Crime and Social Theory* that criminology, as it has begun to take on all the trappings and privileges of a discipline, is in danger of becoming entrenched in an intellectual world that is narrow and parochial, conformist and unreflective. In a highly accomplished and engaging account, Carrabine situates the strengths and weaknesses of contemporary empirical research within the broad contours of what he believes would be a more adequate theoretical framework. His expansive vision of what is needed reacts against weaknesses that have accrued within the long historical formation of criminology over three centuries; against sociology's initial, extended, indifference to the subject matter of criminology; and against contemporary criminology's failure to consolidate the potential opened up to it by various threads of twentieth century social analysis, from Durkheim and the Chicago School to the 'new criminology' of the 1970s. The latter had held out the promise of a 'fully social theory of deviance', which has remained largely, wastefully, unfulfilled. Carrabine's analysis of current research within the sub-themes of transgression, control, geography, and representation is framed by an aspiration towards a combined sociological and criminological imagination. The analysis uses this frame to situate and explore a number of empirical cases under each heading. In the process *Crime and Social Theory* begins to draw together the elements necessary to create a theoretical-empirical paradigm able to rise to the challenges of the age.

It is worth noting that the notion of 'themes' referred to in the series title in fact signals two kinds of themes. The *first* kind is *substantive* and refers to the overall theme of the respective volume – in the present cases, crime or politics – and, more subtly, to the sub-types of thematic content to be found within each of the different clusters of studies highlighted in each volume and indicated through the titles of the more substantive chapters. In *Crime and Social Theory* these are immediately apparent through the chapter headings we've just mentioned – transgression, control, geography, and representation. The substantive themes of *Politics and Social Theory* are gathered around three organizing frames. These are: 'politics from above', where the state and governance are primary themes, allowing the practices of 'Washington', 'Wall Street', and so on, to come into focus; 'politics from below', where reflection on the theoretical themes of identity and participation inform Leggett's empirical focus on consumer identity in an age of economic austerity; and 'politics all around', in which the theoretical themes of culture, ideology and discourse provide an incisive way into some of the key characteristics of neoliberalism.

The *second* type of theme is *methodological*, and refers to the ways in which theory and empirical data are brought together within each of the studies highlighted. I prefer to refer to this set of themes under the label of *conceptual methodology*, rather than just 'methodology', in order to emphasize the ways in which particular theoretical ideas or concepts (and combinations of these) *should* guide more formal methods – such as interviews, observation, documentary analysis, surveys and so on – towards certain types of empirical evidence. Theories, and the interlocking concepts that make them into the theories they are, influence what parts of the world are selected to be of interest. The concepts, also, are shapes that direct us to look for the corresponding bits of empirical evidence, and they allow us to see how much of the (conceptual) shapes are covered by the available evidence, and how much of them remain uncovered, unsubstantiated. In these ways, the theories and concepts can be seen to have clear and identifiable methodological and empirical consequences.

It is relatively self-evident that the **key substantive themes** that emerge in, for example, Fernando de Maio's volume on *Health and Social Theory* – such as those around health inequalities and demographics, the functioning of the sick role, or the practices of pharmaceutical companies, will be distinct from those in other volumes, such as Karen O'Reilly's on international migration or Steve Matthewman's on technology. This is not to say there couldn't be fruitful overlap; it would be very easy to find theoretically informed research projects looking at the health implications of international migration or at the use of technology in health care. However, it is to say that one might expect a series of distinctive thematic concerns to emerge from a focus on studies that have health as their primary concern. It is probable that the lessons to be learnt from the **conceptual methodological themes** can more easily be generalized across the domains of the different books in the series. Here, more commonality is likely to emerge across sub-fields in the ways that theory and the empirical are combined together, notwithstanding their different subject matters.

Each of the authors in the series takes it for granted that particular ways of framing, seeing, hearing, interpreting and understanding – to name just some of the ways we apprehend the world – are involved every time an empirical 'fact' is given that status by somebody. That somebody, in turn, may be any kind of everyday participant within society, deploying their own cultural and social standpoint on the world, whether they are a political power broker, a homeless migrant, a parent, an environmental activist or an academic researcher. Whoever does the apprehending will inevitably infuse the empirical facts they witness with their own perspectives, ideas and ways of seeing, just as they will do something similar in the ways in which they join the facts together into stories and arguments about the social world. Both aspects of their accounts will be affected, in turn, by the texture and contours of their personal biography, by their social positioning, and by the inter-related cultures and sub-cultures they belong to. Embedded within their lived cultural experience are concepts, presuppositions and categorizations that can range from a mixture of the simply inherited and/or confused at one end of the spectrum to a mixture of the systematically reflected upon and/or analytically lucid at the other end of the spectrum. Social theory looks to produce knowledge that sits much nearer the latter end of the spectrum than the former. It aims to identify entities, relations, and processes in the social world that are sufficiently general to be usefully transposed from one situation to another whilst leaving space for the uniqueness of particular circumstances. At its most effective it also strives to find ways of integrating these general concepts with the variations in empirical evidence one meets in the diversity of those specific, unique, circumstances.

The degree of rigour and intellectual seriousness implied by these standards, brought into close liaison with the imaginative ways of seeing that high quality social analysis seeks constantly to renew, are what should make the activities and claims of the social and human sciences stand out. Our claim should be that the accounts we produce add something invaluable to public and civic culture, and to political life, something that damages and undermines less reflective, less systematic forms of knowledge. Social science has its own generic standards: standards that we need to ceaselessly explore, reflect upon, and improve. The relationship between social theory and substantive studies is an especially significant part of this endeavour. It is only by resolutely pursuing this agenda that we can genuinely carry forward the ambitious aspirations of a public social science to make the contribution we so manifestly need it to make in the challenging years ahead.

Rob Stones
Western Sydney University
August 2016

Acknowledgements

I am grateful to Rob Stones for inviting me to write this book, and be part of this series at Palgrave. Both Lloyd Langman and Tuur Driesser have enthusiastically supported the book, and waited patiently for it. Thanks are also due to the two anonymous reviewers who provided constructive advice on how the initial manuscript could be improved. On a personal note, I would like to thank Chrissie Rogers and Sherrie Tuckwell for putting up with me during the writing of it. A number of the chapters draw on previously published material:

Parts of Chapters 1 and 8 draw on:

Carrabine, E. (2015) 'Contemporary Criminology and the Sociological Imagination', in Frauley, J. (ed.) *C. Wright Mills and the Criminological Imagination* (Dartmouth, Ashgate).

Carrabine, E. (2016) 'Changing Fortunes: Criminology and the Sociological Condition', in *Sociology*, 50(5):847–62.

Parts of Chapters 2 and 3 draw on:

Carrabine, E. (2014) 'Criminology, Deviance and Sociology', in Holmwood, J. and J. Scott (eds.) *The Palgrave Handbook of Sociology in Britain* (London, Palgrave Macmillan).

Parts of Chapter 4 draw on:

Carrabine, E. (2016) 'Changing Fortunes: Criminology and the Sociological Condition', in *Sociology*, 50(5):847–62.

Parts of Chapter 5 draw on:

Carrabine, E. (2006) 'Punishment, Rights and Justice', in Morris, L. (ed.) *Rights: Sociological Perspectives* (London, Routledge).

Carrabine, E. (forthcoming) 'Penology', in Turner, B. (ed.) *The Encyclopedia of Social Theory* (New York, Wiley Blackwell).

Acknowledgements

Parts of Chapter 7 draw on:

Carrabine, E. (2013) 'Crime, Culture and the Media in a Globalizing World', in Arrigo, B. and H. Bersot (eds.) *The Routledge Handbook of International Crime and Justice Studies* (New York, Routledge).

Carrabine, E. (2016) 'Doing Visual Criminology: Learning from Documentary, Journalism and Sociology', in Jacobsen, M. and S. Walklate (eds.) *Liquid Criminology: Doing Imaginative Criminological Research* (Dartmouth, Ashgate).

1

Introduction

The aim of this book is simple, even if some of the material encountered in it is not. It sets out to provide an account of the social theories on which studies of crime and its control inevitably rest. Either implicitly or explicitly every such study, no matter how resolutely steeped in narrow, technical issues, is also grounded in larger, more theoretical understandings of how social worlds operate. Indeed, one of the main legacies of the 'new criminology' proposed by Ian Taylor, Paul Walton, and Jock Young (1973) was the way it exposed the nature of these relationships through the promise of 'a fully social theory of deviance'. Written over 40 years ago the book, and the radical intellectual currents surrounding it, challenged the medico-legal character of much orthodox criminology and urged a reconciliation with the key issues animating the sociological imagination. Today, there remains a no less urgent need to address these issues, not least since contemporary criminology has now successfully established itself as an autonomous, independent academic subject that no longer sees itself as a subfield of the legal, medical, or social sciences.

At the same time, the scale of the cultural, economic, and political changes that have gathered pace since the late twentieth century presents additional challenges that are too profound to evade or ignore. As David Garland and Richard Sparks (2000:1) have put it, to wish these difficulties away, 'to carry on regardless, to pursue the conventional agendas of criminological enquiry in the accustomed way, would be to turn away from some of the most important issues that face contemporary social thought and public policy'. These words were written to introduce a collection of essays seeking to renew and invigorate the field, initially published as a special issue of the *British Journal of Criminology* and then as an edited book. Many of the contributors are leading social thinkers (including Zygmunt Bauman, Mary Douglas, Paul Hirst, and Nikolas Rose), but who are rarely thought of as 'criminologists' – even though their work speaks directly to issues at the heart of criminological enquiry. More recently the National Deviancy Conference (NDC) has been revived in 2011 and 2014, as the organizers felt that it was 'very much needed, especially

1

in Britain, as the dominant conferences were once again becoming increasingly administrative and empiricist in nature' (Winlow and Atkinson, 2013:17). The NDC was formed in 1968 as a breakaway faction from official criminology in Britain and gave a formidable platform for critical work to flourish, including Taylor and colleagues' (1973) rallying call for a 'new criminology', before eventually ending in 1979 as the group fractured along the same rifts as sociology more generally, acrimoniously disputing the merits of Marxist, feminist, and Foucauldian approaches then ascendant.

Since then criminology has acquired the organizational trappings of an academic discipline (Loader and Sparks, 2012:8). These include the growth of separate departments, new degree schemes, graduate research funding, large annual conferences, prestigious prizes, and the appointment of researchers whose entire higher education experience has only been in criminology. The following passage captures some of the issues at stake:

> In the last decade or so, and for the first time in its history, criminology has sought to establish firm parameters on what is and what is not classed as 'criminology'. It does this by creating a myth about its own history and then enshrining it as 'fact'. For years criminology was happy to acknowledge that it was essentially an importer of ideas and theories from cognate fields and more firmly established academic disciplines across the social sciences and humanities. It also acted as a meeting place of sorts, an intellectual space into which academics from different disciplinary backgrounds could come to debate the causes of and control of crime and social harm. In recent years there seems to have been a gradual erosion of this very positive intellectual firmament.
>
> (Hall and Winlow, 2012:8)

The central message from these authors is that it is now time for the discipline to recover its vitality and vigour in the face of such obstacles and this book shares their ambitions to renew and extend the theoretical gaze of criminology.

I mention these interventions to highlight from the outset how there are long-standing tensions over the place of theoretical work in this corner of the academic world, where British criminology continues to be wedded to a stolid mix of 'correctionalism, modernism, abstracted empiricism, unprincipled eclecticism and positivism' (Rock, 2011:21). These accusations are regularly levelled against the field and used to denounce the character of much scholarship. At the same time, social theory itself is understood to be in a state of crisis, particularly in relation to sociology, where today there are at best 'highly idiosyncratic treatments of theory in a few sociology departments and a small theory community among the students in those departments' (Turner, 2009:558). Although Stephen Turner is describing the teaching situation in the United States, where the position is undoubtedly extreme, the modularization of courses elsewhere has meant that few students are now acquiring a thorough grounding in the classic, formative debates or a comprehensive sense of the contemporary theoretical landscape. This troubled relationship between social theory and sociology also emphasizes that theoretical traditions exist within and beyond disciplinary boundaries, while the ties to other social sciences also stretch to cultural and literary theory as well. Indeed, the relations between 'classical' and 'modern' social theory also develop and change over time. It is not simply a matter that some theories once considered 'modern' have aged well and entered the 'classical' pantheon; it is often the case that the 'classics' are revisited in an effort to revitalize current thinking (Outhwaite, 2000:3). This is not to suggest that contemporary theorizing must always take the form of recovering and extending 'classical' themes to present conditions; there are genuinely new ideas and approaches needed to meet the distinctive challenges and upheavals of the age.

One of the liberating features of theoretical innovation is breaking with the constraints imposed by traditional ways of thinking. Not unsurprisingly, then, considerable attention has been given to questioning the place of the 'classics' in contemporary social science. Some argue strongly that these texts can only be understood in their historical contexts, while others defend the creative appropriation of inherited ideas that have acquired a privileged status – precisely because they have made a unique and lasting contribution to understanding society (Alexander, 1996). Likewise, self-styled 'new directions' in social theory only gain traction if there is some grasp of the 'old ideas' forming the basis of the quarrel and what they are reacting against (Scott, 2006:3). Although there are many generic attempts to define social theory, they each face the immediate difficulty of accounting for the significant differences between theoretical traditions and positions. These contested views of social theory involve scientific, philosophical, and moral dimensions and have been fiercely debated since the eighteenth-century Enlightenment, where the emergence of the social as something distinct from the political begins to take shape. At root the differences are fivefold and concern: ontology (the nature of social reality), epistemology (what is valid knowledge of this social reality), methodology (what is the best way of researching it), politics (how to change the social reality for the better), and ethics (what is morally just). These philosophical terms capture something of the issues at stake and caution against a superficial synthesis of incompatible, or even irreconcilable, approaches.

Ontological disputes are among the most essential and question whether society has an independent reality in its own right (a 'reality *sui generis*' in Durkheim's famous formulation), or can only be understood through the symbolic and cultural meanings social actors colour the world with. Epistemological questions are bound up with theories of knowledge and rival ways of knowing the world (empiricism, rationalism, and interpretivism are among the competing philosophical positions). Methodological issues stem from what procedures (ethnographic observation, questionnaire survey, or textual exegesis) are thought best equipped to gain knowledge of the world. Politics and political philosophy are at the heart of debates over global crises, democratic principles, and conflicting understandings of what is the 'good' society. Ethics and morality present themselves as preconditions for social life and part of the rich diversity of human experience is a diversity of cultures, practices, and values. Inevitably this leads to antagonisms and calls for a just way of adjudicating between these differences. It calls for a thorough understanding of how social harm arises and what might be done about it. Theories of crime, deviance, and punishment are inevitably bound up with normative judgements on 'what acts *ought* to be crimes and what the criminal justice process *should be* for' (Valier, 2002:1, emphasis in original).

The book will not be structured explicitly around these themes, but they are useful to keep in mind as they indicate the contours of the sociological imagination advocated in it. They suggest the reader will profit from separating out, and paying attention to, four different dimensions of the sociological imagination:

(i) *the dimension of ontology* – this focuses on particular aspects of how the world is, and in the case of the sociological imagination this means focusing on biographies and actions caught up in, and reacting back upon, webs of social structures and the large forces of history;

(ii) *the dimension of epistemology* – this focuses on aspects of knowledge, which here means seeking to acquire *knowledge* about crimes, the biographies of actors involved in them, and their larger contexts, in order to situate crime in the world described by the ontology;

(iii) *the dimension of methodology* – this is quite an amorphous area, when considered in general terms, but an important one as it acts as a bridge between philosophical concepts, technical method, and empirical evidence. It points to the ways in which technical methods such as ethnographic observation, interviews, and surveys need to stay closely in touch with the conceptual direction provided by the ontological focus;

(iv) *the dimension of politics and ethics* – consciously separating out this dimension directs attention to questions around the often neglected area of how to change things for the better.

One of the very key questions addressed by social theory is: 'how is society possible?' There are many different answers, but the situations of persons who are different, disadvantaged, or compromised in some way offer crucial starting points for considering the relationships between biography, history, and social structure.

Although the sociology of deviance emerged in the nineteenth century and is intimately bound up with the broader transformations associated with modernity, the origins of a systematic, comparative, and investigative approach to the problems of crime, disorder, and punishment can be traced much further back in time. Breaking social rules is an inevitable feature of social organization, and is as old as human existence, prompting numerous attempts to make sense of wrongdoing. The various discourses produced on criminality suggest that wherever forms of collective representation have developed to explain human conduct – whether these be 'myths, cosmologies, theologies, metaphysical systems, or vernacular common sense' (Garland, 2002:17) – they have involved some attempt to understand the causes and consequences of lawbreaking. Not all of this vast material should be understood as a form of 'proto-criminology', even if the subject matter broadly resembles some contemporary thinking; it was written in very different times and governed by cultural sensibilities far removed from our own. Theories of crime and punishment do not exist in a vacuum, but emerge in specific historical contexts and often with a substantive empirical focus. The aim of this book is not to lay down a definitive manifesto for an all-encompassing, universal criminological theory, rather it seeks to bring together some of the most significant theoretically informed empirical work in the field. The overall premise is that a renewed commitment to C. Wright Mills (1959) vision of the 'sociological imagination' is the way forward at this decisive moment.

The Sociological Imagination

Mills (1959:3) famously declared that neither 'the life of an individual nor the history of a society can be understood without understanding both', yet the more radical implications of his argument over how the sociological imagination can offer liberation from oppressive conditions are largely forgotten. Today, practically every introductory sociology textbook routinely invokes the first element of Mills' definition, that is, how individuals relate to society, but ignores the second, which uses the 'concept to *overcome* the ties that bind us to social structure, *critique* the work of American sociologists who do not reach the same conclusions he did, and enable us to radically *transform* the status quo' (Goode, 2008:239, emphasis in original). Something of this critical project can be seen in Jock Young's (2011) recent attempt to subject criminology to the kind of withering attack that Mills delivered upon sociology over 50 years ago. Here he condemns the 'abstract empiricism' of mainstream criminology, which is described as one-dimensional, banal, technocratic, and in the deadening grip of quantification, while that which aspires to 'grand theory' is similarly removed from social realities, thriving on trivial, ponderous obfuscation where 'latter-day Foucauldians have taken an outrageous and iconoclastic thinker and turned his writings into some sort of Talmudic parody of contested interpretation' (Young, 2011:6).

These two contrasting tendencies were initially identified by Mills in his scathing assessment of mid-century American sociology, which was ignoring the major issues of the day: how a post-war corporate economy led by a powerful elite, which had forged alliances with the military machine, was corroding social structures and generating profound inequalities. Instead, the profession was content to produce timid, conservative, inaccessible work that lacked any sense of the big picture or the transformative politics required to change the social order for the better. Directing his critique at the leading representatives of each tendency he condemned the 'abstracted empiricism', exemplified in the work of Paul Lazarsfeld, for how it mistakes technical sophistication in method for having something important to say, while the 'grand theory' of Talcott Parsons is famously ridiculed for its lack of intelligibility and for evading urgent political questions surrounding the nature of power. In these different ways the emancipatory promise of sociology had become tragically distorted in the Cold War climate of the era. Distancing himself from those 'colleagues who were busy "choosing the west", otherwise giving aid and comfort to the witch-hunters, or neutering themselves by hiding behind the ideology of value-free scholarship' (Aronowitz, 2003:5), it is clear that Mills wanted sociology to rediscover the classic European thinkers of the nineteenth century who sought to comprehend the entire social condition. This ambition is not without its own problems, such that any attempt to simply apply Mills to the contemporary social science landscape is likely to end up reproducing the assumptions framing his initial critique.

Every text is a product of its times, and *The Sociological Imagination* is no exception, but one of the striking features is just how tame and respectable Mills' indictment has now become. Quotes from it appear so frequently in introductory sociology textbooks that it is as if 'either American sociology had long ago welcomed and favorably absorbed the essence of Mills's critique or, conversely, could stomach only a thimbleful of his tonic' (Dandaneau, 2007, cited in Goode, 2008:250). There is no doubt that Mills would have dismissed these books and the courses they support for so passively accepting the tenets of mainstream sociology, which if anything is today even more thoroughly mired in the troughs he originally identified. In these standard textbook accounts the radical and polemical edge of his work is downplayed and Mills is transformed into a somewhat benign figure, sanctified even, where the rebel becomes a martyr. It is as if he had to 'die young to become a hero in sociology' (Brewer, 2004:318). Of course, this is a further irony as by the time of his death in 1962 he was widely disliked in the profession, having antagonized and quarrelled with most of the prominent members in it, including those who had initially helped him and admired his work.[1]

Several commentators have noted how the book is emphatically modernist in orientation, where the voices of classical social theory provide the language with which Mills can critique post-war American society and the sociologists who inhabit it. Some highlight its Weberian focus on the dangers bureaucratic rationalization presents to human dignity and freedom (Binns, 1977; Hearn, 1985), while others emphasize the influence of Veblen's (1899/1953) searing indictment of the dilettante upper classes on Mills' own understanding of the close ties between analysis, criticism, and style (Aronowitz, 2003; Kerr, 2009). Furthermore, Veblen's satirical reading of the leisure class is firmly rooted in a historical understanding of how conflicts of interest arise macro-sociologically, while giving shape and meaning to an individual's character. This ability to fuse the deeply personal with the larger picture is an approach Mills would deploy throughout his career (Treviño, 2012:9). Yet the book has been denounced precisely because it is so attached to the old grand metanarratives of classical theory that it cannot speak to the post-modern condition. Consequently, it is ill-suited to confront the problems facing contemporary sociology, where Mills is accused of writing 'vaingloriously' and producing a 'hypocritical text with dubious ethics' (Denzin, 1990:4).

These last complaints are not new and were aired in early reviews of the book, charging Mills with messianism, describing him as the 'Billy Graham of sociology' travelling the earth, 'bearing a torch to light our darkness' and finding fault with him for his extreme criticisms, which 'lack profundity' and rendering his own proposals 'lamentably thin' (Fletcher, 1960:169). Many in the sociological establishment, on both sides of the Atlantic, were quick to defend the current state of the profession and the leading figures in it. The most vitriolic review was by Edward Shils (1960:78) who described Mills as a 'sort of Joe McCarthy of sociology, full of wild accusations and gross inaccuracies, bullying manners, harsh words, and shifting grounds', and who had previously fallen out with him over a translation of Weber that would never see publication, for which Shils largely blamed Mills (Oakes and Vidich, 1999), hence the bitter tirade against him. The review remains among the most malicious denigrations in the history of sociology, on one of the finest books to ever appear in it (Becker, 1994). The initial reaction to the book was overwhelmingly negative in the leading American sociological journals. George Homans (1960:517) thought it was nonsense, not least since he 'describes some work that I am familiar with in such loaded terms that I cannot recognize it', while William Kolb (1960:969) accused Mills of dogmatism, inflexibility, and hypocritically generating his own 'abstract mode of sociologism'.

Of course, opinion over the book has shifted drastically over time. Mills' emphatic rejection of American positivist, functional sociology and his endorsement of European social theory chimed with the burgeoning New Left (Hayden, 2006) and he was a decisive figure launching the 'political 1960s, the survivals of which are the few progressive movements that remain, such as environmentalism, and ironically, women's liberation and gay rights' (Goode, 2008:251). It must also be said that Mills' early death helped change perceptions. The book came to be seen as a 'valediction' and his studies anticipated the sociological mood of the 1960s, where the discipline became more 'comfortable seeing itself as a form of critique and debunking' (Brewer, 2004:330). His work was increasingly located in part of a broader attack on positivist sociological methods and the structural-functionalist theorizing then dominant, which would be such a key influence on the development of critical criminology in Britain, as we will see in subsequent chapters. Denzin's (1990) critique of the book is through a post-modern reading that distils feminist, post-colonial, and interactionist approaches to lived experience. He takes Mills to task for claiming to speak on behalf of the oppressed, but nowhere in the book do the 'little people and their personal troubles speak', rather Mills 'speaks for them; or he quotes others who have written about them, usually novelists' (Denzin, 1990:4). Even though fault might now be found with the modernist narrative and muscular posturing in the text, sociology is different today from the early 1960s, and much of this can be put down to the way Millsian ideas were taken up later in the decade.

It is equally clear that *The Sociological Imagination* did not call time on either abstracted empiricism or grand theory. If articles in the leading American sociology journals are any indicator it would seem that 'Lazarsfeldian abstracted empiricism is now even more abstract, more quantitative, more inaccessible to the nonspecialist untrained in statistics, and at least as apolitical as was the case in Lazarsfeld's time' (Goode, 2008:249). There is no doubt that Mills would also have found the pretensions in much postmodern writing a continuation of the high seriousness and utter irrelevance of Parsonian grand theory (Gitlin, 2007). Arguably the real legacy of Mills lies in the way he developed a distinctive blend of perspectives that challenged the competing orthodoxies in the discipline, and it is that critical orientation that needs to be recovered, especially as the relationship between criminology and sociology stands at a crossroads today.

However, it is important to note that in Britain, at least, the close ties between criminology and sociology themselves only really existed from the late 1960s. Such a late marriage requires some explanation, and will be covered in what follows. Efforts to explain crime scientifically began in the late eighteenth century and gathered momentum in the nineteenth century – emerging from an eclectic mix of medico-legal approaches and Victorian social reform movements. Part of what I want to demonstrate is how a particular criminological tradition has been invented in a national context. As the social sciences have developed in different countries they have taken on a distinctive national character, which reflects the historically specific problems addressed in each country. These problems are not always universal, but they do share some common themes, because these more general concerns are often investigated through the particularly pressing cases in each society. Of course, this is not an argument advocating what has been termed 'methodological nationalism', where the nation state is problematically understood to be the natural focal point of disciplinary developments (for a nuanced discussion of these debates in social theory, see Chernilo, 2006), but I will argue that a geographical sensibility is absolutely crucial to understanding the shape of crime and punishment.

Organization of the Book

The book will set out in two opening chapters the main theoretical approaches and debates that structure the field. Chapter 2 will outline the formative positions that have helped shape modern criminology. It will, though, point out that one of the problems with this conventional characterization is the implication that people only began to think about crime 'sensibly' from the middle of the eighteenth century. This is, of course, seriously misleading. Discourses on crime and punishment are as old as human civilization. For example, Bentham's utilitarian reasoning, which judges actions on the grounds of social usefulness and their consequences, can be traced back to the fifth century BC in Plato's dialogues with Protagoras, a Thracian philosopher. At the same time, Kant developed his critique of utilitarian thinking through the ancient concept of *lex talionis* – the 'law of retaliation' and 'eye for an eye' codes of justice. Nevertheless, Enlightenment jurisprudence did seek to establish a rational basis for criminal justice and the rule of law, which emphasized the powers of reason to produce a better vision of social order. The later positivist criminology of the nineteenth and early twentieth century replaced the normative orientation with scientific laws. This chapter will also describe how a minor, applied medical specialism became a professional academic discipline and sets the scene for the encounter with sociology, which will be a major theme running through the book.

In Britain the close relationship between criminology and sociology emerged in the 1960s, with the establishment of a university system that was particularly receptive to the new discipline of sociology. Chapter 3 charts the rise of the American sociology of deviance tradition, which was effectively challenged from the 1970s onwards. Here the fragmentation and proliferation of theories of crime and punishment under the impact of feminism, Foucault's poststructuralism, realist disputes in neo-Marxism, and New Right challenges, through to contemporary preoccupations with governance, risk, and globalization have been decisive. There is now a bewildering range of literature in the field and the design of the book is such that it is organized around four substantive themes. Each of these critically assesses the most significant theoretically informed work in the area, so as to consider new directions as well as fresh uses of the classic positions. A further reason for the choice of the four themes is that, in their different ways, they each situate actors, actions, and reactions in a broader social context. The chapters deliberately concentrate on contemporary work and provide a rough, chronological account of theoretical developments in each theme. The danger with this approach, as one of the anonymous reviewers of the initial manuscript pointed out, is that it can give the misleading impression that there is a fluid development of one set of ideas to the next. Of course, the reality is far more provisional and chaotic than that described in the following pages, and that should be kept in mind, though it is always necessary to impose a degree of narrative order on what is an unruly field. It is not meant to imply that there is some overarching unity or seamless flow in this work, but rather it signals something of its diversity and hints at some of the profound contradictions running through it.

Chapter 4 considers the fate of deviance, which as a concept has declined as an area of sociological interest, while at the same time criminology itself has experienced remarkable growth over the last two decades. In many respects, the metaphor of 'transgression' has come to replace some of the central concerns in the field and these arguments will be assessed in light of the subcultural legacy, which has always sought to portray the distinctive social worlds the different, disenfranchised, and unconventional share with others. Since the 1990s much work has explored the gendered dynamics of offending and examined the ways multiple inequalities intersect and interlock. Crucial here was the recognition of how different epistemologies shape knowledge production, and an early advocate for a 'transgressive criminology' (Cain, 1990:6) urged a break with the confines of conventional criminology in her efforts to unravel the conditions that disadvantage us all.

The theme of 'control' is addressed in Chapter 5, indicating how it encompasses the organized responses to crime and other socially problematic forms of conduct. The main focus is punishment and how it has recently become a multidisciplinary field, where each of the classical traditions in social theory has inspired substantial and innovative ways of understanding crime control. A defining feature of this approach is the detaching of punishment from the legal apparatus and moral arguments that normally surround it to instead reveal the broader structural forces, cultural sensibilities, political conflicts, and social relations sustaining penal systems and patterns of social control more generally. It is a field that is rich with historical and sociological insight, but one telling absence is the lack of a comparative, geographical focus – especially when punitiveness itself varies so starkly across different regions.

Spatial differences are pursued further in Chapter 6, where 'geography' provides the substantive theme, and it begins with a discussion of how the vivid contrasts of urban life have inspired a considerable body of writing on the city as a site of desire, fantasy, and pleasure, as well as a place of anxiety, fear, and violence. The idea of a subterranean 'otherworld' that mirrored and mimicked the more respectable 'upperworld' is a persistent trope in this literature, and helps pave the way for an understanding of the crimes of powerful. The most successful criminal enterprises are loosely structured networks, which also involve 'upright' business people and public officials, and are multifaceted, mutating, and flexible enough to respond to the fast-changing marketplace of illicit goods. Unlike previous eras, contemporary organized crime, which is focused on drugs, fraud, and counterfeiting, is at once both global and local. Today we must consider some, though not all, forms of organized criminal collaboration as involving both local dimensions and international connections and resources. Business and violence are linked in many ways, and suggest a continuity between legality and illegality that is essential to comprehending the criminality of professional elites.

A recent review of the field makes the fundamental point that 'any understanding of the phenomena of "crime" must attempt to comprehend' the
'mediatization of life' (Brown, 2011:413).[2] The full implications of this assertion are followed in Chapter 7 where 'representation' is the central theme. It
opens with the much used and abused concept of moral panic, and while it has
received extensive criticism I explain how contemporary media spectacles do
still foster distinctive moral relations in quite fundamental ways. The crucial
point is that mediated communication fundamentally shapes our experience
of reality. Yet the unexpected and the exceptional still happen and it remains
the job of the media to translate these spontaneous anomalies into neat and
tidy stories. Occasionally, though, these events can produce an electrifying
force that unleashes cultural change and quite profound social transformations. The recent turn to understanding 'iconic power' in cultural sociology
(Bartmański and Alexander, 2012) is of some significance here and echoes
developments in criminology (Carrabine, 2012a), which I spend some time
exploring, not least since there remains hardly any consensus in the social
sciences over how 'the visual' should be analysed or explained (Wilkinson,
2013:262).

The final chapter returns to the relationship between criminology and sociology, but through directly engaging with the sociological condition itself and
identifying two very different directions of travel available. One might be
termed the 'imperial' conceptualization while the other offers a more 'cosmopolitan' vision of sociology and social theory. Clearly I am concerned about
criminology's move away from its sociological roots, and the kind of intellectual parochialism that will result from such independence, but my hope
is that the book will serve as a reminder of the rich theoretical and empirical
work that still exists in the field. Indeed, one of the legacies of Mills is the
way he anticipates Pierre Bourdieu's (1988) criticism of the social sciences and
their perpetuation of the false divide between theory and method, as well as
'the fiction of the autonomous nature of the various social sciences' (Frauley,
2015:25). Above all, the goal is one of bridging the damaging gap between
theoretical and empirical work that remains all too present in social science.

2

Formative Positions

It is no accident that the rise of social theory coincides with the emergence of modern societies. More specifically, the distinctive properties of the 'social' were recognized as having powerful forces by eighteenth-century Enlightenment thinkers, who were initially restricted to rediscovering the works of classical antiquity before radically breaking with the orthodoxies of the past. Such thinking inspired both the French Revolution in 1789 and the Industrial Revolution (a more gradual, but no less profound, transformation in socioeconomic relations occurring at the same time in parts of Northern Europe). The effects of this 'dual revolution' (Hobsbawm, 1973:11) still resonate today, shaping the modern world and giving rise to the concept of modernity, which suggested an altered relationship to historical time and a new understanding of the age as one moving rapidly forward. The promises of modernity – freedom, progress, infinite human advancement – have produced a sense of accelerating history, opening up distinctly new ways of experiencing the past, present, and future (Koselleck, 2004). In this and the next chapter, I chart the development of systematic thinking on crime and punishment as they have emerged in the social sciences over the last couple of centuries, and more specifically I concentrate on how different traditions in social theory have understood criminality, deviance, and social control.

While there are numerous histories of criminal justice institutions – courts, legislation, policing, prisons, and so on – there is relatively little on the history, or the sociology, of criminology. Textbook accounts ritually invoke the same cast of characters, typically beginning with Beccaria (1764/1986) as the originator of the 'classical school' and contrasting this with Lombroso's 'positivist' search for the 'criminal type' over a century later. How these ideas shaped actual practices at the time, or were related to other intellectual trends and institutional settings, is rarely traced in any depth. A sociology of criminological knowledge that examines its structure as an academic and cultural field in which individuals and institutions interact in a web of creative and competing relationships is also largely absent. Efforts to explain crime scientifically began in the late eighteenth century and gathered momentum in the nineteenth century – emerging from an eclectic mix of medico-legal approaches and Victorian social reform movements. Not all of this vast material constitutes a form of 'proto-criminology' (Garland, 2002). Some of it is rather a kind of 'shadow criminology' (Rock, 1994) older than that found in universities, but prefiguring much later approaches and it will be covered in this chapter.

In his account of the origins of social theory Johan Heilbron (1995:3) makes the important point that in the history of the social sciences a distinction between 'disciplinary' and 'predisciplinary' stages in their development should be drawn. This delineation is preferable to identifying a 'prehistory' as these earlier ideas are a vital part of the intellectual formation of academic disciplines in modern universities. The predisciplinary period begins around 1600, in the early modern era, and runs up to the middle of the nineteenth century. Over this time industrial capitalist societies emerged in Europe, and from the beginning they are understood to be in crisis – along various economic, moral, social, and political dimensions – and different diagnoses of these conditions shaped the social sciences. These ideas developed in far more heterogeneous settings than disciplines. Here various 'intellectual genres' with 'specific vocabularies' established a set of discourses and practices where 'intellectual activities were organized in academies and learned societies, which competed with older church organizations'. Heilbron (ibid.) then describes the transition to the later specialization of the modern social sciences, where these 'relatively flexible intellectual genres' give way to 'far more strictly organized university disciplines' from the mid nineteenth century onwards. In this reading the rise of the social sciences is bound up with the process of secularization, where a more 'humanistic' understanding of the world developed during the Renaissance and challenged the authority of the Church.[1] Enlightenment thinkers did not create the scientific revolution, but they certainly popularized it and saw in it a symbol of what human reason might achieve – thereby making the subjectivity of human experience the basis for all knowledge. A crucial dynamic in the predisciplinary period is the emergence of a public sphere enabling such thought to flourish.

The Public Sphere and Enlightenment

The term 'public sphere' was initially coined by the German sociologist Jürgen Habermas (1962/1989) in a pioneering study of communication processes and social change. His argument is that the eighteenth century marked a decisive stage in the development of rational debate. The emergence of capitalism at this time brought with it the commodification of culture and opened up the liberal, democratic possibility of well-informed individuals resolving their differences through enlightened reason rather than brute force. Crucial to the argument is that a new space opened up between the disintegrating feudal authorities (church, nobility, patronage), expanding capitalist markets, urban trade corporations, and newly evolving nation states requiring continuous administration, standing armies, and the legal exertion of authority. The 'public sphere' was much more than a purely discursive realm but was grounded in a network of social spaces and institutions that regulated manners and promoted urbane conduct. These included new, refined sites where conversation could flourish in meeting places such as coffee houses, tea gardens, assembly rooms, salons, spas and resorts, debating societies, and learned associations – all of which had relatively low entry costs and were in principle open to everyone.

It was the energy released by the emerging capitalist markets that stimulated the growth of these public sphere institutions and enabled Enlightenment philosophy to take cultural expression. Moreover, it has been argued that the rise of newspapers, journals, periodicals, and especially literature 'served the emancipation movement of the middle class as an instrument to gain self-esteem and to articulate its demands against the absolutist state and the hierarchical society' (Hohendahl, 1982:52). Although Enlightenment intellectuals inherited many of the assumptions of the classical tradition; they challenged the orthodoxy of the past by looking to the future and founding a new era based on the powers of reason, science, and liberty. The radical idea was that knowledge progressed and that reason would bring liberation from the barbarism of the feudal Dark Ages. They included French philosophers such as Descartes, Montesquieu, and Rousseau who were systematically critical of the despotic regimes in which they found themselves. The light of reason would oppose faith, superstition, tradition, and prejudice to bring about true Enlightenment. Meanwhile, a quarrel raged between 'the Ancients and the Moderns' with various writers arguing that the new science of physics pioneered by Galileo, Boyle, and Newton was far superior to anything produced in antiquity. These developments encouraged European intellectuals to see humanity afresh. Central to the cultural and political project of Enlightenment was the assertion that individuals, through various combinations of reasoning powers and sense experiences, could determine their own destinies. As we will see, penal reformers, among others, drew on these ideas to critique capital punishment and the savagery of the 'Bloody Code', which helped to establish the new system of imprisonment as the just response to crime.

The famous *Encyclopédie*, published in 35 volumes between 1751 and 1765, included Diderot, Voltaire, and Rousseau among the many contributors, and did much to spread and popularize these philosophical ideas. A massive project, it was intended to advance knowledge by bringing together the leading French thinkers and challenged traditional authority through the discovery of new scientific truths. Initially only the very rich could buy the whole series, but cheaper editions followed and were widely discussed in the burgeoning coffee houses and other places of egalitarian assembly. Indeed, the significance of the coffee house was that it provided a radically new kind of social institution, 'at once free from the "grotesque bodies" of the alehouse', and they promoted themselves as '*decent* places to go' where for 'one penny *any* man could sit and drink' (Stallybrass and White, 1986:95–96, emphasis in original). These 'penny universities' claimed moral superiority over the alehouse by being places of productive leisure rather than unruly consumption, thus allowing the protestant ethic of sobriety and profit to be realized in one telling space. Heilbron (1995:51) describes how 'heated disputes broke out' in French 'salons and local and national academies' over the new concept of philosophy that involved a then unique commitment to intellectual and social involvement, where 'men of letters' were playing an increasingly prominent role.

It is important to recognize that the Enlightenment took several trajectories in different parts of Europe. While it is often associated with French and Scottish intellectuals, the English had, a century earlier, experienced their own intellectual revolution when thinkers such as Thomas Hobbes (1651/2008) and John Locke (1661/2003) set out comprehensive social theories of state sovereignty and individual liberty. Their work was written in the midst of civil war, political turmoil, and widespread repression, yet established a view of knowledge as an empirical process where truth is arrived at through experiential observations of facts and their connections. In German-speaking Europe a strong emphasis was placed on traditional values and preserving cultural unity in a hostile reaction against both British empiricism and French rationalism. Even the Prussian philosopher Immanuel Kant, who published his major critiques between 1781 and 1790, which are widely regarded as the finest intellectual achievement of the Enlightenment, remained a somewhat 'isolated figure in his own country', while the 'generation that followed him there rejected precisely that part of his thought which insisted upon these virtues' (Hawthorn, 1987:12). Although there were considerable national variations, these Enlightenment thinkers all shared the view that scientific methods should be extended to the systematic study of human life and social institutions.

By the middle of the eighteenth century Rousseau's proclamation that 'Man is born free, and everywhere he is in chains' controversially reversed the conventional Christian view that humans are intrinsically corrupt and in need of religious salvation while also suggesting the universal right to liberty. Yet it took the French and American revolutions to give legal force to the political theory that declared 'all men are created equal' (except, of course, slaves, women, indigenous populations, children, and so on), while the Terror that subsequently engulfed France at the end of the eighteenth century revealed that populist governments can disregard human freedom as easily as absolutist monarchies. As revolutionaries replaced aristocrats on the guillotine in the years after the French Declaration of the Rights of Man and Citizen, the executions provided 'a practical refutation of its claim that "rights" were natural, let alone inalienable and sacred' (Robertson, 2000:5). It was Jeremy Bentham who mounted an influential liberal attack on natural rights and unjust legal systems, which became a pivotal force driving social reform in the nineteenth century. Even then there was considerable suspicion surrounding a 'standing police force', not least because of fears of Continental systems of police spies interfering in private life and thereby running contrary to English liberty. Contemporary policing developed from a patchwork of parochial systems with towns and parishes relying on the community-based 'watch', local constables, and private 'thief-takers' before the controversial introduction of a metropolitan police force in 1829 to regulate urban life.

Although well known for his literary achievements, Henry Fielding was also a London magistrate and he has been applauded for producing 'arguably the first treatise on criminology published in English' (Sherman, 2011:428). In 1751 he published his *Enquiry into the Causes of the Late Increase in Robbers*, which was based on extensive fieldwork in the city, and included interviews with defendants charged in his court, proposals for regulating the sale of gin and gambling, and a system of rapid response policing, which became known as the 'Bow Street Runners'. His analysis was 'far more sociological than retributive' (Sherman, 2011:429) and the government shortly put his recommendations to the test in the wake of a spate of robbery-murders. His methods proved to be successful, paving the way for the first police force in British history. Fielding questioned the social conditions producing the criminals sent to hang every six weeks at Tyburn, and while his system of policing was based on methods of thief-taking that he had earlier satirized in his *Mr. Jonathan Wild the Great* (1743), the people he hired did manage to swiftly capture the robbery gangs.[2]

Fielding's writing on crime problems has been situated in a wider 'science of police' flourishing in eighteenth-century Europe, which was concerned with the whole art of government and the promotion of the health, wealth, and happiness of the entire population, rather than with the 'suppression of disorder, the surveillance of public space or the protection of private property, which is its contemporary reference' (Smart, 1983:80). As Robert Reiner (1988) has pointed out, this vast body of literature was much broader in scope than that which has come to be defined as 'classical criminology' and deserves much closer scrutiny than it has conventionally received. In England the leading proponent of the 'science of police' was another magistrate, Patrick Colquhoun, who wrote extensively on political economy, crime, and criminal justice. Insisting that each must not be studied in isolation nor separated from wider structural factors, his work should be seen as among the pioneers of criminology. Although the reform of formal policing arrangements is the legacy for which he is now mostly remembered, this was only one small element in the interventions he felt necessary to prevent crime (Reiner, 2012:34).

Typically, it is Cesare Beccaria's (1764) *Of Crime and Punishments* that is taken as the foundational text of the classical school of thought and his influence on Jeremy Bentham, John Howard, and Samuel Romilly is held up as the decisive contribution establishing the key components that would much later shape the modern subject of criminology. It is important to note that Beccaria's work was the result of intellectual exchanges among a Milanese circle that self-consciously modelled themselves on the French *philosophes*, and published the journal *Il Caffè* to disseminate their ideas, while the influence of Scottish thought – especially over the 'science of man' – was significant in shaping Beccaria's text (Beirne, 1993). Although this 'immaculate-conception' account of the birth of criminology can be challenged on a number of levels (Cohen, 1988:3), not least since it constitutes only one of an array of discourses on crime, order, and punishment circulating in the eighteenth and early nineteenth centuries, it did set in motion a set of preoccupations that persist to this day. Most importantly, these writers drew freely from the revolutionary Enlightenment philosophies of Montesquieu, Voltaire, and Rousseau who were highly critical of despotism.

Central to the cultural and political project of Enlightenment was the assertion that individuals, through the powers of their reasoning could determine their own destinies. Such effort, it was maintained, would bring liberation from the barbarism of the *ancient regime*. Thinkers such as Beccaria, Bentham, and Howard developed these ideas in an effort to deliver a more rational and efficient means of delivering justice, that would end the injustice of criminal law as well as condemning torture and capital punishment. Not only is the 'right' to punish very dominant, which is grounded in the liberal notion of the social contract between individual citizens and sovereign state, but also the question of 'how' to punish figured prominently in their efforts to reform criminal justice procedures and institutions.

John Howard's (1777) *The State of the Prisons* did much to popularize prison reform by documenting just how bad conditions were in English prisons when compared to those on the Continent – he especially admired the 'humanity' of Dutch regimes. Although Howard's investigation into the state of prisons was motivated by charity and reform, his methods were 'doggedly empirical', based on comparative measurement and systematic observation, setting up a line of 'penological inquiry' that was to become a defining feature of British criminology (Garland, 2002:21). Among the most significant interpreters of the Enlightenment was the philosopher Jeremy Bentham, a committed individualist who maintained that the state should interfere as little as possible in the liberties of its citizens. He mounted an influential liberal attack on natural rights and the conservative disposition of natural law that upheld unjust legal systems, which became a pivotal force driving social reform in the nineteenth century. Moreover, his utilitarian form of moral reasoning can be seen as a project aimed at securing effective government in a world caught up in the whirlwind of modernization and a new industrial age.[3]

It is in this context that Bentham developed his famous panopticon prison design (later made famous for a very different audience by Michel Foucault), an elaborate inspection apparatus set to 'grinding rogues honest'. He readily acknowledged that it was an omniscient 'way of obtaining power, power of mind over mind' (cited in Evans, 1982:198–9) and could be used as a factory, hospital, school, asylum, and prison. Critics not only worried over the tyranny exemplified in the design, but disliked Bentham's insistence that the panopticon could be run as a profitable commercial business and it was this latter objection that ultimately led to the rejection of his plans. Despite never actually being built, significant elements of his design informed subsequent prison penitentiaries in the nineteenth century (Carrabine, 2012b). The legacy of all these classical thinkers is the belief that archaic laws, repressive institutions, and arbitrary practices can be reformed through a model of instrumental rationality that emphasized an individual's free will and the constitution of a new society. It presented 'on the one side, the free "sovereign" individual acting according to the dictates of reason and self-interest; on the other, the limited liberal state, contracted to grant rights and liberties, to prescribe duties, and to impose the fair and just punishment that must result from the knowing infliction of social harm' (Cohen, 1988:3). It was to be this basic premise of the classical tradition – that a rational subject is responsible for their freely chosen actions – which would later be dismissed as abstract metaphysical speculation and criticized for failing to take into account social conditions and collective structures.

Early Criminologies

Across Europe the early decades of the nineteenth century were characterized by major social upheaval, political instability, and economic crises, while many states began to construct legal and bureaucratic machinery deeply indebted to the rationalized principles of the Enlightenment project. The Industrial Revolution sped up the flow of population from the countryside to the city and helped to establish that pervasive nineteenth-century fear of the seething urban crowd. The free market opened up glaring inequalities, and efforts to contain the social disruptions associated with rising unemployment and new class divisions intensified in the rapidly expanding towns and cities. These conditions were not unique to the nineteenth century, but what was distinctive was the way that journalists, missionaries, novelists, reformers, and others began to analytically document the wretched conditions endured by the urban poor through a mass of detailed observation.

Few thought of themselves as social scientists, but they were pioneering social science methods as they went along in their sporadic forays into the 'unknown continents' of the industrial city. Some of this research remains unsurpassed. Henry Mayhew's remarkable documentation of crime in Victorian London across a series of volumes on *London Labour and the London Poor* (1851–62) was followed by another major study of *The Criminal Prisons of London and Scenes of Prison Life* in 1862 in collaboration with the journalist John Binny. The research innovatively combined ethnographic methods, statistical data, life histories, and maps showing the distribution of social problems – anticipating the famous crime cartography of the University of Chicago's sociology department by some 70 years. A little earlier a young Friedrich Engels (1845/1993) described the brutal *Condition of the Working Class in England* in a searing account of how uncontrolled industrialization, haphazard urbanization, and class apartheid were creating the social problems of the day.[4] The Rev. Thomas Beames's (1850) *The Rookeries of London* is a less well-known, but no less indicative example of the kind of intrepid exploration of slum quarters that appears in contemporary novels, parliamentary reports, and investigative journalism excavating these dangerous places with a clear 'civilizing' mission.

It has also been noted how by the middle of the nineteenth century a form of 'scientific' reasoning about crime had become part of the 'emergent culture of amateur social science' thriving in Victorian England (Garland, 2002:21). Here government officials acting initially in private but then later in a public capacity began to analyse the mass of data that new state institutions had started producing. Many of these Enlightenment reformers had helped to devise them and they included the new police, judicial, and penal authorities, who each produced their own statistical returns from the 1830s, and men such as Rawson W. Rawson, Joseph Fletcher, and John Glyde delivered papers to the Statistical Society of London drawing conclusions about the moral and social causes of crime from meticulously calculated correlations of the data (Morris, 1957). Similar developments were well underway on the Continent and two French-speaking authors, André-Michel Guerry (1833) and Adolphe Quételet (1835), are credited as among the first to develop a distinctly sociological form of analysis that set out to identify the social forces producing crime.

Here a new 'social physics' was pioneered that innovatively applied concepts derived from the natural sciences to social problems and established a positivist tradition that countered the more biological form that the later Italian 'Positive School' of Cesare Lombroso popularized. Guerry and Quételet were both struck by the stability of crime rates, regardless of actions taken by courts or prisons, and in this they prepare themes developed by Durkheim some half a century later. Karl Marx was also impressed, writing in the *New York Daily Tribune* that:

> if crimes observed on a great scale thus show, in their amount and their classification, the regularity of physical phenomena – if as Mr. Quételet remarks, 'it would be difficult to decide in respect to which of the two' (the physical world and the social system) 'the acting causes produce their effect with the utmost regularity' – is there not a necessity for deeply reflecting upon an alteration of the system that breeds these crimes, instead of glorifying the hangman who executes a lot of criminals to make room only for a supply of new ones?
>
> (Marx, 1853, quoting Quételet, 1835, cited in Melossi, 2008:46)

The social mapping of criminality pioneered by these French moral statisticians involved novel cartographic methods in an effort to test hypotheses on the causes of crime that were especially influential in Britain. In particular, empirical findings on the relations between crime and education were much contested, not least since Guerry controversially challenged the popular view that education helped prevent crime, and his analysis of French data revealed that, while virtuous, expanding public education had little effect on crime rates – a conclusion that Joseph Fletcher (1849), among others, rejected and in his lengthy report on 'Moral and Educational Statistics of England and Wales' the focus is broadened from education to other 'social' factors, such as industrialization, pauperism, alcoholism, food costs, and so forth, to contend that 'unregulated capitalism can cause crime' (Rafter, 2009:279) – a view much later articulated by the Dutch Marxist scholar Willem Bonger (1916/1969) who maintained that capitalism is criminogenic as it cultivates a predatory disposition and demoralizes the poor.

Alongside these early sociological studies of crime, which were essentially concerned with collective phenomenon and regularities in the distribution of criminal behaviour, so as to identify the social forces operating over the individual offender, there were a flourishing series of 'cottage industries' (Rafter, 2009:xiii) devoted to the very nature of the criminal mind and body. Initially attention focused on what was termed 'moral insanity' and then later in the nineteenth century the implications of Darwin's evolutionary theory were applied to criminal behaviour. In one important strand the goal became a 'search for *Homo criminalis*, an abnormal being whose characteristics derived from a multiplicity of domains' (Beirne, 1993:6). The psychiatric approach that developed in Britain was based on a system of classification that included such conditions as 'moral imbecility', 'defective', 'derangement', 'incorrigibility', and 'feeble-mindedness', among others, leading some to conclude that criminality was a state of moral insanity, a disease requiring medical diagnosis and treatment.

The growth of private asylums in the eighteenth century led to the development of a new scientific specialism, which was at first termed alienism (that is, it addressed alienated minds) and later came to be known as morbid psychology, then psychiatry. Many superintendents of these asylums also wrote about their patients, producing an 'extensive scientific literature concerned with the description of different mental types, case histories and causal analyses' of how madness developed, which in turn gave rise to a 'new kind of empirical psychology, concentrating upon pathological cases and their rational management' (Garland, 2002:22). A particular concern lay with those offenders who seemed incapable of controlling themselves, repeatedly engaging in violent and dangerous behaviour, often without remorse – suggesting that criminality was rooted in the brain. Moral insanity was understood from within a range of biological conditions rather than as a social problem (Rafter, 2009:xviii). It was this practical experience of managing psychiatric disorders from within institutional settings that was to be a defining feature of British criminology. Here a distinctive 'medico-legal science' developed among prison doctors and psychiatrists that in some ways was 'Lombrosian before Lombroso', but in others careful distinctions were made between the 'wilful' criminal and 'the diseased', emphasizing from the 1860s onwards that for some prison medics 'only a minority of criminals were in any sense mentally abnormal' (Garland, 1988:4). In doing so medical expertise dominated much of the scientific thinking on crime in Britain and much of it was written from within the penal establishment for well into the twentieth century.

The focus on moral insanity in the nineteenth century also informed discussion of habitual criminals, that is, those repeat offenders who appeared to be incorrigible and unable to reform. Once these ideas became bound up with Darwin's theory of evolution in the 1860s they gave a powerful impetus to claims that criminality was caused by hereditary degeneracy. J. Bruce Thompson (1870/2009:95), the resident surgeon at the General Prison for Scotland, was one of the leading proponents of such a view, arguing that criminals are 'moral imbeciles' and constitute a lesser breed, lower down the evolutionary ladder rendering them prey to baser instincts. The concept of degeneration shaped thinking about crime, as well as alcoholism, disability, madness, poverty, and so forth, which were all said to arise from the same hereditary condition – passing from one generation to the next, in any number of forms, and thereby paving the way for eugenics later in the nineteenth century, a movement organized around extinguishing intractable social problems through preventing degenerates from reproducing unfit offspring. Steeped in the prevailing assumptions of scientific racism, which maintained that white Europeans are the most evolved and superior race, the concept implied that criminal characteristics were not only inherited but could also be visibly identified by various signs indicating mental, moral, and physical inferiority. Such themes anticipate Cesare Lombroso's criminal anthropology, which helped to establish a specialist 'science of the criminal' that achieved much fame and notoriety in the closing decades of the nineteenth century.

An Italian physician and psychiatrist, Lombroso is widely regarded as the founder of modern criminology, and his ideas are set out in his 1876 book *L'uomo delinquente* (The Criminal Man). In this study, he observed the physical characteristics of Italian prisoners and compared them to Italian soldiers in an effort to identify different racial types and concluded that many criminals (not all) were atavistic throwbacks to an earlier form of evolution. These stigmata could be found in all kinds of anomalies present in the body: low foreheads, prominent jaws, protruding ears, excessive hairiness, and unusually long arms that, taken together, cause them to resemble the ape-like ancestors of human beings. Accordingly, the born criminal could be recognized through the reappearance of physical and mental characteristics associated with more primitive stages of development. Over time, and in the face of criticism, he refined his theory on the atavistic nature of criminality as he and his associates developed the Italian *scuola positiva* (Positive School) of criminology. The school attracted followers from across Europe and the United States who saw themselves as pioneering a new, positivist knowledge of offenders based on empirical observation and inductive reasoning. The focus lay on the individual criminal, and the particular factors that distinguished offenders from normal, upright citizens.

Although these ideas were very influential and inspired major international congresses, rival national schools of thought (the French remained more sociologically inclined and rejected the biological determinism of Italian positivism), and specialist academic journals, their impact in Britain was modest at best. Here the medico-legal tradition was, by the 1890s, fairly conservative and typically sceptical of Lombrosian ideas, where leading psychiatric figures publicly denounced the 'puerilities of criminal anthropology' and the 'lamentable extravagances' of this new thinking (cited in Garland, 2002:31). Nevertheless, attempts were made to introduce and promote Continental ideas in Britain. Among the most important was Havelock Ellis who published in 1890 *The Criminal*, which accessibly distilled the major ideas of criminal anthropology for the first time in English, and became the key source for British and American readers wanting to learn about the new science. Most practitioners sought to distance themselves from what they regarded as the sweeping generalizations of the Lombrosian tradition, so that the book was greeted with a 'professional scepticism, based not on anti-scientism but upon a rather different scientific tradition – one which was more modest, more acceptable to the institutional authorities' (Garland, 1988:6). It was this pragmatic, medico-legal approach that predominated in Britain for much of the nineteenth century and well into the mid twentieth century.

An important exception is Charles Goring's (1913) *The English Convict: A Statistical Study*, which while rooted in eugenic assumptions was strongly opposed to the Lombrosian anatomical method of impressionistically identifying the various bases of born criminality. Instead, Goring favoured statistical methods and was indebted to Quételet's understanding of 'social mechanics', which could only be revealed through the rigorous analysis of large, carefully collected data sets. From the outset Goring maintained that the criminal did not differ dramatically from the honest citizen, but was rather a variant of the normal, distinguished by the degree to which they inherited certain characteristics. Having dismissed Lombroso's born criminal, Goring eagerly promotes eugenic forms of explanation – concluding that the 'criminal of English prisons is markedly differentiated by defective physique ... by defective mental capacity ... and by an increased possession of willful anti-social proclivities' (Goring, 1913:370).

Instead of Lombroso's atavistic criminal, Goring presents a convict born with inferior stature and low intelligence, leading him to a series of eugenic proposals to reduce crime: segregating the 'unfit' and regulating the 'reproduction of those constitutional qualities – feeblemindedness, inebriety, epilepsy, deficient social instinct, insanity, which conduce to the committing of crime' (Goring, 1913:33). As a number of commentators have noted, members of the penal establishment were critical, not least since the deterministic implications challenged the pragmatic orthodoxy organized around the moral reformation of individual offenders. The Prison Commissioner even warned in his preface to the book that Goring's general theory of defectiveness should not be pushed too far as punishment must remain individualized and based on medico-legal assessments. Ultimately it would be Goring's argument for the superiority of statistical methods and mass data collection that would have the lasting criminological importance. Nevertheless, the debates surrounding the book on publication highlight the degree to which mainstream thinking at this time was dominated by clinical knowledge, which stressed the importance of diagnosing, classifying, and treating individual offenders. For the first few decades of the twentieth century the major studies of crime in Britain were written by doctors, with psychiatric training, holding positions within the prison service.

The first university lectures in 'criminology' delivered in Britain were given to postgraduate medical students in Birmingham by Maurice Hamblin Smith in 1921, in a course entitled 'Medical Aspects of Crime and Punishment' (Garland, 2002:32). Smith was the first to claim the title 'criminologist' and while he was a psychiatrically trained prison medic, he was also an early advocate of Freudian psychoanalysis arguing that the identification of mental conflicts changed the whole course of treatment, making 'every offender a problem to be investigated' (Valiér, 1995:4). Despite official objections to psychoanalysis, there were more enthusiastic proponents outside establishment circles, including the Institute for the Scientific Treatment of Delinquency (ISTD) formed in 1932, which focused on the exploration of individual personalities in clinical settings.

The opening of private clinics, such as the Tavistock (1921), the Maudsley (1923), and the ISTD's own Psychopathic Clinic (1933, later renamed the Portman Clinic, 1937) enabled a new criminological approach to develop that was more preventative in emphasis and operated at a distance from the formal penal system. Crucial in this regard was the spread of child guidance centres, set up in the interwar years as clinics where children exhibiting behavioural and personality disorders could be taken for expert advice and assessment; they became important sites for the discussion of psychoanalytical ideas in relation to juvenile delinquency. Most referrals were from educational sources,[5] and most of the children treated 'were perceived as essentially normal, but having unhappy relationships characterised by anxiety and fear' (Valiér, 1995:6). It is in this context that Cyril Burt's (1925) study of *The Young Delinquent* was formed.[6] Widely regarded as the first recognizably modern criminological work in Britain, it draws together the statistical expertise of Goring with the more clinical experience of Hamblin Smith, but, written for a general audience, it established a model of research that British criminology long remained wedded to: eclectic, multidisciplinary, opposed to single theories, bound up with the penal politics of the day, grounded in the clinical study of individuals, and dedicated to a reformist mission.

Into the British University

Before criminology became a university-based subject in Britain it was regarded as a minor, applied medical specialism practised by a few enthusiasts working in either the penal system or the network of clinics and hospitals that surrounded it. The sociology of deviance, as conceived by Durkheim at the turn of the twentieth century, or as subsequently flourished in Chicago during the 1920s and 1930s barely registered here, and is discussed in the next chapter. Also missing was the 'radicalism of foreign criminologists such as Enrico Ferri and Willem Bonger' and in so far as radical analyses did develop in Britain over this time it was Sigmund Freud, rather than Karl Marx, who provided the inspiration (Garland, 2002:38). What was to prove decisive to the formation of criminology as a professional academic discipline in Britain was the flight of intellectuals from Nazi Europe in the 1930s. The arrival of three outstanding legally trained émigré criminologists at three elite universities introduced almost overnight the criminology that had been advancing separately in Continental universities, and this would dominate for the next few decades.

The appointment of Leon Radzinowicz at the University of Cambridge in 1941 would lead him to establish the first Institute of Criminology in a British university in 1959; Max Grünhut at the University of Oxford in 1940 laid the foundations for a research unit that later became the Oxford Centre for Criminological Research in 1973; and Hermann Mannheim at the London School of Economics (LSE) from 1935 up to his retirement in 1955 pioneered the teaching of the new discipline to undergraduate and postgraduate students alike. Just a generation ago Terence Morris (1988:25) could write of Mannheim that 'there is scarcely a professional criminologist in Britain today who was not either taught by him or taught by someone else who was'. Despite important differences between each, they were pivotal figures transforming criminology into a discipline worthy of government funding (Hood, 2004). Something of the broad, eclectic, and multidisciplinary disposition of the new subject can be gleaned from the following summary of Mannheim's course on the 'Principles of Criminology' taught at the LSE in the 1930s:

> I. The use of Criminal Statistics. History and present character of crime in England and abroad. II. The criminal types and the causes of crime: (1) Physical factors. The anthropological theory (Lombroso). The biological theory. The significance of physical defects. (2) Psychological and pathological factors. The intelligence of the criminal. Insanity and mental deficiency. The psychoanalytical explanation ... (3) Alcoholism. Climate. Race and Religion. (4) The age factor ... (5) The sex factor: Female delinquency and prostitution. (6) Social and Economic factors: Family, broken homes, housing, delinquency areas ... The gang. Profession and unemployment. Poverty. Economic and political crises.
>
> (cited in Rock, 2012:42)

Clearly the 'social' dimension of crime is understood as one set of factors among many others, and when the question has been posed as to why the criminologists of this period appeared to show little interest in the sociology of deviance the following explanation has been given:

> The answer is simple. People were perfectly aware that there were problems about the boundary between criminality and deviance but these were not of immediate concern. The position of sociology itself was not strong. In 1948 the University of London had two Professors – Ginsberg and Marshall, and Marshall was not a member of the sociology department. David Glass was given a personal Chair in 1949. LSE, moreover, was virtually the only place in the country where sociology was taught on a large scale. Then, as later, the department was split between the theoreticians led by Ginsberg and the empiricists led by Glass. Most of the latter were involved in the classic studies of social mobility then under way. Only Mannheim kept an interest in empirical criminology alive ... The intellectual concerns of criminology at the end of the 1940s were dominated by two major themes: capital punishment and psychoanalysis.
>
> (Martin, 1988:38)

There are a number of important points to be taken from this passage. The first is that sociology, as an independent academic discipline, hardly existed. Although there are competing explanations as to why academic sociology failed to develop and expand along the lines of the American, German, or French experiences between 1880 and 1920, it is clear that British universities continued to ignore the academic claims of sociology between the wars. The dominance of the LSE was reinforced by the system of London external degrees 'which carried the LSE definition of the sociology syllabus to the dependent provincial university colleges of Southampton, Nottingham, Leicester, Exeter and Hull' (Halsey, 2004:56). It was only in the 1950s, when these and other colleges were granted independent charters that different approaches began to develop alongside the introduction of new sociology departments at the civic universities of Birmingham, Liverpool, Leeds, and Manchester.

Secondly, the passage identifies the major preoccupations animating criminology. Capital punishment was the defining political issue of the era – the Royal Commission on Capital Punishment, which was set up and worked from 1949 to 1953 was the first Royal Commission on a criminological topic that included a criminologist, Radzinowicz, among its members. Legislation that would eventually lead to the abolition of capital punishment was introduced in 1965. It was not until 1969, at the time of the final debate on abolition in Parliament, that Radzinowicz headed the list of signatories of a letter sent to *The Times* supporting abolition, 'which included the name of every academic criminologist in Britain, save one' (Morris, 1988:32). The other main issue is the extent to which psychoanalysis dominated the 'treatment' of juvenile delinquency. A particularly influential approach was the 'maternal deprivation hypothesis', which maintained that early childhood separations from mothers and mother figures can have damaging effects on a child's mental health and personality development. The assumptions and prejudices informing mother blaming, and other ideas such as 'problem families' that commanded an enormous amount of attention at the time, were subjected to withering critique by Barbara Wootton (1959) in her major assault on the medicalization of social distress.

During the 1950s the new discipline began to take academic shape. A key factor aiding the emergence of criminology as an autonomous subject was the founding of Britain's first specialist academic journal by the ISTD in 1950. The *British Journal of Delinquency* claimed from the outset that it would be a multidisciplinary journal, despite retaining a strong clinical focus (two of the three editors were leading psychiatrists). Controversy over the title eventually led to the name being changed in 1960 to the *British Journal of Criminology*.[7] The British Society of Criminology grew out of another offshoot of the ISTD: the 'scientific group' formed in 1953 as a space where those unhappy with the dominance of psychiatry and psychoanalysis could meet. By the late 1950s they had successfully formed a separate society in an effort to further develop the academic, rather than clinical, focus of their activities.

Over this time the British government began to fund criminological research, giving official and financial backing, thereby further enhancing criminology's scientific status as an academic specialism. Not only did the Home Office establish their own in-house Home Office Research Unit in 1957, but influential government officials and ministers were also key in setting up the Cambridge Institute of Criminology at the elite university in 1959, under the formidable direction of Radzinowicz. Significantly, this figure maintained that criminology could only develop by taking an interdisciplinary approach, and ideally this would involve: 'A psychiatrist, a social psychologist, a penologist, a lawyer, a statistician joining together on a combined research operation' (Radzinowicz, 1961:177). That this list still contained no mention of sociology should not be surprising in the British context, as sociologists of this era remained largely uninterested in crime and deviance, despite the remarkable expansion of the discipline in universities during the 1950s and 1960s.

Sociological Indifference

The reasons for this sociological indifference are complex, and I will try to unravel them in this and the next chapter, but there is much truth in Raymond Aron's assessment of the then state of the discipline: 'The trouble is that British sociology is essentially an attempt to make intellectual sense of the political problems of the Labour Party' (cited in Halsey, 1985:151). Sociologists of the boom period continued to be preoccupied with the consequences, limitations, and failures of the welfare state, where the pragmatism of the Fabian Society characterized much of the thinking. Fabian principles favoured gradual reform over revolutionary change and here sociology was essentially concerned with the constraints social stratification imposed on social mobility and the enduring inequalities produced by the British class structure. In such circumstances crime and deviance were regarded as somewhat peripheral to mainstream sociology and the criminological work that was being produced was unlikely to attract much interest, dominated as it still was by psychoanalysts, psychiatrists, and psychologists rooted in a tradition of predicting delinquency or dedicated to humanitarian penal reform. This field would never look quite the same again once Barbara Wootton's (1959) *Social Science and Social Pathology* had ploughed through the terrain, debunking the myths of value-free social science and demolishing the pretensions to expertise of the medical, psychiatric, and social work professions colonizing how anti-social behaviour was understood.

The book was a major review of the social sciences, funded by the Nuffield Foundation over a five-year period, and was immediately controversial. The rise of psychiatry, Wootton observed, had led more people to be diagnosed as mentally ill, and while some of this labelling undoubtedly had beneficial effects, it also ignored the social causes of mental and social distress. In this her analysis anticipated the anti-psychiatry movements of the 1960s and echoed themes then being developed by Thomas Szasz that attributions of mental illness, like deviance in general, involve moral and political judgements too often disguised by psychiatric labels. Neither denied the pain, discomfort, or distress associated with mental illness, but insisted that it was a serious mistake to classify many psychological conditions and problems as a form of illness. In a similar vein Wootton exposed the dangers of the criminological tradition that had devoted itself to predicting delinquency and exposed how notions like the 'problem family' were irrevocably linked to eugenic class prejudice. The chapter on social work argued that many acted like amateur psychotherapists, trying to discover the personality conflicts of their clients, and it is here she quips that the best way for the social worker to understand her client is to marry him (Wootton, 1959:273).

On publication the book provoked defensive reactions from the professions demolished across 400 pages of text, yet was also greeted as a 'blistering' and 'exhilarating' achievement that 'laid bare the general poverty of criminology, showing it to be a set of rusty clichés and sloppy generalizations' (Downes, 1986:196). Although these words were written much later, David Downes is recalling his own initial response to the book, when he was just starting his own sociological career in 1959. Other commentators on Wootton have noted how all 'this was done in a very pragmatic way drawing on both her own experience as a juvenile court magistrate and on the sceptical traditions of the English empirical philosophers', while the 'use of the term Social Pathology' in the title was an 'attempt to both use a medical term and, at the same time, appropriate it for adoption in a sociological context' (Martin, 1988:42). By attempting to situate criminal conduct in a broader social setting, the clear implication was that many social problems were produced by cultural conflicts in highly differentiated societies and in this the book can be regarded as a forerunner of much that followed.

While it is fair to say that before 1965 there was virtually no British sociological work on crime and deviance, it is important to recognize the contribution of Terrence Morris, who played a significant role introducing American approaches that would later be reworked and transformed by sociologists in and around the National Deviancy Conference. In his study of crime and delinquency in Croydon, a large town in South London, published as *The Criminal Area* (1957), he carefully situated the work in a long tradition of such area studies – stretching back to the nineteenth century and included Guerry, Quételet, and Mayhew among the precursors to his own research. In addition, he set his empirical work in a wide-ranging review of the ecological studies developed by the Chicago School and thereby initiated the rich tradition of distilling North American sociology in distinctively British settings. This is a theme that would last well into the 1970s, only to be partly displaced by a revival of interest in European critical theory. In collaboration with his wife, Pauline, the Morrises (1963) also produced the first home-grown sociology of prison life and introduced to the field concepts, debates, and methods from Donald Clemmer, Gresham Sykes, and Erving Goffman that remain pivotal to this day.

Alongside Morris, David Downes (1966) influentially examined the applicability of US subcultural theory to working-class youth growing up in East London in the early 1960s. Importantly, he found that concepts such as 'status frustration', 'alienation', and 'delinquent subculture' did not readily capture how the boys responded to their situation – they neither envied middle-class lives, nor resented them. Instead, they dissociated themselves from the middle class-dominated worlds of school and work. Leisure provided a collective solution to their problems of experiencing rising expectations, yet remaining socially disadvantaged at a time of post-war affluence. Discontent did arise when their attempts to enjoy leisure were hindered, and their offences were then typically hedonistic, revolving around drinking, fighting, joy-riding, and vandalism. Downes (1988:46) has later explained how this 'attentiveness' to American debates 'reflected the marginality of sociology to the criminological tradition in Britain'. Once the expansion of higher education was well underway in the 1960s, sociology was one of the main beneficiaries, with 28 new university departments of sociology created and accompanied by 'a feverish expansion of staffing' throughout the decade (Halsey, 1985:152). This new generation was becoming increasingly disillusioned with the medico-legal character of much British criminology, while the sociological profession itself remained largely uninterested in questions of crime and deviance.

The prevailing attitudes and climate are nicely conveyed by Stan Cohen, when he describes how those sociologists who were attracted to the margins, themselves were often isolated in the new departments and unhappy with:

the apparent attempt to define criminology as a self-contained discipline that, in Britain, was being dominated by forensic psychiatrists, clinical psychologists, and criminal lawyers. In terms of having congenial people to discuss our work with, we found some of our sociological colleagues equally unhelpful. They were either mandarins who were hostile toward a committed sociology and found subjects such as delinquency nasty, distasteful, or simply boring, or else self-proclaimed radicals whose political interests went only so far as their own definition of 'political' and who were happy to consign deviants to social welfare or psychiatry. For different reasons, both groups found our subject matter too messy and devoid of significance. They shared with official criminology a depersonalized, dehumanized picture of the deviant: he was simply part of the waste products of the system, the reject from the conveyer belt.

(Cohen, 1971/1988:39)

Under these circumstances it is not at all surprising that the American sociology of deviance tradition proved attractive. Two strands were particularly influential: labelling theory, associated with Howard Becker, Edwin Lemert, and Erving Goffman; and subcultural theory, as developed by Albert Cohen, David Matza, and Gresham Sykes. Although the concept of deviance was initially developed by Émile Durkheim in late-nineteenth-century France, where he radically argued that crime and punishment were inevitable properties of any social order, it was in twentieth-century American sociology that these ideas would flourish, as we will see in the next chapter.

3

Sociological Traditions

In Britain the close relationship between criminology and sociology only really emerged in the 1960s, with the establishment of a university system that was particularly receptive to the new discipline of sociology. Up until this point criminology was largely the terrain of forensic psychiatrists, clinical psychologists, and criminal lawyers. Although biological theories dominated in the late nineteenth century and the eugenics movement was especially prominent from the 1900s to 1930s, it is important to note that a strong form of sociological thinking was also developing elsewhere that would decisively challenge the assumptions of these approaches. As we have seen, earlier sociological forms of explanation sought to identify the social forces determining individual offending, but the crucial intervention lay with Émile Durkheim's break with 'analytical individualism' (Taylor et al., 1973:67). This critique of utilitarian political philosophy, which lay at the heart of classical liberal thinking, also undermined the reductionism of psychological and biological understandings of human conduct. And it is here we begin, for these ideas were crucial to the development of an American sociology of deviance tradition, which in turn was decisive for the later break with the medico-legal formulation of criminology that will be described in what follows.

Durkheim and Chicago

Now regarded as one of the 'founding fathers' of sociology, Durkheim's (1895/1966) *Rules of Sociological Method* is a defining statement of the new science he pioneered. Indeed, he was pivotal in establishing it as an institutionalized discipline in France and founding one of the first international journals in the field, *L'Année sociologique*, in 1898, gathering around him, initially in Bordeaux and later at the Sorbonne, an influential circle of collaborators and students. His earliest significant work, *The Division of Labour* (Durkheim, 1893/1960), argued that societies evolve from a simple form, held together by a mechanical solidarity where there is very little specialization of work tasks, to more complex societies where individuals are allocated different social roles and this gives rise to a specifically modern form of organic solidarity through differentiated patterns of mutual dependency. Although he does not offer a very sophisticated account of social change in the book – Durkheim suggests the evolution from mechanical to organic solidarity is explained largely through population growth and density – he does introduce an understanding of punishment as a key dynamic of society's moral order. These are arguments we shall return to in more detail in later chapters in the book, but his insistence that crimes are unsettling because they disturb the collective consciousness (*conscience collective*) is highly significant. Firmly rooted in French intellectual traditions Durkheim was a social theorist who, more than any other, placed crime, law, and punishment at the centre of the sociological enterprise. Indeed, the concept of deviance is born in his writing and is fundamental to understanding how societies work. Ever since, there has been considerable debate over the significance of these ideas, with some depicting Durkheim as a conservative figure interested only in social stability and moral consensus, while others highlight a radical socialist vision in his efforts to identify more just economic relations (Pearce, 1989).

These different interpretations are partly explained by shifts in his thinking, from the early attempts to establish sociology as a positivist science of moral life to the later intellectual positions confronting the dilemmas of modernity, but also arise from the unresolved tensions that run through his work. The ambiguous, yet radical character of his approach is captured in his still striking delineation of crime as a 'social' rather than a purely 'biological' or 'psychological' phenomenon in *The Rules of Sociological Method*. In this book he develops his famous argument on the nature of social facts as things which have an objective reality and exist independently of individual consciousness. Borrowing an analogy from biology he depicts society as a complex organism, capable of experiencing both health and sickness, so that the fundamental task of 'all sciences of life, whether individual or social, is in the end to define and explain the normal state and to distinguish it from its opposite' (Durkheim, 1895/1966:74). Although drawing an analogy between organisms and society, he is clear that sociology must be distinguished from biology, and his fundamental point is that society is more than the sum of the individuals who compose it. Studying individuals alone (as biologists and psychologists do) can never grasp the essence of human experience.

According to Durkheim (1895/1966:65) crime may appear 'pathological', but it is in fact a 'normal' feature of social life, as there 'is no society that is not confronted with the problem of criminality'. Even a society composed only of saints will eventually criminalize some actions or attitudes. Here 'faults that appear venial to the layman will create the same scandal that the ordinary offence does in ordinary consciousness' (ibid.:67). So, for example, bad taste, which might only be frowned upon in 'ordinary' societies, would be strictly punished in such a holy order. Moreover, crime performs a 'necessary' and 'integrative part in all healthy societies', suggesting there is nothing abnormal about deviance. Since there is no society where individuals do not differ from collective norms, it is also inevitable that there will be those who appear with a 'criminal character'. This criminal character is not the consequence of intrinsic criminogenic personality traits, though some may well be mad or bad, but results from the importance attributed to these 'divergences' by the 'collective conscience' (ibid.:70). Durkheim is clearly arguing that deviance is as much the creation of social perceptions as of an objective reality, and this heralds a decisive break with the understanding of deviation as statistically normal (as in the 'social physics' of Quételet) towards one which recognizes cultural differences. It is remarkable that the implications of these arguments would only fully register in Britain in the 1960s, having become increasingly central to American sociology from the 1930s onwards.

Indeed, it is from the old to the new world that we must now turn to track developments and where the Durkheimian legacy has been especially pronounced. North American sociology emerged out of a large and diverse assortment of non-academic reform organizations and philanthropic movements seeking to reduce 'dependency' while advancing 'progressive' causes in the late nineteenth and early twentieth centuries. In this initial phase of the discipline's development an uneasy mix of Christian evangelicalism, social Darwinism, and eugenic thought was drawn upon. One of the significant achievements of what came to be known as the 'Chicago School' of sociology lay in rejecting these early ideas and then dominating the field for the first four decades of the twentieth century, playing a pivotal role in professionalizing and institutionalizing the fledgling discipline. Indeed, it has been said that during this time 'the history of sociology in America can largely be written as the history of the Department of Sociology at the University of Chicago' (Coser, 1978:311). While the importance of Chicago in the history of sociology is rarely challenged, there remains considerable debate over whether it should be characterized as a unified school. Certainly, many of the leading figures had little suspicion they had much – if anything – in common, and it was only by the 1950s that it became retrospectively described by commentators as a school.

In fact, it is the sheer diversity and vitality of studies produced by the Chicagoans that command attention. They include investigations of migration patterns, racial conflict, organized crime, prostitution, real-estate offices, ghettos, local newspapers, motion pictures, hobos, dance halls, intermarriage, the central business district, hotel life, mental illness, chain stores, high society, vice districts, juvenile delinquency, mass transit systems, and much more besides. It is hard to disagree with the view that Chicago in the 1920s is the most studied city of all time. Beginning with Jane Addams and the Hull House research, which extensively mapped the social structure of the city – a method borrowed from Booth's poverty surveys in London and later adopted by the Chicago sociologists as they researched every aspect of urban life. In his collection of writings on the 'Chicago School' Ken Plummer (1997) highlights the importance of Jane Addams and the extraordinary intellectual exchanges at Hull House in the 1890s. These are often left out of the Chicago story but evidently predate and establish the urban interests of the early male sociologists through a distinctive feminist pragmatism, which united liberal values with a cooperative, nurturing understanding of how education and democracy can improve society (Deegan, 1988). A campaigner for the Progressive Party, and then part of a broad liberal reform movement composed primarily of the professional middle classes, such as lawyers, doctors, and teachers, she was critical of the human costs associated with America's rapid industrialization and urbanization. The rise of the social sciences in American universities at this time is part of this movement, as they were seen as a means of alleviating social problems, but tensions quickly arose between those advocating reform and those striving for scholarly objectivity (Turner, 2014).

Chicago itself was an extraordinary city. A modern metropolis exploding with new populations, producing a kaleidoscope of differing social worlds, fuelled by mass migration from all over Europe and the southern states of America. It had grown from a small town of just a few hundred people in the 1830s to over 3 million in the 1930s and became the second largest industrial metropolis in the country. This phenomenal growth brought with it all the signs of modernity – from skyscrapers, dance crazes, movies, and cars through to alcoholism, bootlegging, crime, prostitution, and all the grim realities of urban poverty. It is no surprise then that the study of urbanism is indelibly associated with the Chicago sociologists, but aside from this striking geographical context, the university itself was born from a gift of over $35 million dollars from Rockefeller in 1890 to establish an unrivalled private university. Based on the research seminar tradition of the German university, its first president energetically poached leading thinkers from other institutions, by doubling their salaries, and formed a number of departments almost from scratch. Alongside sociology new departments of architecture, art, economics, and philosophy were also created, bringing a dynamism and innovation to their subjects, and all accompanied by generous research funding.

A key influence on the sociology developing at Chicago was the work of Georg Simmel and his interest in developing a formal sociology of how humans impose form and meaning on the world of experience, while weaving complex webs of interaction. His essay 'The Metropolis and Mental Life' (1903/1950) is among his most well-known pieces, exploring how modern urban social relations shape distinctive personality traits. Robert Park, who led the department of sociology through its heyday, had previously studied with Simmel in Germany and this experience provided him with many of his core ideas. A former newspaper journalist and drama critic Park famously encouraged his students and colleagues to 'tell it like it is' through fieldwork 'out there' on the streets (cited in Sumner, 1994:42). From Park's (1915) defining statement on 'The City' the Chicagoans understood the city as an ordered mosaic of distinctive regions, including industrial districts, ethnic enclaves, and criminal areas. These so-called natural areas evolved in relation to one another to form an urban ecology. Research on juvenile delinquency revealed how certain parts of the city are more crime-prone, irrespective of which ethnic group lived there, and that as these groups moved to other areas their crime rates decreased (Shaw and McKay, 1931). This important finding challenged the then dominant psychological explanations of deviance, which held that crime resulted from individual pathologies and personality defects.

The conclusion that slums had their own social structures and cultural norms, which gave deviant lifestyles validity and normalized criminal activity in gangs, was seen as a response to the more general social disorganization accompanying rapid urban growth. Park (1925) insisted that delinquency resulted from the breakdown of neighbourhood cohesion and the inability of community organizations to integrate adolescents into the wider social order. These themes were developed in a number of studies exploring transitional areas, where these problems were especially pronounced. Frederic Thrasher's (1927) study of *The Gang* maintained they originated in small, informal play groups, with an internal structure and shared traditions passed on from one generation of boys to the next. Conflicts with other gangs and adults was only one type of activity associated with the gangs; they were also athletic clubs and secret societies, as well as having links with local politics and organized crime. Likewise, John Landesco's (1929/1968) account of *Organized Crime in Chicago* explored how racketeers and hustlers became popular heroes in their neighbourhoods, offering thrilling possibilities of escape from the misery of the slums. By describing how the lifestyle offered a 'world where pilfering, vandalism, sex delinquency and brutality are an inseparable part of his play life' (Landesco, 1929/1968:207) the suggestion was that such violations are learned and provide a framework for coping in the hostile struggle for urban existence.

The idea that delinquency was the outcome of ordinary interactions, passed on in particular learning situations and rationalized criminal conduct, was initially proposed by Edwin Sutherland in 1924 in his theory of 'differential association', which highlighted how deviant values are culturally transmitted in social groups. In the decades that followed, he and his students forcefully developed the theory and extended it to 'white-collar crime', revealing how business practices could generate violations of trust and could be found in every occupation. His 'discovery' of 'white-collar crime' (a term he coined) was part of a broader ambition to develop a 'general' theory of crime, insisting that criminal behaviour did not just arise among the poor and disadvantaged, but was to be found across the social structure and in the highest reaches of society. It was especially abundant in what Al Capone called 'the legitimate rackets' (cited in Sutherland, 1940:3) of the corporate world and professional classes. Sutherland's work provided one bridge from the early Chicagoans to the subcultural theory that would become prominent in the 1950s; another is to be found in the sociology of Robert Merton. His thinking was steeped in the classical European tradition of the nineteenth century, which he innovatively fused and enlarged to address contemporary concerns. This is exemplified in his famous essay on 'Social Structure and Anomie' (Merton, 1938) that became one of the most influential essays in American sociology, not least since it highlighted how deviance and crime were rooted in the class structure of society.

Strain, Subculture, and Labelling

Drawing from the traditions established by both Durkheim and Marx, Merton's 'strain theory' of criminal behaviour emphasized the importance of 'structural frustration' in the specific context of American culture between the wars. For Merton the defining characteristic of the post-Depression 1930s was the malaise produced by the tension between the American Dream (based on an egalitarian ideology that anyone can make it, with enough hard work) and the actual reality of extreme economic inequality (where there are only limited legitimate opportunities for achieving the kind of material success that is so culturally exalted). Merton's central thesis is that the disjuncture between culture (the values placed on symbols of success, which are inevitably monetary) and structure (only a few had the means to acquire such prosperity) gives rise to a 'malintegration' at the core of American society (Merton, 1938:673). In developing his argument Merton reworks the concept of anomie – which in Durkheim's (1897/1966) original formulation referred to a lack of normative regulation and an exceptional condition of normlessness, where desires and ambitions run out of control – to describe various forms of deviant conduct generated in the United States. For Merton there were four very different individual responses to such structural strain: 'innovation', 'ritualism', 'retreatism', and 'rebellion' – each depending on the wider context. As he put it, 'Capone represents the triumph of amoral intelligence over morally prescribed "failure" when the channels of vertical mobility are closed or narrowed *in a society which places a high premium on economic affluence and social ascent for* all *its members*' (Merton, 1938:679–80, emphasis in original).

Some maintain that Merton has shifted the meaning of anomie away from the radical implications of the term as used by Durkheim, but there is a very clear sense in which he grounds his analysis in a more Marxist understanding of social contradictions and the commodity fetishism American society produces. In particular, he was keenly aware of the power of advertising and the role of conspicuous consumption in sustaining an intense, competitive pressure on people to keep acquiring status symbols. Merton wrote the paper early in his career at Harvard, where he worked with Talcott Parsons, and both were key figures in promoting a functionalist school of sociology that thrived in the United States from the 1930s to the late 1960s. Significantly, Merton was quite hostile to Parsons' abstract way of theorizing, preferring instead what he later dubbed 'middle-range theory', and his essay on anomie can be seen as an exemplar of this approach. For much of this time the piece was widely accepted and highly regarded, and then from the early 1960s it began to be criticized as part of a broader movement against functionalism. Here the importance the perspective attached to stable social systems, dominant cultural goals, and deterministic role structures came under attack for its inability to explain social change, make sense of conflict, or offer teleological forms of explanation. Consequently, functionalism was tainted with an inherent conservative disposition, so that the concept of anomie was increasingly marginalized and regarded as somewhat dated. It was in the subcultural theory that the Mertonian legacy was to persist most influentially among many ardent followers.

One of these followers was Albert Cohen (1955), who had been taught by both Merton and Sutherland, and his study of *Delinquent Boys* has deservedly become a classic – not least since he maintained that all three of the leading sociological theories of juvenile delinquency had failed to adequately address its causes and had used concepts in largely circular fashion. In his reckoning the Chicago School had overemphasized the social disorganization found in zones of transition, where these areas were not so nearly deprived of community spirit as some had imagined. Merton was criticized for his instrumental understanding of deviant behaviour as a way of achieving culturally approved goals. Instead, Cohen (1955:35–36) argued not all crime was committed in pursuit of wealth; many delinquent gangs engaged in violence simply for 'the hell of it', so the motivations were primarily expressive. Likewise, Sutherland's theory of differential association had taken the existence of gangs for granted, ignoring why some juveniles join and others do not and failing to explain their origins – where they come from, why gang members do what they do, and why gangs persist in some places but not others. Cohen answered these questions through the concept of subculture, insisting that the social world of the juvenile delinquent provides an alternative means of acquiring recognition and respect among disadvantaged youth.

Although the term 'subculture' had been used by anthropologists since the 1870s, it is Cohen who is often credited as the first to systematically apply it to delinquency. For Cohen, subcultures typically borrow elements from the dominant culture, but rework them in distinctive ways. His understanding of culture is resolutely functionalist, in that it sees culture as a way of solving problems, but the emphasis is on the difference between a particular social group and the larger collectivity. The prefix 'sub' highlights the way the groups are subordinate, subversive, or subterranean, and thereby viewed as beneath, but still within a wider culture. Accordingly, the gang was defined as a subculture with a value system at odds with mainstream culture, distinguished by specialized vocabulary, shared beliefs, and distinctive fashions. Subcultures were then regarded as collective solutions to the structural problems posed by class location and the experience of anomie. Cohen pioneered the idea that boys became delinquent through a process of 'status frustration'. In schools especially, he noted that boys from deprived backgrounds often found it an alienating place as they were judged against prevailing middle-class standards (what he called the 'middle-class measuring rod').

Against these standards some children are doomed to fail, as their cultural differences have not prepared them for school life. In their frustration working-class boys invert the values of the school – achievement, hard work, planning for the future, and deferring gratification – and develop an exaggerated hostility towards them. Through a process of 'reaction formation' academic success is redefined and the vices of the middle classes become virtues in the working-class gang: hedonistic, malicious, disrespecting property, and instant pleasures are among the defining features of this milieu. Drawing on Merton he described three different responses working-class boys could adopt: the 'college boy solution' offers to the bright 'conformists' a way of achieving upward mobility; 'stable corner boys' are 'retreatists' who accept their inferior position and adjust to middle-class values without attaining them; while the 'delinquent subculture' is for the 'innovators' who invert the rules of respectable society and reject them. The book was written in the midst of post-war anxieties over urban gang delinquency and gave rise to a whole raft of studies in the 1950s and 1960s testing and modifying various elements of the theory in various metropolitan settings (Cloward and Ohlin, 1961; Short and Strodtbeck, 1967) as well as prison (Clemmer, 1958; Sykes, 1958).

An early critic was David Matza (1964, 1969) who in his account of delinquent drift provided some sense of the seductive, 'invitational edge' that transgression offers. He objects to the sharp distinction drawn between the criminal and the law-abiding, and forcefully argues that subcultural theorists are mistaken in seeing the relationship between the values embodied in delinquent subcultures and the conventional mainstream as set in opposition. There are many points of 'subterranean convergence', and conventional culture is often not quite as conventional as it is made out to be (Matza, 1964:36–37). It consists not only of ascetic puritanism, middle-class morality, the boy-scout oath, and so forth, but is also hedonistic, frivolous, and exciting, especially where toughness is equated with masculinity, as in cowboy frontier mentality, or the bohemian celebration of demi-monde excess. A key component of his theory of drift is that boys can commit delinquent acts when their commitment to the moral order is weakened, which is accomplished through 'techniques of neutralization' (Sykes and Matza, 1957) that operate to deflect disapproval from authority figures. The process of drift helps to explain the fluid, episodic character of much delinquency and why there is such an alluring pull to make things happen in a mundane world.

At the same time as this subcultural tradition was evolving a second approach was also developing – later described as 'neo-Chicagoan' by Matza (1969) and associated with a new, younger group of scholars who settled in the city in the late 1940s and early 1950s. They revived a commitment to immersive empirical research, in an effort to understand how social realities are constructed through meaningful interactions with others. The leading representatives include Howard Becker, Erving Goffman, and Joseph Gusfield, among others, who reworked the path opened up by George Herbert Mead a generation earlier. Mead had pioneered a distinctive type of social psychology at Chicago in the 1920s called 'symbolic interactionism' by his students, which emphasized process and interpersonal relations. He insisted that society and the self were mutually dependent and the product of dynamic, human-generated meanings and interconnected experiences. These insights formed the basis of a perspective that would provide a challenge to the functionalism then dominant in sociology, so that by the 1960s interactionist studies of deviance and social control were profoundly reshaping the field.

The central idea unsettling orthodox thinking was that deviance was not a property of the act committed, but is rather a category constructed in the course of interaction between the self and others. Howard Becker's (1963:9) famous studies of *Outsiders* popularized this approach by describing how deviance is a process created through the 'application by others of rules and sanctions to an "offender"'. This labelling process, as it soon became known, was by no means inevitable or irreversible as Edwin Lemert's (1951, 1967) influential distinction between 'primary' and 'secondary' deviation emphasized. Secondary deviation is more than simply a response to passing episodes of primary deviance. It is meant to describe the ways in which societal reaction (through stigma, punishment, myth, and so on) can shape crime or deviance by obliging offenders to reorganize their self-identity in accordance with the public symbols, designations, and interpretations of their conduct. Subsequent studies explored how drug use (Schur, 1963), homosexuality (Hooker, 1963), and mental illness (Goffman, 1962; Scheff, 1966) were constructed through labelling dynamics. Social problem construction also needs some form of individual and collective moral enterprise, and this pattern of discrediting certain classes of conduct was recognized by Becker (1963), while Joseph Gusfield's (1963) account of 'symbolic crusades' makes it central to his analysis.

Gusfield's discussion of the rise of the temperance movement in the United States in the nineteenth century, which resulted in national alcohol prohibition in 1919, reveals how the traditional middle classes viewed abstinence as a defence against their declining prestige and a form of status protest in response to the world changing around them. Kai Erikson's (1966) study of deviance in seventeenth-century Massachusetts was another key text. The Salem witch trials, he argues, resulted from deep crises within Puritan society so that the witchcraft threat was created by the community to provide an outside enemy against whom society could unite against as well as vividly demonstrating the shapes the devil could assume. Both Gusfield and Erikson crucially located deviance in broader social structures and community conflicts, rather than within specific individuals. This constructionist approach has been enormously influential and has led to intense debates between strict, contextual, and objectivist proponents of social problem formation (see Jenkins, 1992:1–3). Studies of labelling thus concentrated on social reaction, while subcultural theory focused on deviant action, and it was the fusion of these two American traditions that would transform British criminology.

The National Deviancy Conference

The 1960s was a watershed decade. It was an era when all kinds of established authority came to be challenged; from popular culture to civil rights, revolutionary upheaval was in the air and academic disciplines too experienced profound changes. When British sociologists began to study such topics as drug-taking, sexual proclivities, youth cultures, and mental illness, they found themselves 'doubly marginalized' (Downes, 1988:46) by both their own discipline and orthodox criminology. In his indispensable essay on the development of criminology and the sociology of deviance Stan Cohen recalls how a more radical approach to crime and deviance was conceived:

> In the middle of the 1960s, there were a number of young sociologists in Britain attracted to the then wholly American field in the sociology of deviance … Official criminology was regarded with attitudes ranging from ideological condemnation to a certain measure of boredom. But being a sociologist – often isolated in a small department – was not enough to get away from criminology; some sort of separate subculture had to be carved out within the sociological world. So, ostensibly for these reasons (though this account sounds suspiciously like colour-supplement history), seven of us met in 1968, fittingly enough in Cambridge in the middle of a Institute of Criminology conference opened by the Home Secretary. We decided to form a group to provide some sort of intellectual support for one another and to cope with collective problems of identity.
>
> (Cohen, 1981/1988:80)

The National Deviancy Conference (NDC) was thus formed as a breakaway faction and while there was no shared view of what it was for, it was very clear what it was against. This opposition enabled the remarkable flourishing of radical work that would have a lasting impact. It transformed the field into the site of exciting, formidable, and urgent political questions that remain central to critical criminology.

The seven founding members were Stan Cohen, Kit Carson, Mary McIntosh, David Downes, Jock Young, Paul Rock, and Ian Taylor, each of whom would go on to make major contributions to shaping sociological understandings of crime, deviance, and social control. One indication of the incredible intellectual ferment is that in the first five years of the NDC, from 1968 to 1973, there were 63 speakers from Britain at 14 conferences, who between them produced a little under 100 books on diverse topics (Young, 1998:16), ranging from the phenomenology of suicide to industrial sabotage, as well as a series of classic analyses of class and youth that are among the main legacies of the NDC. The initial aim was to establish a forum that would include not only academics, but also activists involved in militant social work, radical prisoners' groups, the anti-psychiatry movement, and campaigners against state violence. Soon conflict and division would characterize the group as tensions rose over the different directions critical work should take – but not before the approaches pioneered at the NDC became established and institutionalized themselves. By the time of the last conference in 1979 they had fractured along the same rifts of sociology more generally, acrimoniously disputing the merits of Marxist, feminist, and Foucauldian approaches then dominant. Ironically, this was just as Margaret Thatcher came to power with a radical right-wing government, which was intent on advancing a free market vision of society, where the pursuit of private gain becomes the organizing principle of all social relations, while successfully capturing the terrain of law and order politics for the coming decade.

It is also no accident that the NDC was born in that other tumultuous year of 1968, when revolutionary uprisings and street demonstrations helped forge a cultural utopian optimism among radical political movements. From the outset the group was a dynamic mix of anarchists, interactionists, Marxists, and phenomenologists committed to transforming the field of criminology from a science of social control into a struggle for social justice. Indeed, many would define themselves as anti-criminologists, so strong was the opposition to the establishment orthodoxy. Similar radical approaches were also developing across Europe, especially in Scandinavia, and in North America, most notably at the Berkeley School of Criminology at the University of California where the Union of Radical Criminologists was founded in 1971. Although the sociology of the NDC was at first quite derivative of American deviancy theory, there was also a strong New Left influence, especially from British socialist historians such as Perry Anderson, Eric Hobsbawm, Sheila Rowbotham, and E. P. Thompson, each of whom provided a 'history from below' and understood culture as a 'way of struggle' between classes.

While not sharing the entire thrust of Anderson's (1968) argument on English intellectual culture, Cohen (1981/1988) did find his diagnosis helpful in explaining why sociology in Britain showed such little interest in crime and deviance up to the late 1960s. This was partly owing to a distinctive parochialism characterizing much thinking, but also a fundamental failure to grasp what sociology is about. In Anderson's withering assessment the conservative, pragmatic, and individualistic traditions of British history have not produced a creative or critical intellectual elite:

> To this day, despite the recent belated growth of sociology as a formal discipline in England, the record of listless mediocrity and wizened provincialism is unrelieved. The subject is still largely a poor cousin of 'social work' and 'social administration', the dispirited descendants of Victorian charity.
>
> (Anderson, 1968:8)

According to Cohen (1981/1988:70), the weakness of sociology is overstated here, but he endorsed the accusation that not only is there lacking a tradition of revolutionary thought, but there is a lack of any major intellectual traditions at all – resulting in the 'amateur, muddling-along ethos of British life combined with the Fabian type of pragmatism' conspired to associate the study of crime and deviance with social work and humanitarian reform.

Since there was no indigenous classical sociology, that which did develop in the 1960s took two different directions. One sought intellectual credibility and aspired to fit 'scientific, academic, or professional self-images into which certain topics were not responsible enough to be fitted', while to the 'hard radicals ... deviants were not really politically interesting' (Cohen, 1981/1988:78). By the end of the decade, as sociology rapidly expanded in British universities, the 'great appeal of the NDC was not only to sociologists of crime in search of a congenial forum, but also to younger sociologists who saw in deviance an escape route from the positivist methods and functionalist orthodoxy of much British sociology' (Downes, 1988:47). It is clear then that for a new generation caught up in the heady political and cultural upheavals of the 1960s the NDC offered a genuinely emancipating setting for those committed to social justice.

Among the rich diversity of approaches, theories, and methods developed in and around the NDC the strand focusing on youth and class has proved to be especially influential. In both Stan Cohen (1972/2002) and Jock Young's (1971) work there was an emphasis on the much publicized conflicts between youth subcultures and establishment forces in the 1960s. Both were early formulators of the concept of moral panic. In Cohen's study the notion of deviancy amplification is used to explain how the petty delinquencies of rival groups of mods and rockers at seaside resorts were blown up into serious threats to law and order. Cohen goes to some length to situate the mediated moral panic over mods and rockers in a social context. In particular, the hostile reaction revealed much about how post-war social change was being experienced – the new affluence and sexual freedom of teenage youth cultures in the 1960s fuelled jealousy and resentment among a parental generation who had lived through hungry depression, world war, and subsequent austerity.

Likewise, Young's (1971) account of drug-taking in bohemian London details how the mass media transformed marijuana use into a social problem through lurid and sensationalist depictions of hippie lifestyles. Crucially, he notes how the high-pitched indignation contains a potent mix of fascination and repulsion, dread and desire that moral guardians exhibit towards the objects of their anxiety. There is a strong Durkheimian theme here, in that the boundaries of normality and order are reinforced through the condemnation of the deviant, but what Cohen (1972) and Young (1971) were both emphasizing was that this process only occurred in modernity through a considerable distortion of reality. It would be Stuart Hall and his colleagues at the Birmingham Centre for Contemporary Cultural Studies who went on to explain how the process of defining a social group as deviant was a result of political struggle and ideological coding. The collection *Resistance through Rituals* (Hall and Jefferson, 1975) brought together papers stressing the creativity of subcultures, as opposed to the wooden determinism of earlier American theorization, in a sophisticated understanding of class conflict. Here post-war youth cultures are seen as collective responses to the material conditions and problems the young, especially those from the working class, negotiate in their lived social realities of structural disadvantage. These, and other themes, are later developed in *Policing the Crisis* (Hall et al., 1978), which is perhaps the landmark text of the Centre, and I will return to it shortly as it develops an explicitly Marxist account of crime that was initially suggested in *The New Criminology* (Taylor et al., 1973).

It is worth pausing here to consider the achievements of *The New Criminology* in a little more detail, as it is arguably the most well-known and certainly the most controversial product of the NDC. Written by three sociologists, Ian Taylor, Paul Walton, and Jock Young, it was a major exercise in ground-clearing and succeeded in differentiating radical European analysis from the American study of deviance. Their method was one of 'immanent critique', which was to accept the main axioms of each major theoretical perspective and then expose its internal contradictions. In doing so it demolished the orthodox positions in criminology (especially of the positivist kind and the focus on individual or social pathology), sociology (here the target was the abstract empiricism of post-war British Fabianism and the mandarinism that accompanied it, as well as the functionalist, labelling, and subcultural traditions of American sociology), and Marxism (acknowledging that Marx himself paid hardly any systematic attention to crime, instead the critique concentrates on classical Marxist understandings of crime as a demoralized response of the 'dangerous classes' to their bleak economic situation). In effect all prior conceptions of crime and deviance were to be abandoned, to be replaced by their vision of a 'fully social theory of deviance' sketched out in the conclusion of the book.

The 'formal elements' of the theory are listed and involve 'a political economy of criminal action, and of the reaction it incites, and for a politically informed social psychology of these ongoing social dynamics' (Taylor et al., 1973:279). Few did attempt to completely deliver on the radical manifesto, but many were drawn into the collision with the latest developments in European Marxism that the book inspired. Much later Jock Young (1998:28) has conceded that 'by far the most complete expression of such an approach' is to be found in *Policing the Crisis* (Hall et al., 1978), not so much because the authors set out to rigorously follow their requirements, but rather because of the combination of deviancy theory with Marxist analysis. The book sets out to examine 'why and how the themes of *race, crime* and *youth* – condensed into the image of "mugging" – come to serve as the articulator of the crisis, as its ideological conductor' (Hall et al., 1978:viii, emphasis in original). It draws together the Birmingham Centre's work on youth subcultures, media representation, and ideological analysis in a magisterial account of the hegemonic crisis in Britain that began in the late 1960s and anticipates the victory of Margaret Thatcher's authoritarian 'law and order' programme in the 1980s. The book ostensibly explores the moral panic that developed in Britain in the early 1970s over the phenomenon of mugging. Hall and his colleagues demonstrate how the police, media, and judiciary interact to produce ideological closure around the issue, leading black youth to be cast as the folk devil in police and media portrayals of the archetypal mugger – a scapegoat for all social anxieties produced by the changes to an affluent, but destabilized society.

Taking Sides

Critics from all sides were quick to highlight some of the flaws involved in these radical directions. Socialists worried that the 'romanticism of crime, the recognition in the criminal of a rebel "alienated" from society is, for Marxism, a dangerous political ideology' (Hirst, 1975:218). Others felt that the failings of radical criminology exposed a much broader inability of the Left to produce any compelling solutions to the problems facing Britain (Mungham, 1980). Mainstream voices retorted that the radicals have ignored 'the large measure of consensus, even among the oppressed, in condemning the theft and violence that makes up the bulk of traditional crime' (Radzinowicz and King, 1979:87). Under these kinds of criticisms a bitter divide would come to split the Left during the 1980s and much of the 1990s along an 'idealist–realist' polarity. Left realists claimed a renewed commitment to social democratic principles and emphasized the need to take crime seriously. They insisted that the left idealists regarded 'the war against crime as a sidetrack from the class struggle, at best an illusion invented to sell news, at worst an attempt to make the poor scapegoats by blaming their brutalizing circumstances on themselves' (Lea and Young, 1984:1). Left realism was seen as a 'Labour party criminology, produced by socialists moving from sectarian left groupings into the central political arena' (Cohen, 1988:22). It advocated reformist, not revolutionary change and was committed to improving social relations in the inner city.

However, those identified as 'idealists' fiercely rejected the label and associated criticisms. Arguing that their version of a 'criminology from below' against the authoritarian state was a response to the realities of life under Thatcherism and pointed to how left realist policies 'accept rather than challenge the terrain of the powerful' (Sim et al., 1987). One of the main legacies of radical criminology has been the extensive analysis of the role and use of power by the state and the changing nature of class rule over this time. Further work developed the insights from *Policing the Crisis* to reveal and challenge the intertwining of popular racism with notions of black criminality. Paul Gilroy (1987:113) went on to describe how the rule of law and the maintenance of public order mobilized racist common sense to maintain support for a state in crisis, and criticized left realists for their 'capitulation to the weight of racist logic' despite all the 'polite social democratic rhetoric'. Divisions remain between the different strands of critical criminology, and further radical understandings of crime and punishment soon challenged the NDC approaches.

Among the most damaging was the almost complete absence of women from the field, and a lack of any structural analysis of the consequences of male domination. Instead, as one critic put it, concepts 'of "man" were to the fore, and NDC portraits of soccer hooligans, "paki-bashers" and industrial saboteurs as proto-political deviants did nothing to dissipate a sense that the masculine was a privileged concern within even a radical sociology of deviance' (Sumner, 1994:287). The beginning of feminist scholarship in British criminology is usually dated from the publication of Carol Smart's (1976) *Women, Crime and Criminology*, which documented how women had largely been neglected by the 'malestream' and the small amount of research that had been carried out on female offenders either reinforced sexual stereotypes or was outright misogynistic. For Smart (1976:227), the task of a 'feminist criminology' was to 'find alternative modes of conceptualising the social world', while Mary McIntosh (1977:396), in contrast, saw it as bringing to centre stage 'the question of gross differences between male and female crime rates'. This gender imbalance had been earlier recognized by Wootton (1959:318) when she observed that 'the sex difference far outweighs any other factor' yet no 'one seems to have any idea why; but, hardly anyone seems to have thought it worthwhile to try to find out'. Those that did tended to address why women were more conformist, rather than attempt to explain why so many more men committed crime than women, let alone consider how conceptions of deviance and control systematically distorted experiences along gendered lines.

It has become conventional now to describe the impact of feminist scholarship in criminology in a number of distinct phases and different approaches, yet there is much evidence to suggest that feminist perspectives still lie outside mainstream criminology. By Ngaire Naffine's (1997) reckoning criminology remains a male-dominated discipline, largely involving academic men studying criminal men. It is hard not to disagree with her view that questions surrounding gender have been subjected to effective ghettoization, where 'the standard case is the study of men as non-gendered subjects and the speciality is the study of women as gendered beings' (Naffine, 1997:2). Although the emergence of a sociology of masculinities has had some impact in recent decades, especially in the work of Messerschmidt (1993) and Jefferson (2002), it is clear that such a topic remains on the margins of the discipline. To take one telling example, it is notable that the editors of *The Oxford Handbook of Criminology* chose not to include or update Jefferson's (1997) excellent essay in any of the three subsequent editions of this major textbook – and in the most recent edition the discussion of masculinities occupies just two pages (Heidensohn and Silvestri, 2012:348–350) in the chapter on 'Gender and Crime', in an edition that is some 1,029 pages in length.

The final fault line exposed in the radical turn lay in the impact of the French philosopher Michel Foucault's poststructuralist deconstruction of the entire criminological enterprise. In a now much-cited passage he remarks:

> Have you read any criminological texts? They are staggering. And I say this out of astonishment, not aggressiveness, because I fail to comprehend how the discourse of criminology has been able to go on at this level. One has the impression that it is of such utility, is needed so urgently and rendered so vital for the working of the system, that it does not even need to seek a theoretical justification for itself, or even simply a coherent framework. It is entirely utilitarian. I think one needs to investigate why such a 'learned' discourse became so indispensable to the functioning of the nineteenth century penal system.
>
> (Foucault, 1980:47)

It needs to be emphasized that Foucault's target here is not the sociological approaches associated with the NDC, but rather the psychiatric and medico-legal frameworks that were central to the development of criminology in the nineteenth and twentieth centuries. By the time Foucault (1975/1991) published his major work *Discipline and Punish*, he was already a well-known intellectual, and the book is much more than a history of punishment, not least since he makes a broader argument about the disciplinary character of modern society.

From the late 1970s onwards there has been much debate over Foucault's ideas on the significance of surveillance on patterns of social control and 'penality' (Cohen, 1979, 1985; Garland and Young, 1983; Garland, 1985). Stan Cohen, for example, maintained that the development of community corrections and the decarceration movement marks both a continuation and an intensification of the social control mechanisms identified by Foucault (1975/1991). This 'dispersal of discipline' thesis insists there is now a blurring of where the prison ends and the community begins, with an overall increase in the total number of offenders brought into the system. While Cohen (1985) chronicled the recruitment of friends, relatives, and neighbours into the web of surveillance through curfews, tracking, and tagging, a debate ensued over the applicability of Foucault's ideas to contemporary patterns of punishment (Bottoms, 1983; Nelken, 1989; Taylor, 1999). Other developments since the 1990s include the rapid expansion of electronic, information, and visual technologies, all of which greatly enhance the surveillance capacities of the state. At the same time, a number of authors were drawn to Foucault's later writing on 'governmentality' to influentially describe a 'new penology' (Feeley and Simon, 1992, 1994) transforming criminal justice and the very nature of democracy. A point Jonathan Simon (2007) went on to make in his analysis of how the United States is increasingly 'governing through crime', a view also shared by Richard Ericson (2007:1) in his diagnosis of how neo-liberal politics encourages 'treating every imaginable source of harm as a crime' to be managed by the intensification of surveillance networks and the elimination of procedural safeguards in criminal law.

Taking Stock

This brief review can only point to a few of the main directions taken in the 1970s, but it should be clear that this was a turbulent, productive, and exciting era. According to one of the central figures, it 'was a dizzying scene, more a paradigmatic kaleidoscope than a clear-cut progression of superior paradigms delivering a knock-out blow to the inferior' (Downes, 1988:49). It would be misleading to give the impression that all the changes described above are all bound up with the NDC, even though it can rightly claim to have had a considerable impact in British sociology. Cohen (1981/1988:84–86) concludes his review of the then state of criminology and the sociology of deviance by pointing to some of the other subfields of sociology that were hospitable to new deviancy ideas. These include education, medicine, mass media, welfare, and social policy, as well as cultural studies and a revival of interest in the study of law as a social institution – which mirrored developments in critical legal studies. At the same time the mainstream institutional bases of British criminology remained largely untroubled by the theoretical quarrels and political disputes associated with the new perspectives.

If anything administrative criminology, that is empirical research funded by and largely conducted within government, grew in size and significance over this period. Most notably at the Home Office Research and Planning Unit, but also the research branches of the Prison Department, Metropolitan Police, and 'allied state agencies have all expanded and become more professional and productive' (Cohen, 1981:83). At the borders patterns of reflexive accommodation and creative exchange could certainly be identified between administrative practitioners and more critical criminologists, but the sense of conflict and schism helped to give a 'useful order to an emerging field' (Rock, 1988:191). In a further irony, it was the impetus of radical, sceptical, and critical versions of criminology that would fuel the remarkable growth of the discipline in the decades to come. As Pat Carlen (2011:98) recently put it, 'it was only as result of the advent of critical criminology that, in the United Kingdom at any rate, the discipline of criminology was reinvigorated sufficiently to put up a successful fight to become recognized and institutionalized as a university discipline independent of its parent disciplines of law and/or sociology'. This expansion has been particularly striking in Britain. Although Carlen was instrumental in setting up the first undergraduate degree programme in criminology at Keele University in 1991, she would never have predicted that today some 94 universities teach criminology and criminal justice in single or joint schemes.

Such an expansion would have appeared even more unlikely in the 1980s, when the decade saw major cuts to the level of funding across the social sciences and the period can best be described as one of consolidation. Academic criminology remained a small social world, while teaching was restricted to a handful of postgraduate courses and specialist options in the final year of law or sociology degrees. Indeed, some have recalled how it was still possible to read all that was published in the field. Much of it was produced by a few dozen or so active researchers, while those who were now entering the profession found they had missed the great wave of recruitment to teaching posts. Their choices were either to take up more precarious research contracts in applied criminology (in various agencies such as the Institute for the Study of Drug Dependence and the National Association for the Care and Resettlement of Offenders, as well as left-wing municipal authorities open to radical criminological argument and conducting critical victimization surveys) or emigrate to Australia, Canada, or the United States in pursuit of academic careers. Towards the end of the 1980s Paul Rock (1988:63) described how the 'central terrain of the sociology of deviance is no longer subject to bellicose dispute, most criminologists having become more conciliatory and catholic', where many of the 'fortunate generation' (those recruited to university posts in the 1960s and 1970s) had now attained 'respectability and influence' in their own institutions.

Later in his essay on the then state of the discipline, Rock depicts a quietly contented corner of the social sciences:

> British criminology itself is the work of only two hundred or so scholars. It revolves around the doings of one pivotal generation and a smaller second generation who were trained principally in Cambridge and London and then in Sheffield and at much the same time. British criminologists know one another, they educate one another, they sometimes marry one another, they read each other's work and they gossip about each other ... But quite strenuous efforts have been made to suppress the acrimony which once marked British criminology and, indeed, an unstable pattern of agreement has started to emerge.
>
> (Rock, 1988:67)

No doubt this passage reflects a particular view of one of the 'fortunate generation', but it does also reveal how a shared interest began to consolidate around a vision of criminology as a discrete, mature scientific discipline that would soon come to fruition. By any measure the rapid expansion of criminology since the early 1990s has been quite remarkable.

The major stimulus for this growth has been the successful creation of criminology as an autonomous, independent subject that no longer regards itself as a subsidiary of the legal, social, or medical sciences (Peters, 2006). Criminology has very quickly established itself within mass higher education systems, exhibiting an impressive ability to attract students, scholars, and research grants. In Britain, this has fuelled a rapid expansion of academic posts over the last 20 years or so and has been accompanied by a publishing boom where handbooks, textbooks, monographs, edited collections, and journal articles now proliferate. As Ian Loader and Richard Sparks (2012:8) have suggested this is partly owing to the pressure of various government research assessment regimes, but the period has also seen increasing internal specialization of the subject, which they point out is bound up with criminology taking on the organizational qualities of an academic discipline. Such institutional forces include the growth of separate departments, new degree schemes, graduate research funding, large annual conferences, and the appointment of researchers whose entire higher education experience has only been in criminology. The creation of such specialist journals as *Policing and Society* (founded in 1990), *Theoretical Criminology* (1997), *Global Crime* (1999), *Punishment and Society* (1999), *Criminology and Criminal Justice* (2001), *Youth Justice* (2001), *Crime, Media, Culture* (2005), and *Feminist Criminology* (2006) is an indication of this trend and offers a sense of the diverse subfields in the discipline.

Indeed, the sociology of deviance had come under sustained attack for its internal contradictions and inability to confront larger questions of power, control, and ideology. These issues were exemplified in Alvin Gouldner's scathing critique of the 'zookeepers of deviance' who presented 'man-on-his-back', rather than 'man-fighting-back' (Gouldner, 1968/1973:38–9), which was a major influence on *The New Criminology*. The demise of the concept is also captured in books such as Geoffrey Pearson's (1975) *The Deviant Imagination*, which argued that the romanticization of crime, deviance, and illness in what he called 'misfit sociology' was ultimately a dead end. Although the concept of deviance was further reworked at the Birmingham Centre, it quickly became subsumed under broader debates surrounding culture, ideology, and politics. By the 1980s it was clear that cultural studies had moved on to questions of difference, identity, and postmodernism, while a major 'obituary' from the 1990s claimed the entire 'field had died' (Sumner, 1994:ix).

As we will see in the next chapter, the metaphor of transgression has come to replace some of the central concerns in the sociology of deviance, where old questions are put in a fresh light. These still speak to the relationship between the centre and the margins, identity and difference, the normal and the pathological, order and excess, and ultimately the desire to transcend limits (Jenks, 2003:5). It is also no accident that these ideas have recently resurfaced in cultural criminology (Ferrell et al., 2008), which has done much to emphasize the role of image, style, and meaning in subcultures and the mediated processes through which crime and punishment are constructed. At the same time, cultural criminology becomes yet another instance of the internal specialization and increasing fragmentation of the criminological enterprise, where the 'field of inquiry seems at risk of sinking into a set of cliques where criminologists read the work of others who think like them, write for those very same people and publish only in the journals that they and their colleagues are already reading' (Bosworth and Hoyle, 2011:3).

The rapid expansion of criminology is not just restricted to Britain; it has also been especially pronounced in the United States. According to the American Sociological Association (ASA), criminology and criminal justice majors now outweigh those enrolled on sociology programmes by some two-thirds (Hannah-Moffat, 2011:450). In the United States the movement towards independent criminology and criminal justice programmes was already well advanced and many tend to be vocational rather than academic in orientation. State universities and colleges led the way in providing professional criminal justice education, where sponsorship from the Justice Department's Law Enforcement Assistance Agency has been pivotal, but poses awkward questions over what criminology is for and whether it is actually an academic discipline at all (Garland, 2011). The institutional separation of criminology from sociology has also occurred at graduate level, while the major professional associations have grown much larger than the crime-related sections of the ASA and these have been instrumental in strengthening the organizational base of their new discipline (Savelsberg and Sampson, 2002:101).

It is not simply that criminology has divorced itself from sociology in the United States. Although there are some important exceptions, sociology has also 'pulled away from criminology, particularly as taught and studied at elite institutions' (Short, with Hughes, 2007:632). The expansion of an applied, vocational criminology has adversely impacted on the subject's intellectual status and hastened the demise of the specialism in the sociology departments at the leading research universities (Garland, 2011:311). Despite the centrality of research on crime and deviance in many of these departments in the first half of the twentieth century, a certain disdain for the subject matter has long been in evidence, as the sociologist Gilbert Geis (1974:287) observed: 'scholars at so prestigious an institution as Columbia University barely deign to work in the field of crime' – recalling Merton's (1957:17) earlier blistering condemnation of the 'slum-encouraged provincialism of thinking that the primary subject matter of sociology was centred on such peripheral problems of social life as divorce and delinquency'. Indeed, the separation of criminology from sociology in general in America was symbolically and institutionally realized by Merton's insistence on situating the study of crime in the Department of Social Administration at Columbia and his role in founding the Society for the Study of Social Problems in 1951 for those sociologists disillusioned with the directions taken by a new elite in the ASA, who were moving away from Chicago-style research to the 'abstractions of structural functionalism' (Short, with Hughes, 2007:624).

In Europe the pattern is more mixed. Some countries, such as the Netherlands, have experienced rapid growth along similar lines as Britain, while others have seen hardly any institutional autonomy emerge and are still dependent on 'parent' disciplines (as in Germany and Italy). Scandinavia continues to have relatively small, but influential criminological traditions. Since 2000 the European Society of Criminology has been an important site helping to expand criminology across some 50 countries, hosting a large annual conference, and publishing the *European Journal of Criminology*. Aside from these developments, it has also been noted that criminology departments and degrees have rapidly increased in Canada, Australia, New Zealand, and South Africa, with many beginning to appear in India, China, and Asia (Loader and Sparks, 2012:9–10). Criminology is now taught around the world, and while the history, character, and disposition of the subject varies considerably across time and place (Becker and Wetzell, 2006) it is important to consider the implications of these changes.

Criminology as Discipline

From the outset many of the leading figures have insisted that criminology is not a discipline, and the entire NDC movement can be seen as a form of 'anti-criminology', which has gradually had to 'absorb the implications of its own creations' (Cohen, 1988:16). One influential definition has it that criminology is a 'rendezvous subject', where various branches of learning gather around a shared substantive theme, sometimes overlapping, more often moving past one another in different directions (Rock, 2011:20). On this reading criminology is simply a meeting point for the traffic in ideas between researchers schooled in the more fundamental disciplines of economics, history, law, philosophy, psychology, and sociology, and is constantly enriched and rejuvenated by the appropriation of ideas and concepts from these other disciplines. For some, contemporary criminology has all the organizational trappings of an academic discipline, but it has no intellectual core around which diverse approaches and speciality areas can cohere. It has a 'subject matter but no unique methodological commitment or paradigmatic theoretical framework' (Savelsberg and Sampson, 2002:101) and the worry is that an 'independent criminology' will further 'fragment into distinct specialisms', with an increasingly inward focus resulting in 'negative consequences for collective learning' (Garland, 2011:312). Criminology's growing isolation from the more basic disciplines comes with great costs; as it disengages from them it has opened itself up to greater government intrusion and runs the risk of losing academic status as a university subject.

These changes have also been accompanied by a growing political scepticism towards certain kinds of scholarly expertise, altering the once close relationships between policy-orientated criminologists and government officials, provoking a 'growing rift between Home Office and academic researchers' (Newburn, 2011:512). If central government is no longer as important a patron of criminological research as it once was, then other sponsors have risen to prominence (including the police, penal professionals, pressure groups, private security firms, and other non-governmental organizations), yet dangers remain over the readiness of criminologists to produce 'serviceable knowledge for rationalizing the operations of the already powerful' (Loader and Sparks, 2012:15). The struggle is a long-standing one and confronted by every discipline that seeks to maintain academic integrity while pursuing research funding and some degree of real-world relevance. On this last point, one of the defining features of British criminology has been a humanitarian commitment to reforming the system and this aspiration continues to attract many to criminology. Equally the 'romantic, voyeur-like appeal of the subject matter' (Cohen, 1981:81) should not be underestimated. Indeed, one of the earliest critics of the sociology of deviance concluded that it was simply the study of 'nuts, sluts and preverts',[1] which problematically ignored crimes of the corporate economy and the state's own violence (Liazos, 1972). This was an important critique and drew attention to the limits of state-defined criminality, which then as now, is the result of political processes and offered a reminder that legal categories are social constructions.

It should be clear that I am against the increasing 'independence' of criminology from sociology, but it is worth asking just what should a sociological criminology look like? Here Edwin Sutherland's (1924:3) definition of criminology as a body of knowledge that regards crime as a social phenomenon, which studies the 'processes of making laws, of breaking laws, and of reacting toward the breaking of laws', remains unsurpassed. Sutherland raises three deceptively simple questions: Why are laws made? Why are they broken? What should be done about this? This formulation calls for an 'intellectual perspective that lies outside the ideology and interests of those who run the crime-control system and the academics they hire to help them' (Cohen, 1988:9). Crime and punishment are bound up with wider social processes, and while there will always be contested views of what criminology is, these are state-defined categories and practices, which intimately tie criminology to government in quite troubling ways (Garland, 2011:305). One of the central tasks of a sociological criminology is identifying these links and the problems that flow from them, even as the relationships change and become more obscure.

None of this is to say that sociology is the only discipline criminology should be seeking a renewed relationship with; there are no doubt productive encounters to be had with its other constitutive disciplines. In the effort to establish its own disciplinary credentials, criminology has lost some of its intellectual energy and it is worth remembering that it has nearly always been animated and enlivened by ideas imported from elsewhere. The metaphor of 'rendezvous subject' is a well-used one, and it is the traffic in multidisciplinary approaches that has sustained post-war British criminology, but which has also left it prone to a bewildering eclecticism and disorganized fragmentation. Under these circumstances the growing separation of criminology from sociology is to be resisted; instead, a renewed focus on how dialogues across many disciplines can be facilitated is the way forward. The remainder of this book is dedicated to exploring one invaluable way to do this – through the rich intellectual resources of social theory.

4

Transgression

One of the lessons learnt from the previous chapter is that the concept of deviance has declined as an area of sociological interest, at the same time as criminology has experienced remarkable growth since the 1990s. For some, the term transgression is to be preferred, especially in cultural criminology (Presdee, 2000; Ferrell et al., 2004). The emphasis in much of this work is on the foreground experience of action and the alluring spell that wrongdoing casts. Among the attractions of this revived interest in the concept of 'transgression' is the way it takes 'us along a series of continua, both vertical and horizontal, such as sacred–profane; good–evil; normal–pathological; sane–mad; purity–danger; high–low; centre–periphery and so on' (Jenks, 2003:2). The key dynamic is the sense of 'trespass', of stepping beyond prescribed limits, breaking rules and exceeding boundaries, where the 'trouble' is as much 'inside' as it is 'outside' (Jervis, 1999:3). I will examine the implications of these arguments in more detail in what follows, but it is important to note that one of the consequences of the recent expansion of criminology has been the proliferation of seemingly new theories of criminality.

Often these new approaches are revisiting older sociological ideas, but with sophisticated quantitative research methods and the aim of working through statistically testable propositions. The list would include the way that anomie has been revived in 'general strain theory' (Agnew, 1992), social disorganization is reincarnated as 'collective efficacy' (Sampson et al., 1997), deviant careers are now understood through the lens of 'life-course criminology' (Bonistall and Ralston, 2014), differential association underpins 'social learning theory' (Akers and Jensen, 2003), and the ascendancy of rational choice in all manner of 'control' theories (Clarke and Felson, 2008). If the earlier sociologists could be accused of romanticizing deviance, then these newer theories have gone too far in portraying crime as 'mundane' (Best, 2004a:75).

The major task remains one of constructing 'a fully social theory of crime and deviance that does not maintain that there is a sociology of "normal" people and another discipline seeking to explain crime and deviance' (Young,

2013:xiv). These words were written by Jock Young in an essay introducing the 40th anniversary of the publication of the *New Criminology* where he goes to some lengths to situate the book in a critical sociology that was inspired by C. Wright Mills' (1959) *The Sociological Imagination*. They serve to remind us that the problems generated by crime, deviance, and punishment should not just be situated at an individual level of motivation or whim, but in wider social structures and historical processes. These insights need to be borne in mind as we turn to consider why it is that some people break social norms and commit criminal acts ranging from minor incivilities through to highly offensive and disturbing acts, such as serial killing and other forms of what might be called 'radical evil'.

Disreputable Pleasures

Although I am suggesting there is a dynamic range here – from the mundane and trivial to extreme and unthinkable acts of cruelty – it is important to be aware of the difficulties posed by relativism and the interpretive pluralism encouraged by the appreciative legacy of studying people from the standpoint of their own constructions of reality. One way through these definitional problems is provided by John Hagan (1977:12) who maintains in his book *The Disreputable Pleasures* that 'deviance consists of variation from a social norm', and crime is simply one special instance of deviance, as it breaks 'a social norm that is proscribed by criminal law' (Hagan, 1985:49). In doing so he distinguishes between four basic types of public attitude towards problematic conduct, ranging from those about which there is a 'consensus' (most serious crimes, such as murder and rape), through 'conflict' (where there is some disagreement, as in political violence and public disorder), to 'social deviations' (where there is generally low agreement on seriousness and the social response is often variable), and finally 'social diversions' (broadly acceptable variations in lifestyle, though other societies may deem them as unacceptable). Most of the book explores the conceptual contrast between conflict and consensus crimes to conclude that it is the values and standards of those groups who have the power and authority to define certain acts and actors as disreputable, unwanted, and unacceptable who ultimately determine the process of criminalization. There is some very helpful conceptual clarity here, yet the focus remains on the social construction of deviance and the enduring persistence of group interests in the designation of disreputable statuses; it does not address the motivations to commit wrongdoing and engage in banned conduct.

Despite the title of Hagan's (1977) book bringing attention to the pleasures of the dissolute and the desperate desires that lead some to break the law, the term 'pleasures' itself is left curiously unexamined. In his account anomie, neutralization, and control theories exemplify the consensus paradigm, while subcultural, labelling, and radical criminologies illustrate the conflict model.

Significantly, he subsequently endorses control theory as the most promising avenue for criminological theory to pursue (Hagan, 1985) and in this he antici-pates the extraordinary revival of this perspective since the early 1990s. Key here was the publication of Michael Gottfredson and Travis Hirschi's (1990) *A General Theory of Crime*, which emphatically sought to return criminology to its classical roots by maintaining that crime resulted from an offender's self-interested choices, committed for immediate short-term gains and satisfac-tions. Their general theory was not just restricted to crime and delinquency, but offered a universal explanation of criminal offending at all ages, and in all places, as well as explaining activities that shared the same conceptual space but were non-criminal (in Hagan's terms these would be 'social deviations' and 'social diversions') such as gambling, smoking, drinking, and obesity.

The defining feature explaining them all was the attribute of low self-control, a trait that distinguishes some impulsive individuals from others. Gottfredson and Hirschi (1990) argue that self-control is formed primarily through sociali-zation in the family and is learned early in childhood, remaining fairly stable throughout life, and once acquired is difficult to undo. Children who do not learn to curb selfish impulses, delay gratification, and plan for the long term are much more likely to engage in activities that are risky, thrilling, and reck-less. Consequently, they are likely to stay indifferent to others and self-centred throughout life, remaining careless 'in the sense that they care less about the responsibilities of work and family or being law-abiding' (Best, 2004a:73) than those who behave in socially approved ways. The biggest problem facing such a universal theory is how to explain the declining rates of criminality in adult-hood. If low self-control is an enduring feature over the life course, then why do most adolescents mature out of delinquency? (This was also a telling criti-cism Matza had earlier levelled against strain and subcultural theories.)

To answer this question other control theorists turned to an examination of the social bonds that tie some people more than others into respectability. In Robert Sampson and John Laub's (1993) *Crime in the Making* and their subsequent study of *Shared Beginnings, Divergent Lives* (Laub and Sampson, 2003) their central findings were that delinquents had weak ties to their fami-lies and schools, but strong bonds with other young delinquents, which gener-ate social networks that facilitate and embed criminal activity. Their work was an attempt to explain why some individuals both become involved in crime initially, and then subsequently desist from delinquency as they get older. Those that did go 'straight' usually find adult respectability through critical turn-ing points, whether these be developing intimate partnerships, finding steady employment, or entering military service, they each offer new sets of social relationship and invite self-reflection. Others achieved 'desistance by default' through unwittingly following rules and only later realizing they have left the game. Their work is nuanced and perceptive, always emphasizing how contin-gent the maturational reform process is and the part played by active human agents negotiating complex social worlds.

Seductions and Edgework

In some respects, the focus on the situational factors that precipitate criminal activity is shared with Jack Katz's (1988) important account of the *Seductions of Crime*. But here it is the very sensuality of crime that becomes the focus of attention across a diverse range of acts. The book was highly provocative and intended to restore the rich, interpersonal drama of the illicit by focusing on what he terms the 'moral emotions', such as shame and humiliation, in a nuanced phenomenology of the moment. As he explains:

> Follow vandals and amateur shoplifters as they duck into alleys and dressing rooms and you will be moved by their delight in deviance; observe them under arrest and you may be stunned by their shame. Watch their strutting street display and you may well be struck by the awesome fascination that symbols of evil hold for the young men who are linked in the groups we often call gangs ... The careers of persistent robbers show us, not the increasingly precise calculations and hedged risks of 'professionals,' but men for whom gambling and other vices are a way of life, who are 'wise' in the cynical sense of the term, and who take pride in a defiant reputation as 'bad'. And if we examine the lived sensuality behind events of cold-blooded 'senseless' murder, we are compelled to acknowledge the power that may still be created in the modern world through the sensualities of defilement, spiritual chaos, and the apprehension of vengeance.
>
> (Katz, 1988:312)

What unites all these very different experiences is the transformative force of shame and humiliation. Yet Katz is careful to acknowledge that different people respond differently to these existential feelings, and they do not always result in violent crime; many turn the pain inward and endure it. In the example of violent crime he maintains that in 'virtually all robberies, the offender discovers, fantasizes or manufactures *an angle of moral superiority* over the intended victim. The stickup man knows that dominance requires more than brute force' (Katz, 1988:169, emphasis in original). Armed robbery involves a strong interactional dynamic, laced with danger and uncertainty, yet to be successful the offender needs to take unambiguous control of the situation from the start and convince the victim they are not in a position to resist.

By attending to the wilful and sensual Katz also highlights the excitement involved, often for no material gain. Such actions are not just restricted to particular groups, for the sensual attractions of transgression reside within us all. While his work has been influential (especially in cultural criminology) it has not escaped criticism on the grounds that it disregards the wider social context in which all action takes place (O'Malley and Mugford, 1994; Young, 2007), fails to secure 'serious distance' (implying that offending stories are taken at face value), and lacks any 'systematic explanation' of the various 'motivational' accounts (Taylor, 1999:224). Yet, as Keith Hayward (2002:83) suggests, these objections ignore 'the failure of "background" structural theories of crime to address the fundamental question of why (under shared social conditions) one person rather than another commits crime'. This is a crucial point and suggests that there remains a troubling split between structure and agency and a need to reconcile the rich, existential focus of his work with an understanding of structural dynamics and historical processes giving shape and meaning to lives that transgress. In this regard Stephen Lyng's (1990) concept of 'edgework' has proved to be especially helpful, not least since he attempts to combine both Marx and Mead in an attempt to understand voluntary forms of risk-taking in a broader social context where the 'problem of consciousness' is a decisive link between macro-level economic forces (Marx) and social interaction at the micro-level (Mead).

The 'edgework' concept itself is taken from the journalist Hunter S. Thompson and his depiction of anarchic, excessive conduct, most famously in his hallucinatory account of *Fear and Loathing in Las Vegas*, where 'negotiating the boundary between life and death, consciousness and unconsciousness, and sanity and insanity is a central theme' (Lyng, 1990:855). Various types of dangerous sports (rock climbing, skydiving, downhill skiing, motor racing, and so on), risky occupations (firefighting, test piloting, combat soldiering, and police work) and illicit sensations (binge drinking, drug use, body modification, sadomasochistic sexualities, eating disorders, and outlaw bikers) are among the practices that have been identified as involving edgework. The unifying feature they all share is that they each carry recognizable and significant threats to personal safety and surrounding environments.

By shifting the focus of attention onto the anarchic, impulsive, and spontaneous qualities of the edgework experience, Lyng highlights how the current socio-economic context gives rise to distinctive ways of being in late modernity. A key opposition he identifies is between 'spontaneity' and 'constraint' in an effort to link with Marxist and Meadian social theory. In particular, Lyng derives from Marx an understanding of 'creativity' that distinguishes between forms of work that enlarge human endeavours and those that do not, while from Mead he grounds an interactional analysis of how individuals become social. The argument is that people do not 'always remain passive in the face of alienation and oversocialization', but that for many 'the central dynamic of day-to-day existence is an incessant search for the self' (Lyng, 1990:870). He is careful to acknowledge that this pursuit can take many forms in the capitalist marketplace, but a pivotal one is consumption and the *Culture of Narcissism* (Lasch, 1978) it generates, where an infatuated preoccupation with the self is having corrosive consequences on American life.[1] The quest for spontaneity and freedom from constraint through edgework summons up an ability to master situations that verge on total chaos, and this involves the deployment of highly specific skills.

In contrast to random chance activities such as gambling, or other situations where one's fate is placed in the hands of others, edgework requires a measure of control and never pure luck. Some of these themes can be clearly seen in Richard Wright and Scott Decker's (1997) *Armed Robbers in Action*, which, as the title suggests, is based on studying active violent crime in St Louis, Missouri. Their book moves through the initial motivations to commit stickups, through choice of targets, and then to the mechanics of the act. Most of their participants are described as living in a 'street culture' based on 'desperate partying', for while they are poor the cycle of desperate partying leads them to robbery to maintain this lifestyle and it is this that sets them apart from other poor people. The active offenders they interviewed recount that they typically have to make it explicitly clear that the scene is turning into a crime, forcing the compliance of intended victims by creating a convincing illusion of impending death. This is created by catching their prey off guard, and then using tough talk, a fierce disposition, and the display of a deadly weapon to scare them into unquestioning obedience. The intention is to preserve the illusion for as long as possible without having to turn the robbery into murder, and reassuring victims that submission will not bring further jeopardy. Armed robbery is a fraught, interactive event and situational troubles can easily arise. Victims may fail to respond in the desired way. When this happens, the offenders usually respond with severe, but non-lethal, violence, relying on brute force to bring the victim back into line. Very few want to kill their victims, although some were prepared to resort to deadly force if need be.

The authors are clearly influenced by Katz and his depictions of the moral and sensual attractions of crime, but their findings highlight instrumental rather than expressive motivations for doing stickups. Although some described being thrilled by the sense of power, most committed robbery for the money. Few expressed regret, but fewer still seemed to be driven by inner convictions to do harm or to dominate. The expressive side of their motivations was linked to participating in desperate partying and contempt for the world of conformity, where their skills and education could only lead to low wages and social marginality. In contrast, Roger Matthews (2002) in his study of armed robbers argues that many of the mundane offender depictions of crime, particularly those coming from prison, are learnt responses designed to play down the attractiveness of robbery. He suggests these justifications are strategically developed in prison in an effort to secure an early release, yet he notes that when it comes to describing the actual robberies the participants would suddenly liven up and recall the adrenaline rush of the crime. This happened a number of times, but the following quote conveys the feeling:

Always high, always on a high like, getting off on doing the buzz, the buzz of actually doing the whatever like, job, 'cos we do burglaries as well, like, get off on that get off on whatever. To actually do a job and walk out of a sort of like bank, post office, when you got sort of like twenty or thirty grand, you can't get a better buzz than that.

(Matthews, 2002:36)

To explain this dynamic he turns to the concept of edgework in an effort to critique rational choice theory and its attempt to explain criminal behaviour in terms of mundane shifts in the routine, everyday patterns of life.

Not unsurprisingly the focus in edgework studies on prototypically male, high-risk endeavours has been criticized by several feminist criminologists, who see it as a further instance of the essentially gendered character of risk research (Chan and Rigakos, 2002; Halsey and Young, 2006; Walklate, 1997). One of the earliest and most perceptive critics of the concept highlighted how Lyng's (1990) examples are almost all 'activities that are engaged in primarily by white men with attachment to the labor force' (Miller, 1991:1531). Drawing on her own research with African-American, female street hustlers Eleanor Miller contends that their daily oppression is such that they have to engage in edgework to a far greater extent than working- or middle-class men and because of their structural location they rarely do so voluntarily. Miller's work can be seen as an early attempt to think through how the axes of race, class, gender, and sexuality intersect in particular ways to produce subordination.[2]

Again the 'tension between foreground practices and background structures' (Ferrell et al., 2008:73) is raised and Miller does concede that 'experientially and in terms of social psychological impact, edgework might be functionally equivalent across these groups' (Miller, 1991:1533). The key concern is how human agency is shaped by social structures, enabling what is and what is not possible in particular cultural contexts, and how certain patterns of conduct reproduce structures of domination.

One way in which foreground experiences and structural conditions can be seen to operate is through the process of 'transcendence', which is a distinctively modern phenomenon and it has been argued that the 'disenchantment of the modern world generates the routinized, despiritualized world of calculative rationality, and an attendant order of time, space, and society to which Romanticism, edgework, and crime (of the kind discussed by Katz) are transcendent responses' (O'Malley and Mugford, 1994:198). But as these authors recognize, escaping the dull monotony of everyday life is not open to everyone to the same degree:

As a consequence of the inequality of resources in society, some of the ways of transcending mundane life are more open to some groups of people than to others. Skydiving, for example, may offer a transcendent experience, but is unlikely to be available to many young black members of the urban underclass. Crack on the other hand, may provide a similarly transcending experience, but unlike skydiving is available to all, rich and poor.

(O'Malley and Mugford, 1994:209)

In an important article Mike Collison (1996) went on to highlight how drug use, drug dealing, and predatory crime provide significant resources for mobilizing a powerful form of masculine subcultural capital on the street. The research reveals some of the pleasures and pains of being an underclass male youth on the margins of civil society in Britain at the end of the last century. These are primarily tales of social exclusion and attempts by young men to reinvent themselves through the seductions of cultural consumption, risk-taking, and crime.

In Collison's account predatory street crime and excessive lifestyle are not simply embraced by some young men as a response to poverty, nor are they due to faulty socialization, but rather earning the reputation as 'mad' is absolutely central. As he explains:

> 'Mad' is a common street term. It carries a meaning of prestige much like the word 'bad' in America, but more often it is used directly to capture a self (or situation) which pushes it further than others; does more crime, breaks more rules, uses more violence, is more wrong. The mad joy-rider, street-fighter, thief, drug user, leisure worker makes a statement in chaotic deviance which both signifies difference from normative orders and over-socialization, and belonging within a peer group. 'Sad' may be used tragically to describe the intrusions of mundane reason into daily life: getting arrested, excluded (from school, the home), addicted, going honest, and worse, wearing cheap 'imitation' clothes.
>
> (Collison, 1996:440)

The hedonistic thrill of pushing it to the edge with seemingly reckless abandon is what is decisive here and there is no doubt that the drug economy offers for these young underclass men a chance to live life in the fast lane. It is significant that the sensual delights of excessive consumption are also echoed among accounts from older, professional criminals. In particular, Dick Hobbs (2013) has explained how armed robbery offers a way of enjoying a lifestyle of conspicuous consumption and escape from the drab routines of working-class employment. As one of the professional criminals he cites sums it up: 'well I'm a natural. I mean, I am a natural. I love it, I love the high life … I love the … going out to wine and dine, the fucking champagne and the birds, and living it up, and first class on the aeroplanes. Champagne fucking Charlie. You know. Ducking and diving; and, you know, wining and dining' (in Hobbs, 2013:145). Armed robbers rarely used the income generated by their crimes to build stronger underworld alliances or to extend illegal networks, but were more concerned with long holidays in Spain and enjoying the good life (Taylor, 1984).

We will return to consider the dynamics of organized crime in Chapter 6, not least since it 'is a category of transgression that invokes extraordinary levels of hype, excitement, and anxiety, and with little consensus regarding its definition'

(Hobbs, 2013:4). While there are conceptual difficulties surrounding the term 'organized crime' it remains prominent in and beyond criminology, and not simply because it seems to differ completely from 'opportunistic individual' crime, but through its combination of both interpersonal networks and social menace (Levi, 2014). What is clear from this discussion is that certain crimes offer a set of resources and practices that enable men to accomplish their masculinity, whether this is on the urban street or in the business suite. Much work since the 1990s has explored the gendered dynamics of offending and examined the ways multiple inequalities intersect and interlock to render some subordinate while reinforcing the privileges of others. Crucial was the major shift in feminist scholarship that recognized differences among women and the different epistemologies shaping knowledge production. Indeed, Maureen Cain (1990:6) was an early advocate for a 'transgressive criminology' urging feminists to step outside the confines of conventional 'criminological discourse' and instead 'raise questions about our constitution of gender itself' in an effort to unravel the conditions that disadvantage both men and women. It is to such developments that we now turn.

Doing Difference

It has long been recognized that the criminal woman inhabits an unsettling cultural space. She not only violates society's legal codes, but also defies its gender norms by challenging conventional understandings of feminine conduct. This has given rise to the concepts of 'double deviance' and 'double jeopardy', which were coined by Frances Heidensohn (1985), to describe how female offenders are stigmatized in the criminal justice system and are vulnerable to harsher punishment on account of their anomalous position as deviant women. Moreover, Heidensohn highlights the importance of formal and informal controls regulating gender in other areas of social life, where what happens to girls and women in courts and prisons is connected to what happens in the family, at school, and at work. Much attention has been given to the continuities in social control across a whole range of institutions and settings, and while these will be explored in more detail in the next chapter, it is important to note that the shame involved in the loss of reputation to women is considerable and damaging. Yet by the end of the 1980s it became increasingly apparent that describing girls or women (or, for that matter, boys and men) as essentially unified categories was problematic. Since then the emphasis has shifted to addressing the multiple inequalities that structure identities and shape action.

Initially associated with the struggles of black women in the civil rights movement in the United States, the theoretical approach has come to be termed 'intersectionality', which highlights interlocking influences of class, gender, race, and other forms of difference such as age, dis/ability, sexuality, and so forth. In many respects intersectionality complicates and deepens Mills' (1959) arguments on the need to understand biography in relation to the whole society, and that the character of intersectionalities will vary geographically – suggesting the importance of a comparative dimension to the sociological imagination. The term intersectionality has become popular because it 'aims to make visible the multiple positioning that constitutes everyday life and the power relations that are central to it' (Phoenix and Pattynama, 2006:187). But how to conduct an intersectional analysis is open to some debate, as all the contributors to a special issue of the *European Journal of Women's Studies* on 'intersectionality' make clear. Most challenge Judith Butler's (1990:143) mocking of the 'etc.' that often appears at the end of lists of social divisions, and her claim that it signals both 'exhaustion as well as of the illimitable process of signification itself'. Nira Yuval-Davis (2006:2002), for example, disagrees with Butler and instead maintains that it is vitally important to keep separate 'the different analytical levels in which social divisions need to be examined' and explore 'the ways different social divisions are constructed by, and intermeshed in, each other in specific historical conditions'. She questions Butler's premise – that the process of signification is illimitable – by suggesting that some particular social relations are more salient in some specific contexts than in others. Or to put this another way, 'differences like gender, colour and class do not add but multiply: a Black woman is not oppressed "twice" but many times' (Ludvig, 2006:246). This is a crucial point of intersectionality analysis – the socially structured systems of race, class, and gender have different organizing logics, but they are not a series of discrete variables, and their combined effects are multiplicative rather than additive. The three systems interlock and while 'race, class and gender can be seen as different axes of social structure, individuals experience them simultaneously' (Anderson and Collins, 1992:xxi). They are analytically distinct, but concretely and historically they are inseparable.

In criminology one of the finest examples of the approach remains Lisa Maher's (1997) ethnographic study of white, black and Latina female drug users in three Brooklyn neighbourhoods. Her research was undertaken at the height of the crack cocaine drug trade and revealed the cultural distinctions, social hierarchies, and economic opportunities operating in the city and how these worked to exclude women from the most lucrative jobs, leaving sex work as the only reliable way of generating money. Yet she highlights how racialized dynamics structured participation in these illegal economies and demonstrates how crack changed the nature of the sex trade – lowering the price of sexual exchanges and increasing the levels of violence faced on the strolls. In response the women developed violent presentations of self in an effort to defend themselves:

> 'Acting bad' and 'being bad' are not the same. Although many of the women presented themselves as 'bad' or 'crazy' this projection was a street persona and a necessary survival strategy ... unlike their male counterparts, for women, reputation was about 'preventing victimization'.
>
> (Maher, 1997:95–6)

Throughout the book Maher emphasizes how poor minority women are active agents working in the informal economy, where the combined effects of class, gender, and the racialized power structure of the street shapes their life worlds.

By highlighting the ways in which women were likely to resort to violence in particular contexts Maher is focusing attention on how crime is a situated action, and in this she echoes other developments in feminist scholarship that had begun to see gender itself as a 'situated accomplishment' (West and Zimmerman, 1987:126). Crucial to this 'doing gender' approach is the understanding that gender is performed and is 'produced' through interaction with others.[3] Consequently, gender is not simply a trait, role, or individual characteristic, imposed on us, but is rather an ongoing accomplishment that is 'both an indication and a reproduction of gendered social hierarchies' (Miller, 1998:38) shoring up sexual differences between men and women. This ethnomethodologically informed position was subsequently developed to address how race and class are also achieved and patterned over time, as in 'doing race' and 'doing class', and ultimately 'doing difference' (West and Fenstermaker, 1995). These ideas were central to subsequent feminist explanations of why there are such stark differences in women's and men' offending and victimization, where men commit the overwhelming majority of serious crimes and it is this glaring fact that has been either ignored or misunderstood by much 'malestream' criminology.

It is important to recognize that while there are at least a dozen different feminist perspectives in the discipline (Maidment, 2006) they each seek to question the conventional boundaries of criminological scholarship and broaden its horizons. Despite the differences between them they all share a concern with gendered forms of oppression and a commitment to social change. Patriarchy is both a structure and an ideology derived from the 'law of the father' in which men have more power and privilege than women. Yet the concept has always been controversial and although it is less often used today its meanings and the debates surrounding gender inequality continue to appear in 'disguised language' (Hunnicutt, 2009:553). One major development has been a focus on masculinities, where crime has been understood as a resource for accomplishing gender:

> The robbery setting provides the ideal opportunity to construct an 'essential' toughness and 'maleness' it provides a means with which to construct that certain type of masculinity – hardman. Within the social context that ghetto and barrio boys find themselves, then, robbery is a rational practice for 'doing gender' and for getting money.
>
> (Messerschmidt, 1993:107)

Drawing on Connell's (1987) influential discussion of gender, which emphasized how there are hierarchies not only between men and women, but also among men, the book popularized the concepts of 'hegemonic masculinity' and 'emphasized femininity'. They are the dominant forms of gender, organizing other masculinities and femininities into positions of subordination or opposition.

The depiction of a hierarchy of masculinities sprang from gay men's experiences of violence and vilification from straight men. These concepts were later refined by Connell (1995) to emphasize the importance of psychoanalytical ideas in demonstrating the range of possibilities in developing gender identities, as well as the contradictions and tensions in conventional masculinities, which are always provisional accomplishments as they unfold over time. James Messerschmidt (1993) pioneered this approach in criminology and since then a considerable amount of attention given to the idea of 'doing gender' in theoretical and empirical work. For example, Messerschmidt (1997) subsequently drew on Giddens' (1984) structuration theory, which attempts to overcome the agency/structure divide in social theory, in his examination of crime as 'structured action'. Here he sought to grasp how race, class, and gender are 'made' by the social structural constraints that channel agents to act in specific ways. Following Giddens he maintains that social structures are neither external to human actors, nor are men and women simply passive victims of structural conditions, but rather social structures are realized by 'knowledgeable' people as they act in specific social situations. Often agents reproduce social structures in their routine interactions but sometimes they can change them through improvised and innovative conduct.

One difficulty with this approach was that hegemonic masculinity was used tautologically, in that it employed circular reasoning, to explain both the cause and the effect of crime (Collier, 1998:21). A further complaint was that the framework overdetermined men's offending and could not answer why it is only a minority of young men from a particular ethnic group or social class who choose to accomplish their masculinity by 'doing crime', while the majority do not (Jefferson, 1997). Such a criticism is also levelled at explanations arguing that 'poverty causes crime', but as Kathy Daly (2013:238) suggests, while the idea of 'doing masculinity' has 'some intuitive appeal, most people would find "doing poverty" to be in bad taste'.

Others challenged the gender dualism underlying the assumptions of this perspective (Miller, 2002:441). Jody Miller's critique builds on her research with young African-American women in gangs in two contrasting North American cities, St Louis and Ohio, in her book *One of the Guys* (2001). She is well aware that the title is provocative, for it recalls outdated 'tomboy' stereotypes that feminist research has challenged for decades now. Yet the phrase 'one of the guys' was an epithet the young women strove to acquire, which they achieved by 'gender crossing' and policing each other's sexuality by vilifying those they regarded as 'hos' and 'sluts'. It served to both distance them from 'a denigrated sexual identity and maintain an identity as a "true" member' (Miller, 2002:446). The book highlights how gender inequality – male leadership, double standards over sexual conduct, the sexual exploitation of some girls, and most girls' exclusion from serious gang crime – continues to organize the mixed-gender gangs Miller studied. Overall, her research reveals that girls and young women deploy a flexible repertoire of situated actions that may (or may not) be primarily concerned with accomplishing normative femininity. To be 'one of the guys' is not the result of being similar to boys, but is rather achieved by being different from other young women through successful 'gender crossing' that places them on a more equal footing.

In her earlier work Miller (1998) had compared the motivations for and accomplishment of street robbery in St Louis and found that while there were few gender differences in the accounts women and men gave for why they commit robbery (money, status, and/or excitement), the way they enacted the crime was strikingly different. Men overwhelmingly deployed the same method – using physical violence and/or a gun to target other men involved in street life, such as drug dealers, drug users, and gang members. The women mainly used three methods: targeting female victims in physical confrontational robberies (often around nightclubs); setting up male victims by appearing sexually available; and working with male street robbers of other men. The women do not 'do robbery' differently from men 'in order to meet different needs or accomplish different goals', but rather the robbery styles employed by women emerged from 'practical choices made in context of a gender-stratified environment' where 'men are perceived as strong and women are perceived as weak' (Miller, 1998:61). These insights informed a subsequent study of the gendered dynamics of street robbery in the United Kingdom and how gender moulds enactment patterns (Brookman et al., 2007). For both men and women the prime motivation was the acquisition of money for drugs and hedonistic pleasure. Closely tied to this culture of 'desperate partying' was the use of violence to secure reputation and status, while the 'buzz' or 'kick' of interpersonal violence was highlighted as the main motivation for robbery by some. Others were motivated by a deep desire for 'payback' to rectify perceived wrongs (for example, revenge for status challenges, or debt collection) and which constituted a form of retaliatory 'street justice'. This research provides further confirmation that men and women share similar motivations to offend, but how they approach and accomplish their crimes is frequently different.

One important finding from Brookman and colleagues' study was that the social distance between robbers and victims tended to be greater in the United Kingdom than in the United States, which suggests the significance of 'doing' a class-based gender performance during a robbery. The targets tended to be 'tourists, clubbers, suburbanites and shop keepers' in cosmopolitan commercial districts who 'are easier to intimidate, regardless of gender, than the robbers' peers' and drew upon 'victim's more general fears of crime and victimization' perceiving 'the class source of the threat as serious despite the gender of the robber' (Brookman et al., 2007:881–2). By locating the embeddedness of UK street robbery in what the authors term 'networks of hedonistic partying' their work also implies that the 'codes of the street' (Anderson, 1999), by which the urban young live, can cause and justify violence.

Messerschmidt (2005) has also refined his position, arguing that we should not reify gender by focusing solely on gender differences, but rather should explore gender diversity (that is explaining both similarities and differences) in the commission of crime. His more recent work has offered further theoretical complexity by exploring how criminal action arises from the dynamics of gender, race, class, and sexuality across four case studies, namely an examination of racist lynching during the Reconstruction era (1865–1877), the life history of Malcolm X as an account of a 'reformed hustler', a study of 'murderous managers' and organizational deviance at NASA, and finally an analysis of the 'perilous president' – George W. Bush and his attempts to construct a regional and global 'heroic hegemonic masculinity in an attempt to "sell" his war against Iraq' (Messerschmidt, 2014:97) in the aftermath of 9/11. Running through *Crime as Structured Action* is a sustained argument challenging simplistic notions of gender and highlighting the paradoxical nature of social life, in that it is both uncertain at every moment and made over time, yet also highly patterned and conditioned by social structures.

This is a crucial point, and in the next section we will see how forms of action remain social, even when the activities themselves seem resolutely antisocial and push at the very limits of a culture. As we saw in the last chapter it was the concept of subculture that sought to explain how differences between a particular social group and the mainstream come to be defined as deviant, defying the beliefs, lifestyles, manners, and values of the larger society. In what follows I trace the legacy of the subcultural tradition as it was developed by Stuart Hall and his colleagues at the Birmingham Centre for Contemporary Cultural Studies (CCCS). This is well-worn ground and I do not intend to cover all of it, rather I want to focus on how the notion of transgression emerged as central to the experience of profane otherness and marginalized cultural practices. The key book here is Peter Stallybrass and Allon White's (1986) landmark text *The Politics and Poetics of Transgression*, which offered a nuanced sense of the politics of popular cultural forms and the antagonisms that surround them. In doing so we can see how the concept of deviance and the subcultural terrain became subsumed under broader debates surrounding culture, ideology, and politics, so that by the 1990s it became clear that cultural studies had moved on to questions of difference, identity, and postmodernism. In response, the last 10 to 15 years have seen the growth of what have been termed 'post-subcultural' studies that have emerged to address the criticisms associated with the Birmingham tradition (Sweetman, 2013). These new perspectives have difficulties of their own, not least since the outright rejection of this past leaves a 'valorizing of individual consumption' that fails to grasp 'the generation or articulation of deviance as social experience' (Blackman, 2014:506). It is to such matters we now turn.

The Subcultural Legacy

The subcultural tradition, as it evolved through the Chicago School up to the Birmingham Centre, always sought to portray subcultures as distinctive social worlds – deviant, disenfranchised, and unconventional, but forming ties with others sharing similar values, practices, and geographies. At root what is emphasized is the social aspects of difference and affiliation in increasingly pluralized, fragmented societies. The subcultures group working at the Birmingham CCCS in the 1970s established an approach that was framed by broader theoretical debates circulating at the Centre. These were a lively and volatile mix of 'two paradigms' shaping the overall cultural studies project, one is often termed 'culturalism' and is a distinctly British perspective associated with socialist historians and literary critics, while 'structuralism' is the second paradigm and was strongly influenced by European thinkers where the 'linguistic turn' proved seismic (Hall, 1980), as was the legacy of the Italian Marxist theorist and interwar Communist activist Antonio Gramsci – especially his concept of 'hegemony' that would have a profound influence on Stuart Hall's thinking. Also decisive were developments in critical criminology, where symbolic interactionism and labelling studies insisted that deviance was not so much an action but a 'transaction' given a particular meaning by those with the power to define. These different strands enabled subcultures to be understood in fresh ways – no longer seen in terms of a frustrated readjustment to dominant middle-class values, but a defiant opposition to them. The rise of spectacular youth subcultures in post-war Britain was read as signifying the predicament of social change and distilling the bitter dynamics of class conflict in the shift to a modern, consumer society.

An early account studied the emergence of 'mods' and 'skinheads' in the East End of London during the 1960s through a distinctive class analysis of the destruction of working-class community and the erosion of its traditional culture. In his influential essay Phil Cohen (1972:23) maintained that youth subcultures do not solve the crises in class relations, rather they 'express and resolve, albeit "magically", the contradictions', which are experienced at various levels: at the ideological they are caught between 'traditional working class puritanism' and the 'new hedonism of consumption'; while at the economic the future is either 'part of the socially mobile elite' or joining 'the new lumpen'. This approach was further refined in the chapter 'Subcultures, Cultures and Class' (Clarke et al., 1976) from the collection *Resistance through Rituals* (Hall and Jefferson, 1976), which is informed by developments in Marxism (most notably from Althusser and Gramsci). The various subcultures discussed in the book are seen as attempts to win back space through challenging the status quo. However, this resistance is played out in the fields of leisure and consumption so that it ultimately fails to challenge broader structures of power. This theme is developed in Paul Willis's *Learning to Labour* (1977), an ethnographic study of how a 'counter-school culture' among a group of working-class 'lads' ultimately serves to prepare them for menial, unskilled employment and thereby reproduces inequalities.

The meanings of subcultural style are explored with considerable verve by Dick Hebdige (1979) through a mix of textual analysis and case studies where the interest in the working class is retained, but is now situated in the subversive potential of Continental avant-garde aesthetics. Although he saw subcultures as creative and mobile sites of resistance, in their innovative and improvised use of objects, they were also vulnerable to two kinds of 'incorporation'. One is through the 'commodity form' where the styles become mass-produced commodities and part of conventional, mainstream fashion. The second is the 'ideological form', and here Hebdige (1979:97) is attentive to the ways 'folk devils' are defined as 'deviant' in the media, but also to the subtler processes in which their threat is tamed: 'the Other can be trivialized, naturalized, domesticated' or 'transformed into meaningless exotica ... consigned to a place beyond analysis.' Nevertheless, the lasting impact of the book, and the CCCS approach more generally, is to pit youth subcultures against the incorporating logics of mass culture and the 'sustained ideological onslaught of "affluence"' (Clarke et al., 1976:25).

Critics were quick to dispute the political significance attached to subcultures in the approach and were troubled by the elitist focus on the original, authentic moment at the expense of any sense of a lived culture (Clarke, 1981/1990). Others found fault with the tendency to romantically read youth style as internal to the group, with commercialization only coming later, which underestimates the way changes in youth subcultures are manufactured by culture industries (Cohen, 1980/1988). Concerns were also raised over the preoccupation with white, male, and working-class subcultures, where the celebration of the spectacular ignored the racism and sexism in them. However, the Marxist emphasis on class was contested by feminists at the Birmingham Centre, most notably by Angela McRobbie (1981) who highlighted how Willis and Hebdige had implicitly privileged masculinity and ignored relationships in the family, households, and sexuality. Working-class culture is not just the school and workplace; it also includes the bedroom and breakfast table, indicating how writing women into subcultural arguments radically changes them. Indeed, much of McRobbie's work ever since has been a sustained, gendered interrogation of social change and a tracking of how consumerism borrows some of feminism's central concerns, while at the same time diluting and undermining their critical meaning and impact (McRobbie, 2009).

The relative neglect of ethnicity is a criticism that needs to be addressed in more detail, not least since Stuart Hall and his colleagues begin to track the politics of race in their major work on *Policing the Crisis* (Hall et al., 1978). Likewise, Hebdige (1979:45) had a keen eye for the cross-cultural exchanges between black and white communities, seeing, 'played out on the loaded surfaces of British working-class youth cultures, a phantom history of race relations since the War'. Yet the very 'Englishness' of the cultural studies project remained largely unexamined until the publication of the collection of essays *Empire Strikes Back* (1982) which argued for a more critical encounter with the complexities surrounding the social construction of race and how the political meaning of terms such as 'black' are contested and fought over.[4] As Paul Gilroy (1987b:12) subsequently maintained, it is nationalism rather than class that is the main reason why race is marginalized in scholarship and he condemned the 'morbid celebration of England and Englishness from which blacks are systematically excluded' in the discipline. By this point it is also clear that Hall was turning from a preoccupation with class and ideology to the 'politics of difference' and 'hyphenated identity'. In his account of 'New Ethnicities' he argues for 'an awareness of the black experience as a *diaspora* experience, and the consequences which this carries for the process of unsettling, recombination, hybridization and "cut and mix" – in short, the process of cultural *diaspora-ization*' (Hall, 1996:447, emphasis in original).

Gilroy (1993, 2000) also questioned absolutist forms of racial and cultural difference through his approach to diaspora, which becomes the key to understanding the relationships between culture, time, and place. The idea of the *Black Atlantic* is developed as a complex unit of analysis, transcending 'both the structures of the nation-state and the constraints of ethnicity and national particularity' (Gilroy, 1993:15). He remains resolutely critical of essentialist accounts of black cultural formations, insisting they produce 'camp mentalities' echoing not only fascism but also the commercialization of African-American music and urban, ghetto styles. In the latter, new claims of ethnic authenticity chime with twenty-first-century corporate multicultural commodification: when 'hip-hop's marginality' becomes 'as official and routinized, as its overblown defiance, even if the music and its matching life-style are still being presented – marketed – as outlaw forms' (Gilroy, 2000:180). His critique of the exclusivist bio-politics at work here is extended to the ways the black body is coded as either super human in the black athlete or as less than human in the violent black criminal. Notions of 'ghettoness' have become synonymous with forms of transgressive 'otherness' (Jaffe, 2012), but Gilroy's more recent work has explored the 'convivial culture' of multicultural cities, where forms of tolerance jostle with racism and yielding fresh insights into the relationships between the metropolis, colony, and the 'immigrant' (Gilroy, 2004).

In important respects this focus on identity and difference was bound up with broader changes across the intellectual landscape, where the era of 'the Post' came to characterize these new times: post-colonialism, post-feminism, post-fordism, post-marxism, post-structuralism, and looming over all, the post-modern. Postmodernism originated in architecture but spread throughout the arts, becoming a distinctive aesthetic movement inflected with irony, pastiche, and a knowing self-referentiality, while in the humanities and social sciences the ideas developed from the 'linguistic turn' among Continental thinkers such as Jean Baudrillard, Jacques Derrida, Michel Foucault, and Jean-François Lyotard. The key proposition is that the fundamental assumptions of modernity now no longer hold, but are fracturing and fragmenting, transforming social life in profound ways. A sense of these dizzying dislocations was provided by Hebdige (1988) where he sets out to overcome the weaknesses of subcultural analysis by exploring the positive possibilities afforded by the debates over postmodernism. Yet early on we learn that this will be an 'obituary' for his initial 'theoretical models' where the 'idea of subculture-as-negation grew up alongside punk, remained inextricably linked to it and died when it died', so the opening chapters constitute his 'attempt at a farewell to youth studies' (Hebdige, 1988:8). This idea was subsequently developed by Steve Redhead (1997) and others who argued that the subcultural moment had now passed into history (between the death of punk and the rise of rave later in the 1980s), and the movement to 'club cultures' required fresh postmodern theorizing. At the same time the metaphor of transgression became central to understanding the experience of otherness and a disordering of conventional categories.

The key text exploring these issues is Peter Stallybrass and Allon White's (1986) *The Politics and Poetics of Transgression*, which introduced the concept of the carnivalesque and the ideas of the Russian literary theorist Mikhail Bakhtin to cultural studies. The book explores the persistent hierarchical mappings of 'high' and 'low' culture in Europe and 'the process through which the low troubles the high' (Stallybrass and White, 1986:3). This process is transgression and is grounded in Bakhtin's (1984) understanding of the carnivalesque, which is a metaphor for the temporary, licensed suspension and reversal of order – when the world is turned upside down and inside out, when the low becomes high and the high turns low – on occasions of popular festivity at fairs, festivals, and Mardis Gras, and all for a brief period of time. It is on these occasions that transgressive desires can be temporarily enjoyed, strict hierarchies reversed, and vulgar excess indulged. As Hall (1996) recognizes, it is the 'sense of the overflowing of libidinal energy associated with the moment of "carnival" that makes it such a potent metaphor of social and symbolic transformation'. For, in Bakhtin, the notion of carnival is not simply a metaphor of inversion, whereby the 'low' replaces the 'high', it is instead the purity of this binary distinction that is transgressed, blurred, and made 'grotesque'. Much of their book is an account of the life and death of the carnival and the battle for popular culture, charting how 'a fundamental ritual order of Western culture came under attack – its fasting, violence, drinking, processions, fairs, wakes, rowdy spectacle and outrageous clamour were subject to surveillance and repressive control' (Stallybrass and White, 1986:176). Although the earlier practices of carnival diminished in Europe, largely as a result of Church persecution and subsequent Puritanism, its symbolic significance continues to persist and elements of the carnivalesque can still be found almost anywhere.

Rob Shields (1991) develops this point by examining how the carnivalesque is resurrected in 'places on the margin' and encountered in liminal zones. One of the examples he gives is of the seaside town and how they became sites of leisure, but also of trouble and excess (dirty weekends, saucy postcards, rowdy

bank holidays, youthful misdemeanours, bodies scantily clad, and so forth).
Here the carnivalesque is pushed to the spatial edges, but in other accounts
these unruly pleasures have been sublimated through a modern civilizing process, only to reappear in the form of bohemian lifestyles (Featherstone, 1992).
The implications of these arguments for criminology have been put as follows:

> the more that there are efforts to map out a world of morality and permis-
> sibility and the more the impermissible is repressed, the more perversely
> attractive it becomes and the more that liminal zones (space-time locations
> where the impermissible occurs) become covertly valued and pursued. So
> it is that red-light districts, especially during the darker hours (compare
> Melbin, 1978) become places of disreputable pleasure in which otherwise
> reputable people dabble, reproducing the divisions that lie at the heart of
> modern culture while playing with the (moral) edge between them ... This
> raises the familiar point that that the deviant and the reputable are inextri-
> cably intertwined and the right side of the tracks can exist only in contrast
> to the wrong side of the tracks.
>
> (O'Malley and Mugford, 1994:210)

It was Mike Presdee (2000) who sought to set out the complex fragmentation
and reworking of carnival in his now classic work on cultural criminology.
In particular, he argued that in 'the acts of body modification, S&M, raving,
recreational drug-taking, hotting and rodeo, gang rituals, the Internet, festivals and extreme sports, lurks the marginal performance of carnival fragments
in the late twentieth century' (Presdee, 2000:47). Of course, this is quite a
disparate list of practices and not all by any means are criminal but what
they share is the ludic pleasures of performance counterposed to the respectable values of sobriety, propriety, and restraint. It is a line of argument that
drew him to the sensual dynamics of edgework, as outlined above, and the
emotionally charged, lived experience of transgression. These ideas challenge
the way much contemporary criminology has reduced crime to a mundane,
instrumental activity.

Instead, the underlying premises are completely reversed to reveal 'the *intensity* of motivation' in a 'world where pleasure has to be seized despite the
intense commodification of consumer culture, where control must be struggled
for in a situation of ever increasing rationalisation and regulation' (Young,
2007:20, emphasis in original). No doubt this is a romanticized view of the sur-
viving fragments of carnival in contemporary culture, and in this it has echoes
of Michael Maffesoli's (1996) account of neo-tribal sociality in the midst of a
rigid, alienating mass society. His approach has been enormously influential in
shaping the 'post-subcultural turn' (Bennett, 2011) over the last 20 or so years
and can be contrasted with more resolutely unromantic accounts of youth cultural practice. The most important work to emerge in this latter vein is Sarah
Thornton's (1995:8) work on club cultures, which emphatically declares it is

'post-Birmingham' in a number of distinct ways. Chief among them is the way that discourses of the young have too often been taken at face value: where 'youth have celebrated "underground", the academics have venerated "subcultures", where young people have denounced the "commercial", scholars have criticized "hegemony"; where one has lamented "selling out", the other has theorized "incorporation"' (Thornton, 2007:185).

Thornton's approach looks back to much earlier Chicagoan schooled sociologists Howard Becker (1963) and Ned Polsky (1967/1998) and their research on jazz musicians and the beat scene in New York. Both drew attention to insider and outsider dynamics, where the 'hip' define themselves against ignorant 'squares'. Among beatniks the term 'hipster' had acquired a 'pejorative connotation' and was used to describe 'one who is a mannered show-off regarding his hipness', indeed the beats regarded themselves as 'hip' but most 'definitely not hipsters' (Polsky, 1967/1998:145). From this work on the fine-grained classifications and hierarchies operating in unconventional social worlds Thornton innovatively develops the French sociologist Pierre Bourdieu's (1984) notions of cultural capital and distinction to British clubbers. Her key move is to reconceptualize club cultures as 'taste cultures', where being 'hip' and 'in the know' constitute forms of 'subcultural capital' and 'confers status on its owner in the eyes of the relevant beholder', while nothing depletes it more than 'someone trying too hard' (Thornton, 1995:12).

By attending to the internal divisions and stratifications of dance clubs and raves Thornton is able to explore how social differences are classed and gendered. During her fieldwork, for example, there were frequently disparaging remarks made towards 'raving Sharons', 'Techno Tracys', and 'handbag house', each of which denotes a feminized denigration of an unsophisticated mainstream. But what is highly significant about her work is that she insists these classifications should not be equated with the actual dance cultures of working-class girls, rather these euphemisms reveal a lot about the elitist values of hardcore clubbers, and she quotes Bourdieu's point that 'nothing classifies somebody more than the way he or she classifies' (cited in Thornton, 1995:101). In this way the social logic of subcultural capital is performed through what it dislikes and what it is not. The majority of clubbers distinguish themselves against an imagined mainstream and these distinctions are a means by which young people jockey for social power, assign social status, and presume the inferiority of others. Her work stands in some contrast to the post-subcultural turn which denounces 'modernist theory' as too 'class-centred' (Muggleton, 1997:200) and unable to grasp the new postmodern meanings of style where 'there are no rules, there is no authenticity, no ideological commitment, merely a stylistic game to be played' (Muggleton, 2000:47).

Consequently, terms like 'tribe', 'scene', and 'lifestyle' have been advanced to deal with the problems associated with subcultural theory, where the suggestion is that these are better equipped to capture the proliferation, fragmentation, and individualized character of contemporary youth cultures (see Bennett,

2011, for an overview). Others criticized CCCS subcultural approaches for over relying on theoretical abstraction at the expense of empirical data (Hodkinson, 2012), which has become a regular complaint over the decades. Significantly, Hall and Jefferson (2006) have responded to these criticisms in a wide-ranging survey of how their approach has fared. In discussing some of the main post-subcultural contributions they note they certainly provide:

> fuller accounts of the lived accounts of the lived experiences of their subcultural 'bearers' better than we did in *RTR*, thereby meeting the main thrust of the 'lack-of-ethnographic-authenticity' critique. But, beyond that, what do we learn of the larger picture? How well are these empirically grounded subcultures 'grounded' in relation to the political, economic and socio-cultural changes of their respective times? The answer is 'not very well', if at all.
>
> (Hall and Jefferson, 2006:xiv)

This is partly owing to an 'endemic problem with ethnographic accounts' where insider accounts 'told from within is taken to be the privileged level of enquiry and of explanation' and some are fundamentally 'opposed to ... making connections between lived experience and structural realities' (ibid.) Their line of critique here is to accuse the post-subculturalist ethnographers of offering up a 'hollow empiricism' that fails to grasp the larger, structural condition and ties to historical developments (Sweetman, 2013:2).

Conclusion

The tensions exposed here between cautious, ethnographic work and big picture, sociological theorizing were echoed in Loïc Wacquant's (2002) polemical review essay of three books exploring urban poverty in North American cities.[5] In his withering assessment:

> these three books illustrate well the perennial pitfalls of ethnography as embedded social research when it is carried out under the banner of raw empiricism. It can get so *close* to its subjects that it ends up parroting their point of view without linking it to the broader system of material and symbolic relations that give it meaning and significance, reducing sociological analysis to the collection and assembly of folk notions and vocabularies of motives.
>
> (Wacquant, 2002:1523, emphasis in original)

His extensive assault on the appreciative stance of the ethnographers included finding them guilty of a 'sanitizing thrust' and uncritically accepting 'informants' self-portraits' (ibid:1478) while failing to connect the deindustrialization of the city with the conduct found on the streets. Each of the three authors responded to Wacquant's charges and found him guilty of distorting their arguments, misrepresenting their findings, and creating absurd caricatures of their books. According to Anderson (2002:1534) his 'distortions' result from a 'peculiar view of the role of social theory in ethnographic work' that insists on a 'rigid commitment to a theory' and then a readiness to 'subordinate the cultural complexity he or she finds in the field to that theory'. His rebuttal then points out that 'Wacquant is no Bourdieu' and 'this is readily shown when he applies Bourdieu's ideas in dogmatic and ill-suited fashion to the Philadelphia ghetto' (ibid:1535). The misreading results from a top-down structural theory that cannot grasp the messy complications of daily interactions on the street and this quarrel played out in a review symposium gets at some of the fundamental differences between microsociological approaches, each of which are opposed to the kind of grand theorizing in structural sociology.

These tensions are never likely to be resolved as they are asking very different questions of what theoretical work should do, but it is significant that they have arisen again recently in the controversies surrounding Alice Goffman's (2014) ethnographic account of disadvantaged life in a Philadelphia neighbourhood. Above all what seems to have 'frustrated her critics was the fact that she was a well-off, expensively educated white woman who wrote about the lives of poor black men without expending a lot of time or energy on what the field refers to as "positionality" — in this case, on an accounting of her own privilege' (Lewis-Kraus, 2016:1) that served to reinforce popular stereotypes and trade in sensationalism. By getting 'too close' to her subjects she is accused of lacking rigour and accepting at face value the accounts her subjects give of themselves. Worse still than being impressionistic, her research is criticized for being exploitative – complaints that have haunted ethnography for over a hundred years. There is no doubt that the current controversies over the book condense unsettled disputes that reach far beyond this particular case. As Johnny Ilan (2015:9) has argued, 'street culture is rife with complexities, contradictions and dissonances' to the extent that it is best understood as a continuum. The messy reality of street collectives and their hierarchies stands in stark contrast to how they are conceived in state and popular imaginaries (Hallsworth, 2013).

All of which is to suggest that we need to be able to distinguish between good and bad ethnography – from 'thick' and 'thin' description – and Matthews (2014:208) spends some time setting out what to 'critical realists a good ethnography' should look like and argues it should include a number of key attributes, and insists they must:

> be evaluative of social action and aim to better understand human capabilities, vulnerabilities, and values. People's involvement and response to different forms of transgression are not reducible to the search for excitement, engaging in 'edgework', the experience of resistance, or even the joy of transgression. We need to understand more about the ethical dimensions of social life and the complex mix of values, aspirations and concerns of

those we study ... Some account also needs to be taken of public opinion and social norms to understand why different forms of crime and deviance matter to people.

(ibid.)

The two exemplars he chooses to support his case are Willis's (1977) *Learning to Labour* and Goffman's (1962) *Asylums*, both of which begin with particular situations and move out to more general forms of explanation, through a process of abstraction that identifies the essential features of the processes and institutions under study. In this article Matthews is emphasizing the role of theory, and his overall project is geared towards building a critical realist approach that goes beyond 'so what' criminology (see also Matthews, 2009). There is no doubt criminology is in urgent need of theoretical renewal, but a complaint is that 'he moves us further away from genuine critical realism and closer to the administrative pragmatism that bogged down left realism in the 1980s' (Hall and Winlow, 2015:63). I will return to these arguments later in the book, but what should be clear is that the collective dynamics of street life are complex and illustrate the need for further exploration of the vast terrain on which social theory and empirical research meet.

5

Control

If sociological criminology can be reduced to three questions – why are laws made, why are they broken, and what can be done about this? – then this chapter is explicitly concerned with the first and third questions. At the time Edwin Sutherland was writing, in the 1920s, these questions would have been addressed by the concept of social control, an idea then closely tied to particular visions of democracy and social order, where the construction of a consensus among a great many different people in worlds sharply divided was pivotal. The central issues were how do social interactions come to be patterned, conforming to norms and rules of conduct, rather than be chaotic, and what happens when there is some wayward departure from these routines and practices? By the 1970s and 1980s the concept of 'social control' stood at the centre of important theoretical debates, largely prompted and provoked by Foucault's (1975/1991) influential account of the emergence of the 'disciplinary society' in Western Europe in the early nineteenth century. Since then it has fallen from favour, partly over concerns that it was being used too vaguely and loosely, describing all the ways in which conformity might be secured – ranging from child socialization through to more repressive mechanisms of state coercion.

In a decisive contribution Stan Cohen (1985:2) warned that the term was in danger of becoming a 'Mickey Mouse' concept.[1] He condemned lifeless sociological explanations on the necessity of social-systemic integration (as in earlier structural-functionalist accounts on how the different parts of society are bound into a more or less coherent whole) and crude historical contrasts between pre-industrial and modern societies, as well as looking beyond the narrow, technical terrain of the formal mechanisms used in the official control of crime. To bring greater analytical precision to the concept he defined social control as:

> those organized responses to crime, delinquency and allied forms of deviant and/or socially problematic behaviour which are actually conceived of as

such, whether in the reactive sense (after the putative act has taken place or the actor identified) or in the proactive sense (to prevent the act).

(Cohen, 1985:3)

This tighter definition has the advantage of conveying how social control is also a flexible process, involving not just criminal justice agencies, but also those involved in education, health, the military, welfare, and other professions regulating troubling conduct.

At around this time a distinctive academic field concentrating on 'punishment and society' began to take shape. It was given fresh impetus in David Garland's (1990) survey of the different social theorists who have highlighted the institutional complexity of punishment, and how it plays a range of penal and social functions, in which crime control is only one objective – albeit an important one. This strategy of detaching punishment from the legal apparatus and moral arguments that normally surround it to instead reveal the broader structural forces, cultural sensibilities, political conflicts, and social relations sustaining penal systems was a crucial one and has helped to establish a new multidisciplinary field in recent decades. The chapter begins by charting the origins and development of this approach, where each of the three 'founding figures' in sociology have asked some fundamental questions on the social foundations of punishment. Yet, with the arguable exception of Durkheim, punishment did not constitute a prime theoretical focus for either Marx or Weber, rather each has provided their followers with explanatory frameworks that differ widely and have often proceeded with considerable disregard for rival perspectives.

Revisiting the Classics

Durkheim's theory of punishment is initially advanced in his most famous book *The Division of Labour in Modern Society* (1893/1960), is then extended in the article 'Two Laws of Penal Evolution' (1901/1984) to give a more nuanced understanding of historical change, and is further refined in his lectures on *Moral Education* (1925/1961). In *The Division of Labour* he develops his classic theory on the emergence of specialized work in modern societies through distinguishing between simple pre-industrial societies, in which there is little division of labour, and more advanced societies, where people perform complex, specialized tasks. In each type of society he saw punishment playing an important role in the creation of solidarity as it arouses furious moral indignation and a ritualized expression of social values against those who violated the sacred moral order. The later essay 'Two Laws of Penal Evolution' accounts for historical changes in the 'quality' and 'quantity' of punishment, highlighting the tendency for brutal bodily practices (torture, mutilation, execution, and so on) to be gradually replaced by the more 'lenient' and less severe sanction of imprisonment, as evidence of trans-formations in the *conscience collective* towards the privileging of human dig-nity and liberty in modern societies. Here the 'cult of the individual' acquires a sacred status, and a concern for the plight of the criminal is a hallmark of civilization. Durkheim's lectures, given in 1902 and 1903 and collected under the title *Moral Education* (Durkheim, 1925/1961), include several chapters exploring the purpose of punishment in the classroom in a broader discussion on the uses of authority and the virtues of civic republicanism. In these last words on the topic he places a strong accent on the communicative aspects of punishment – how it plays a constructive role in collective rituals and rein-forces social morality.

Durkheim recognizes that punishment is not a particularly effective way of controlling crime – in fact he insists this is a modern fantasy – but its significance lies in publicly declaring that a wrong has been committed and that it is right to feel outraged by this violation of the social order. In his final major work *The Elementary Forms of Religious Life* his attention shifts from the 'conscience collective' (shared norms and beliefs) to 'collective representations' (shared ways of thinking) and classifications, where the distinction between the sacred and profane is crucial. Durkheimian themes have informed insightful analy-ses of how penal rituals provoke symbolic and emotive effects. For instance, the Danish sociologist Svend Ranulf argued that criminal law developed as a consequence of middle-class moral indignation (for a nuanced discussion of Ranulf's ideas, see Barbalet, 2002), while Harold Garfinkel (1956:420–4) insisted that the rituals of the court room should be understood as a 'degrada-tion ceremony' as 'moral indignation serves to effect the ritual destruction of the person denounced' by defining the accused as an enemy of all that is good and decent in society – a view subsequently developed by Pat Carlen (1976:17) in her analysis of *Magistrates' Justice*, where she describes 'the material geneses and symbolic forms of the coercive surrealism and absurdity' permeating the rituals of trial procedures.

In the 1960s Kai Erikson (1966) influentially explained the religious perse-cutions and witch trials in seventeenth-century Massachusetts in Durkheimian terms of community boundary maintenance and deep, structural crises in Puritan society. At the same time, the anthropologist Mary Douglas (1966) in her account of *Purity and Danger* emphasized that evils often take the shape of cultural pollution, and the control of these threats is fundamental to all human societies. Violations of symbolic classifications provoke disgust and fear, giving rise to disorder, and while different cultures define 'the pure' and 'the dangerous' in distinct ways, such codes are always present and every culture must come to terms with anomalies that defy its basic assumptions. How the threat is con-ceived, and the way in which it is met, tells us much about the structure of the community itself. More recently, Philip Smith (2008) has ambitiously sought to reinterpret every significant penal institution – from public executions, through the panopticon and guillotine up to the electric chair and supermax prisons – through a neo-Durkheimian framework. As these examples indicate there is a rich tradition exploring the structural relationships between deviance and control, indicating how they are fundamental features of social organization and function to shore up the normative order of particular communities. The radical claim is that punishment works not to control crime but to reinforce social solidarity. Critics wonder how widely shared collective values are and point to the numerous divisions in society, so that it should be no surprise to learn that Marxist analyses of punishment not only address a whole range of themes ignored by Durkheim, but also reinterpret many of those that are.

Neither Marx nor Engels wrote extensively on penal institutions, rather the legacy of the Marxist tradition has been to consider punishment in relation to economic structures and examine the class interests served by social control. The key argument is that such systems maintain and strengthen the position of the ruling class, rather than benefiting society as a whole, and that punishment as a social institution plays an important political role as a repressive state apparatus. The foundations of a distinctive materialist framework were laid initially by the German Marxist scholar Georg Rusche in the early 1930s. His arguments were later written up with the assistance of Otto Kirchheimer and published in 1939 through the exiled Frankfurt School of Social Research in New York, as *Punishment and Social Structure*, but did not receive much attention until a second edition was published in 1968 and prompted a revival of their thinking in the nascent radical criminology then taking shape. The book presents a detailed analysis of the changing relationship between labour markets and penal discipline in Western Europe across distinct epochs: the early Middle Ages (characterized by penance and fines) where land was abundant and labour was in short supply, giving rise to a relatively lenient penal system; the later Middle Ages (a harsher regime of corporal and capital punishment) where there was now a labour surplus and increasing urban poverty; the age of mercantilism in the sixteenth century changed labour market conditions once more and led to new forms of punishment (galley slavery, transportation, and penal servitude in houses of correction are each focused on enforcing labour); the emergence of capitalist modes of production in the eighteenth century prompted further changes, including the rise of imprisonment as the dominant form of punishment.

In Rusche and Kirchheimer's analysis, the modern prison as it developed through the nineteenth and early twentieth centuries was not simply a warehouse for the temporary confinement of the unruly and undesirable, but a new form of regulating economic and social relationships. It emerged as a coercive instrument of ruling-class control 'disseminating an acceptance of the work-discipline demanded by the wider, unequal capitalist market place' (Taylor, 1999:192). Crucial here is the principle of less eligibility, by which they refer to 'the standard of living within prisons (as well as for those dependent on the welfare apparatuses) must be lower than that of the lowest stratum of the working class' (Rusche and Kirchheimer, 1939:108). Their basic thesis

has been developed by Dario Melossi and Massimo Pavarini (1978:145) in an argument highlighting the close ties between factory discipline and the new penitentiary, which is 'like a factory producing proletarians not commodities'. The capitalist organization of labour is created by the factory, and is reinforced by other institutions such as schools and prisons, so that 'the entire system of social control is modelled on the relations of production' (Melossi, 1979:98). Although this variant of Marxism does rightly emphasize the importance of economic relations on penal practices, it does so in a way that minimizes the significance of other crucial factors and has been criticized for its reductionism and functionalism (the objections are detailed in Garland, 1990:106–10). Nevertheless, this political economy approach has been revitalized in Alessandro de Giorgi's (2006) nuanced attempt to provide a materialist explanation for the development of new technologies of control since the 1970s up to the present day.

In contrast, other Marxists have stressed the role of punishment in ideological class struggles and the maintenance of state power rather than labour market conditions and systems of economic production. This approach is associated with a radical group of social historians led by E. P. Thompson (1977), who challenged what became known as the Whig view of history (one that champions progressive reform and constructs history 'from above') by studying the eighteenth-century Bloody Code, which specified the death penalty for a vast array of offences such as hunting, poaching, and damaging property. He revealed how customary rights in the countryside and workplace were being eradicated and in doing so illustrated the class interests served by these statutes. Likewise, Douglas Hay (1975) highlighted how the discretionary character of capital punishment empowered local elites in his analysis of eighteenth-century criminal law, by drawing attention to its dual functions of ideological legitimation and class coercion. In particular, Hay regards the expansion of capital punishment as a 'rule of terror' on the part of the landed aristocracy over thousands of landless poor, with the exercise of clemency (where the lord of the manor speaks to fellow gentry on behalf of a tenant at risk of severe punishment) regarded by Hay as a central factor contributing to a culture of deference among the rural peasantry. Displays of mercy were a crucial factor in allowing the ruling class to maintain power long after the social ties of feudalism had collapsed and well before a modern system of rule had developed. It was the criminal law, above every other social institution, that enabled England to be governed by a small elite with little administrative or military capacity, and that the ideology of law 'was crucial in sustaining the hegemony of the English ruling class' (Hay, 1975:56).

The 'revisionist historians', as they were known, were writing from within a humanistic tradition of Marxism, contending that the law can function ideologically to legitimate the existing order, but took issue with more structural forms of Marxism influential at the time:

people are not as stupid as some structural philosophers suppose them to be. They will not be mystified by the first man who puts on a wig ... If the law is evidently partial and unjust, then it will mask nothing, legitimize nothing, contribute nothing to any class's hegemony.

(Thompson, 1977:262–3)

The clear implication is that the law is an 'arena for class struggle' rather than the exclusive possession of a ruling class (Thompson, 1977:288). However, critics point out that the criminal law and penal sanctions command a wide degree of support from the subordinate classes (the very population said to be controlled and regulated by such mechanisms of class rule) and that such practices afford a degree of protection previously unrealized (Fine, 1985). Nevertheless, one of the strengths of Marxist analysis is that it invites us to think of punishment not as a simple response to crime but as an important element in 'managing the rabble' (Irwin, 1990:2) – matters that are developed in the work of Michel Foucault who, for some, marks a decisive break with Marxism. In other respects, Foucault develops some Weberian themes, but in truth the work stands alone as a strikingly original contribution to modern social theory and was crucial in the formation of 'punishment and society' scholarship.

Of the three founding figures of sociology Max Weber concerned himself the least with punishment, but it is clear that many of his arguments and themes have informed a number of influential studies. In his major work on *Economy and Society* (Weber, 1968a, 1968b), written between 1910 and 1920, he develops a sociological understanding of domination that differentiates between charismatic, traditional, and rational-legal types of authority. Examples of each are to be found in historical and contemporary societies. Charismatic leadership is based on the ruler's possession of extraordinary abilities to transcend the everyday and personally inspire obedience, while the traditional form is based on custom, habit, and the rule of elders. Patriarchalism is a pure form of traditional domination, based on the power of the father over the household, while patrimonialism is the extension of this authority over large areas of land and feudalism is an instance of a more formalized system governed by status honour. Under rational-legal authority the rule of law is paramount and bureaucracy is the organizational form of domination. It is the form of rule that Weber regarded as the best for modern industrial states, not least since those granted the right to rule must themselves obey laws, rather than pursue their own interests. The spread of reason was especially important in developing the administrative capacities of the state through establishing formal rights and duties.

These ideas informed James Jacob's (1977) *Stateville*, which charts the changes at the Illinois prison over a 50-year period (1925–75). The key shift is from structures of authority based on personal dominance (in the charismatic guise of Warden Joseph Ragen) to a corporatist bureaucratic organization by the mid-1970s. The book belongs to a rich tradition of empirical sociological research on prison life prominent from the 1950s onwards, yet also anticipates how the rationalization of punishment would become an important theme in the literature (Spitzer, 1983). The argument is now that:

> developments such as regular paid police forces, a professional judiciary, rules of evidence and due process, penal codes with graduated punishments, the move from torture, mutilation and death to imprisonment and fines, are not so much progress in humanitarianism as progress in bureaucratized rationalism, necessary to meet the social control needs and legitimacy conditions of modern societies.
>
> (Hudson, 1997:90)

A Weberian approach is one that emphasizes how instrumental rationality penetrates deeper into the social fabric and becomes a defining feature of modernity.

Disciplinary Power and Societies of Surveillance

Weber's bleak view that the 'iron cage' of rationality and bureaucracy will ultimately imprison us all is expanded in Michel Foucault's (1975/1991) *Discipline and Punish*. A key inspiration for both was Nietzsche who insisted that all interpretation is selective and partial while all forms of reason are particular expressions of the will to power. This is not to suggest, as some critics do, that any of these thinkers advocates a naïve relativism incapable of distinguishing between interpretations of the world. This enduring theme of highlighting the relativity of knowledge to the interests of those concerned is developed by Foucault who dissects every body of knowledge for traces of the will to power it epitomizes. Although Foucault reworks some important Weberian themes, the French intellectual landscape in which he developed his ideas was dominated by the pillars of Marxism and phenomenology. He has explained how 'people of my generation were brought up on these two forms of analysis, one in terms of the constituent subject, the other in terms of the economic in the last instance, ideology and the play of superstructures and infrastructures' (Foucault, 1980:116). In making his break with these orthodoxies Foucault drew on the emerging structuralist forms of analysis that extended ideas in linguistics to cultural and social phenomena. Important examples of this new approach include the anthropologist Claude Lévi-Strauss's examination of the underlying structures of kinship relations, while the literary critic Roland Barthes applied structuralist methods to popular culture and the philosopher Louis Althusser radically reinterpreted Marxism to develop a theoretical 'anti-humanism' that profoundly influenced Foucault.

At the heart of his thinking lies certain key themes, which Foucault later claimed had been driven by the goal of creating 'a history of the different modes by which, in our culture, human beings are made subjects' (Foucault, 1982:208). Closely tied to this questioning of the human subject lies the joint concerns of power and knowledge. In his early work Foucault sought to grasp how the human and social sciences historically became possible, while his later writings came to regard power as a discursive system of knowledge that shapes institutional practices in specific sites (such as asylums, barracks, factories, prisons, and schools). It is in this context that Foucault's (1975/1991) *Discipline and Punish* should be situated. The book is far more than a history of punishment. It is rather a wide-ranging account of how power operates in modernity. The book opens with a striking juxtaposition of two entirely different styles of punishment that illustrate the fundamental transformations that had taken place in penal practices, namely the disappearance of the public spectacle of violence and the installation of a different form of punishment by the early nineteenth century, which is captured in a bland listing of the rules from an institutional timetable used in a Paris reformatory. The juxtaposition immediately highlights the importance of discontinuity. In what is now a defining feature of Foucault's approach, he uses the strangeness of past practices to call into question the supposed rationality and legitimacy of the present.

Foucault's overall argument is that the disappearance of the public spectacle of torture and its replacement by the prison is not a sign of progress and enlightenment. It is instead a sign of changing techniques of power, which aim to punish more deeply into the social body through discipline and surveillance, and he sets himself the ambitious task of 'writing the history of the present' (Foucault, 1975/1991:31). Cohen summarizes his argument in the following way:

> the 'Great Incarcerations' of the nineteenth century – thieves into prisons, lunatics into asylums, conscripts into barracks, workers into factories, children into school – are to be seen as part of a grand design. Property had to be protected, production had to be standardised by regulations, the young segregated and inculcated with the ideology of thrift and success, the deviant subjected to discipline and surveillance.
>
> (Cohen, 1985:25)

The new disciplinary mode of power which the prison was to represent belonged to an economy of power quite different from that of the direct, arbitrary, and violent rule of the sovereign. Power in a capitalist society had to be exercised at the lowest possible cost, both economically and politically, while its effects had to be intensified and extended throughout the social apparatus.

Although Foucault's work continues to be influential, as we will see throughout the chapter, it has been criticized for its 'appalling' historical inaccuracies (Braithwaite, 2003:8); 'impoverished' understating of subjectivity (McNay,

1994:22); preference for 'ascetic description' over normative analysis (Habermas, 1987:275); and for not being able to tell the difference between prison and life outside. Edward Said (1988:9–10), whose own work has drawn heavily on Foucault's ideas, has criticized his Eurocentrism through failing to grasp 'the fact that history is not a homogeneous French territory' while remaining silent on how 'discipline was also used to administer, study and reconstruct – then subsequently to occupy, rule and exploit – almost the whole of the non-European world'. Clearly these are multifaceted criticisms, but it is difficult to dispute the view that his work provided criminology with a new theoretical framework to understand social control in modernity. Yet at the very moment when Foucault's (1975/1991) analysis of the 'Great Incarcerations' was published many Western societies seemed to be radically reversing this pattern through decarcerating the confined and deploying alternative sanctions in the community.

Community corrections came to be regarded as a more humane and less stigmatizing means of responding to offenders, while treating mental illness in the community was generally seen as preferable to the asylum. However, a number of authors were sceptical and argued that treatment in the community amounted to malign neglect, with the mentally ill left to fend for themselves in uncaring environments (Scull, 1977). In criminology, Stan Cohen (1979, 1985) influentially maintained that the development of community corrections marks both a continuation and an intensification of the social control patterns identified by Foucault (1975/1991). This 'dispersal of discipline' thesis insists that there is a further blurring of where the prison ends and the community begins, with an accompanying increase in the total number of offenders brought into the system.

While Cohen (1985) chronicled the recruitment of friends, relatives, and neighbours into the web of surveillance through curfews, tracking, and tagging that now pervade the 'punitive city' (Cohen, 1979), a debate ensued over the applicability of Foucault's ideas to contemporary patterns of punishment (Bottoms, 1983; Shearing and Stenning, 1985; Nelken, 1989). As one perceptive critic put it:

Like Foucault's own work on the prison, Cohen's analysis of the juvenile justice system is noticeable for its generally anti-institutional posture and its unswerving dislike of all forms of social control – often on the fundamentalist premise that social control is in some sense inhumanitarian, and always underpinned by a libertarian assumption that seems unable to countenance any form of institutional restraint of individuals under any circumstances.

(Taylor, 1999:204)

Since the 1990s there has been a rapid expansion of electronic, information, and visual technologies, all of which have greatly enhanced the surveillance capacities of the state. Surveillance operates in so many spheres of daily life that it is impossible to avoid, and is embedded in the routines of everyday life, regulated by hidden forms of computerized dataveillance (Garfinkel, 2000). These range from 'the Electronic Funds Transfer at Point of Sale (EFTPOS) machine for paying the supermarket bill or the request to show a barcoded driver's license, to the cellphone call or the Internet search, numerous everyday tasks trigger some surveillance device' (Lyon, 2001:146).

Likewise urban fortress living has quickly moved from a dystopian vision (Cohen, 1985) to become a reality, particularly in Los Angeles (Davis, 1992, 1999), so that contemporary surveillance is both inclusionary – offering a sense of safety, security, and order for some city dwellers – and exclusionary for others – prohibiting certain teenagers from entering panoptic shopping centres while planners develop sadistic street environments to displace the homeless from particular localities. John Fiske (1998) has further analysed the video surveillance of the American city to reveal how it is a rapidly developing control strategy focused on the young black male and is a disturbing instance of the totalitarian undercurrents in late modern democracies. The experience of surveillance varies considerably depending on social location and grouping, for some it enhances convenience, while for others it is an invasive and relentless feature of everyday life (Goffman, 2014; Rios, 2011). Ray Coleman and Joe Sim (2000:636) have argued that the deployment of CCTV in city centres is not simply a crime-prevention technology but is a troubling response to 'gaps left by a series of legitimation deficits around policing and in urban governance generally'. A key shift is that today everyone is likely to be the subject of surveillance, to a greater or lesser degree, as a result of socio-technical developments.

In response, the concept of 'surveillant assemblage' (Haggerty and Ericson, 2000) has been developed to capture the contemporary logics of social control. Here the philosophical work of Gilles Deleuze and the psychoanalyst Félix Guattari has been pivotal, as it suggests systems of social control have become more fluid and permeable than in the centralized panoptic or Orwellian visions of the totalizing surveillance apparatus. Indeed, Deleuze (1992) maintained that we now live in 'societies of control' that are in the process of replacing the 'disciplinary societies' identified by Foucault, where different types of loosely linked control systems flow into one another, intermingle, and overlap unsteadily. The emerging character of these current developments has been described as follows:

> The assemblage is all about linking, cross-referencing, pulling threads together that were previously separate. This also hints at its mode of growth. It is like the weed 'Creeping Charlie' that sends out horizontal shoots which in turn become new nodes in a constantly growing network. It is, as Gilles Deleuze and Felix Guatarri would say, "rhizomic." In the assemblage, surveillance works by abstracting bodies from places and splitting them into flows to be reassembled as virtual data-doubles, calling in question once again hierarchies and centralized power.
>
> (Lyon, 2003a:31)

These new forms of 'digital rule' (Jones, 2000), which have become possible with the rise of electronic technologies and the 'social sorting' (Lyon, 2003b) that accompanies them, do suggest that further theoretical work is needed to grasp the current patterns of control. There has since been a lively quarrel over the extent to which the disciplinary model has been superseded by more decentralized and non-hierarchical modes of surveillance (the recent edited collection by Ball, Haggerty and Lyon, 2012 gives a sense of the range of the disputes).

Deleuzian ideas also inform Marc Schuilenburg's (2015) study of the shifting terrain of hybrid, public–private security practices that now proliferate across urban landscapes. The 'rhizomatic meanings of security and care' (Hallsworth and Jones, 2014:58) offer fresh insights into a topic that has become a key subject in criminology. It is mobilized in a number of ways: '"governing security", "governing through security", "selling security", "civilizing security", "imagining security" and tackling "insecurity", as well as making concrete reference to "security management systems", "private security", and the "security industry"' (Zedner, 2009:1) are just some of the examples that have preoccupied criminologists since the turn of the century. In his *Against Security* Harvey Molotch (2014) has described how the forces of security and the command-and-control regimes they inspire are often counterproductive. Writing primarily in a US context he explains why one of the main reasons for the elaborate concentrations of security at airports is not because they are especially effective, but because they can be concretely arranged. Even then there are frequent failures to detect trouble:

> A particular problem is detecting bomb parts; because bombs disassemble into individual elements, each of which will appear innocent to a screener. But screeners also miss grossly inappropriate artifacts. A report leaked to the press on TSA's [Transportation Security Administration] own undercover operations ... at Newark Airport (conducted in October 2006), found that screeners failed twenty of twenty-two security tests, missing numerous guns and simulated bombs (these tests are not about liquids or scissors). There had been previous and repeated failures of 100 percent at some U.S. airports ...
>
> (Molotch, 2014:107)

Instead of these tactics, which not only annoy but intimidate, Molotch does offer genuine alternatives to the claims and practices marshalled in the securitization of the state. In this, his approach chimes with attempts to produce a 'counter-conduct of security' that can connect to new forms of civic life, ethics, and obligations not grounded in 'fear and enmity' (Carney and Dadusc, 2014:71).

Among the most influential attempts to explain crime control developments from the 1970s up to the present has been David Garland's (2001) *The Culture of Control*, which analyses how the changing social relations and cultural sensibilities of late modernity have undermined an older 'penal-welfare' model of crime and punishment. Two contradictory tendencies are at work, one he describes as 'criminologies of everyday life' that stress 'the modification of situations and opportunity structures rather than the reform of deviant individuals' (Garland, 2001:182). He explains that under the modernist, penal-welfare practices the goal was social integration, whereas the late modern approach regards the problem of social order as one of system integration and minimizing the opportunities to commit crime. The second is decidedly 'anti-modern' and is described as a 'criminology of the other', where 'the language of warfare and social defence' is deployed to define offenders as dangerous, threatening strangers who are 'intrinsically evil or wicked' (Garland, 2001:183). These arguments build on his discussion of how the *control* of crime had come to be regarded as a matter that lay beyond the state and requires the institutions of, and individuals in, civil society to manage, while the *punishment* of crime remains the business of the state and a significant symbol of state power (Garland, 1996). By tracing the developments as cultural adaptations to the emerging political landscape, which combined free market neo-liberalism with an authoritarian social conservatism and came to dominate in the United Kingdom and the United States, Garland's analysis provides a compelling account of the punitive turn in these societies, to which we will return in the section on mass incarceration. Yet it is worth noting that his most recent writing has been on the welfare state (Garland, 2014, 2016) and it suggests that there are important connections to the body politic in security described above.

Different Voices and the Civilizing Process

It will be clear that these main sociological traditions have largely ignored the punishment of women and it is only in the last 30 years or so that studies of the control of women have appeared. Nevertheless, it is important to emphasize that the study of gender continues to be marginalized and criminology remains a male-dominated discipline consisting largely of academic men studying criminal men, while the 'costs to criminology of its failure to deal with feminist scholarship are perhaps more severe than they would be in any other discipline' (Naffine, 1997:5). A clear instance of this is the widespread finding that when women are punished, this is as much about upholding conventional gender stereotypes as penalizing criminality (Carlen, 1983; Edwards, 1984; Howe, 1994). Moreover, the control of women is predicated on processes of transcarceration, where offenders move between different institutional sites (Lowman et al., 1987). Feminist studies have shown how there is a continuum of regulation in women's lives that encompass the penal system, mental health and social welfare systems through to informal social (and anti-social) controls (Cain, 1989; Smart, 1995).

The decisive intervention is Maureen Cain's (1989) edited collection *Growing Up Good*. Policing here means something more than the police force. The argument is that the criminal justice system is usually the last domain through which girls are policed because the everyday scrutiny which they are subjected to is far greater than that applied to boys. Moreover, very few girls can escape these lower levels of control, such as in the school and family, and one of the key sites for the policing of young women is through sexual reputation (Lees, 1989). The overall picture that emerges from this work is a more nuanced understanding of disciplinary control once the uneven experiences of women and men are considered. For instance, it is clear that women are much more likely to be controlled by psychiatry and social work while men are more readily incarcerated; it then follows that gender divisions are as fundamental to structuring punishment as those of class and race.

The issue of alterity arises in the history of women's struggle for rights and feminists have exposed how abstract universal norms are in fact partial male constructs. For instance, Simone de Beauvoir (1949) explained how women are oppressed by being a secondary Other to man's primary Self, whose existence is determined by being unlike men. The patriarchal subordination of the feminine is discussed further by Luce Irigaray (1985) who argues that the polis, from Plato's ideal republic to Hegel's universal sphere, is founded on exclusion through which women are forced to resemble men and reject their specificity in order to participate in civic life. Consequently, she is critical of liberal feminists who have called for the power imbalances between women and men to be reversed by struggling for equality as ultimately it involves accepting the existing terms of debate and forces women to become like men. The difficulties in the liberal feminist position were similarly revealed in the struggles over equality in criminal justice practice, as the best that can be achieved is the right to be treated like men (MacKinnon, 1987). Thus, Carol Smart (1989:139) argued that the early feminist struggle over equal rights had become problematic as the language and institutions built to protect rights are based on male ways of understanding the world.

Consequently a number of proposals for a 'feminist jurisprudence' (Carlen, 1990; Daly, 1989; Naffine, 1990) have been made on two main premises. The first is that legal categories which are supposedly gender-neutral reflect male dominance (MacKinnon, 1987); the second is that there is a kind of reasoning characteristic to women, which is excluded from criminal justice decision-making. While feminists continue to emphasize the need to bring women's experiences into legal theorizing through advocating 'woman-wise penology' (Carlen, 1990), there is widespread dispute over whether there is a universal 'female voice'. The tensions between 'different voice' (Gilligan, 1982) and 'male dominance' (MacKinnon, 1987) perspectives have structured much debate. One influential approach was Frances Heidensohn's (1986) use of the care/justice dichotomy in the criminal justice system. She defines the logic of justice in terms of the *Portia* principle: rational, judicial, and masculine; and the ethics of care as the *Persephone* principle: relational, informal, and feminine. Her conclusion was that both approaches have been used at various times in ways not always beneficial.[2]

The idea that women have a distinctive form of moral reasoning that is more concerned with finding solutions to specific and concrete problems, while men are more drawn to the application of general abstract rules, is primarily associated with the work of Carol Gilligan (1982) in her book *In a Different Voice*. She termed the female moral style 'the ethic of care' in contrast to the male 'logic of justice' and argued that both voices should have equal weight in moral reasoning, but in practice 'women's voices were misheard or judged as morally inferior to men's' (Daly, 2002:65). Consequently, feminist criminologists have called for legal processes to admit expert witnesses with specific feminist viewpoints to qualify masculine constructions of crime and punishment (O'Donovan, 1993; Valverde, 1996).

The concept of feminist moral reasoning proved to be controversial as it sought to replace one distorted unitary view of the world, the male, with another unitary female view (Walklate, 2001), while the term care has been criticized by disability activists and postmodernists for its oppressive and 'carceral' undertones (Hughes et al., 2005:263). Nevertheless, these debates effectively demonstrate that criminologists need to examine crime and punishment from a gendered perspective. This point has been put in the following way:

> Feminist criminology has prospered by focusing on the plight of women – women victims and potential victims and women offenders – and instead avoided the arguably more pressing work of bringing feminist analyses to bear on the old penological question of the rehabilitation of (largely male) offenders, especially violent offenders.
>
> (Valverde, 2012:248)

There are no easy answers, and while gender differences are important, there is no consensus over what these actually are and how these might shape practices of punishment, treatment, and control. Mariana Valverde (2012:247) also makes the telling point that those 'of us who popularized phrases such as "the medicalization of women's deviance" in the 1980s do not find it easy now to turn on a dime, intellectually, to protect psychiatric services for women in conflict with the law from austerity campaigns and budget cuts'. Her overall point is that there remain some problematic tendencies in theoretical work that excels in critique, but flounders in the painful world of practice.

In addition, feminist historians and criminologists have revealed how the ideological practice of institutional confinement began much earlier for women than for men. Mary Bosworth's (2000) analysis of the Hôpital de la Salpêtrière – the main hospital-prison complex for women in Paris from 1656 up to 1916 – indicates that many of the practices commonly held to originate in nineteenth-century penitentiaries in fact emerged far earlier in the seventeenth and eighteenth centuries. Likewise, Sherrill Cohen (1992) emphasizes how the existence of separate institutions for women across Europe from the sixteenth century onwards, such as Magdalene houses for 'repentant' prostitutes, combined penitence, religious instruction, and reformative labour in ways that anticipate developments in the nineteenth century. It has even been estimated that for much of the seventeenth and eighteenth centuries in London the number of women confined in 'houses of correction' was often greater than the number of men (Matthews, 1999:14), while Victorian responses frequently 'drew attention to "crimes of morality" committed by women, such as prostitution or public drunkenness' (Zedner, 1991:309). Clearly the lessons to be learnt from 'herstory' are not only that the confinement of women in the early modern period challenges conventional and revisionist histories, but also that women were central to the burgeoning practices of institutional exclusion, segregation, and control.

So far I have outlined some of the classical and contemporary positions in 'punishment and society' scholarship but there remains one important strand yet to be discussed. The work arose from the renewed attention given to the social theorist Norbert Elias's (1939/1984) understanding of *The Civilising Process*. His approach describes and explains how what we experience as 'civilization' is shaped by particular cultural sensibilities and psychic structures that have changed over time. In Elias 'civilizing' does not theoretically equate with 'progress' nor is it a 'value judgement', rather his study of European etiquette reveals how 'manners and personality in Western society gradually evolved from the late Middle Ages and was related to changes in state formation and the monopolization of power within them' (Pratt, 2000:185). In his *The Spectacle of Suffering*, the Dutch historian Pieter Spierenburg (1984) drew on Elias's account and established it as a rich alternative to both Foucault's analysis and Whig histories celebrating the rise of humane punishment in his study of the decline of public executions. The book is based on a detailed description of changing attitudes to the use of capital punishment and other torments inflicted on the human body in Amsterdam from 1650 to 1750. Over this time many of the brutal excesses gradually begin to decline or disappear altogether and similar patterns are found across Europe, which are owing to a growing repugnance and disdain among social elites for the infliction of suffering on powerless victims. These heightened emotional sensibilities are situated in a broader Eliasian argument on the pacification of social life through the increasing ability of nation states to effectively impose law and order over their territory.

Garland (1990) was also crucial in placing Elias's potential in the sociology of punishment canon, not least since he highlighted how certain aspects of life disappear from the public arena. As he explains:

Sex, violence, bodily functions, illness, suffering, and death gradually became a source of embarrassment and distaste and are more and more removed to various private domains such as the domesticated nuclear family, private lavatories and bedrooms, prison cells, and hospital wards. Lying behind this process is the tendency to suppress the more animalistic aspects of human conduct, as being signs of the crude and uncultivated.

(Garland, 1990:222)

One example of this approach is Vic Gatrell's (1994) analysis of public executions in Britain, which explores the complex ways in which the sentiments of compassion, sympathy, and pity developed over time. These cultural sensibilities helped distinguish the feeling, refined bourgeois self not only from the primal, unfeeling mob but also from an arrogant and exclusive aristocracy. These refined sensitivities eventually led nineteenth-century elites to express 'squeamishness' over the sight of capital punishment and played a prominent role in the campaign that led to the abolition of public hanging in 1868. Yet one of the many ambiguities he leaves unresolved is whether the polite classes actually felt revulsion and shame over judicial execution, or if sympathetic sentiments were emotions they felt they ought to express. Furthermore, he emphasizes that the movement ended up sanitizing capital punishment by removing the spectacle of suffering from public view. It is important to remember that for a further century 'murderers continued to be strangled on ropes too short or too long, dying more dreadfully in private than in public' (Gatrell, 1994:590) behind prison walls.

A more recent attempt to develop Elias's thesis in relation to contemporary patterns of punitiveness is to be found in John Pratt's (2002) *Punishment and Civilization*. The work maintains that for much of the modern period, penal practices have followed the contours of the civilizing process (the demise of public punishments; abolition of the death penalty; the 'disappearance of the prison'; and the gradual improvement of prison life over much of the twentieth century). In addition, he highlights the key role of bureaucratic governance in determining both the quality of prison life and the control of knowledge about it, noting from the 1980s how the appearance of new forms of punishment (boot camps, chain gangs, and the like) run counter to the technocratic rationalism driving penal development. That much of this 'new punitiveness' looks back to premodern punishment, depending on community participation and public humiliation to achieve their effects, and is taken as indicative of 'decivilizing' forces disrupting the civilizing process.

Again Elias (1996) is drawn on to explain how civilization and decivilization can exist simultaneously, and lead to the most barbaric outcomes, as he explained in his later work on the holocaust. He argues that the mass slaughter can only be understood in the context of the distinctive social processes of the German configuration. The concentration camps depended on bureaucratic efficiency, with few asking questions about what was going on in them and Elias emphasized the speed with which civilized conduct can disintegrate once social conditions become precarious, hostile, and fearful. As Pratt (2013:94) has recently put it, 'the reality of the genocide was successfully hidden from public view, in much the same way that mass incarceration in some Western societies and its attendant consequences (not least being its racial overtones) has become a non-issue in the 21st century'. The late modern penal explosion did not spark the formation of the 'punishment and society' field, but it has attracted considerable scholarship over the last two decades and it is to such matters we now turn.

Mass Incarceration and the New Penology

The American 'prison experiment' is characterized by a dramatic growth in the prison population as penal practices shifted from those grounded in the rehabilitative ideal to policies grounded in retribution, deterrence, and incapacitation. Through implementing mandatory minimum sentencing laws, 'Three Strikes and You're Out' legislation, and restrictions on parole, a 'punitive turn' set in motion the huge growth in prison populations and expenditures. After 50 years of relative stability, the incarceration rate began to rise exponentially – in 1970 there were 196,000 prisoners in state and federal prisons in the United States, but by the turn of the new century the figure exceeded 2 million and it has been estimated that if current US trends continue '30 per cent of all black males born today will spend some of their lives in prison' (Garland, 2001:6). Critics argue that the 'experiment' has been funded by the diversion of public expenditure from welfare to the prison, while the level of violence, particularly among the young and disadvantaged, continues to devastate life in many North American cities (Currie, 1996). Others point to the alarming racial dimension to this strategy of containment (Wacquant, 2001; M. Alexander, 2010; Tonry, 2011). Two decades ago it was revealed that one in nine African-American males aged 20–29 was in prison at any one time, and that a staggering one in three was either in prison, on probation, or on parole (Mauer, 1997).

The question of why the United States has embarked on such a divisive social policy of mass incarceration has received considerable attention. It is clear that the prison explosion has impacted disproportionately on young, less educated African-American men and has deepened already entrenched inequalities. Many are critical of the idea that the cause is simply due to an increase in crime committed by that particular population. Bruce Western's (2006) analysis of national data sets reveals that despite the huge increase in the incarceration rate of black men in the last quarter of the twentieth century, they were less involved in crime in 2000 than in 1980. Moreover, the data suggest that the racial disparities in imprisonment for drug offenders (the 'War on Drugs' is often said to be the key driving force fuelling penal expansion) are not primarily due to race differences in offending. Indeed, the actual evidence suggests that the current prison boom is not a simple and straightforward response to crime, given that crime rates were *declining* before the massive prison expansion even began (Gilmore, 2007). It is to broader cultural, institutional, political, and structural forces that recent scholarship has turned so as to grasp the factors shaping criminal justice policy.

Among the most provocative has been Loïc Wacquant's (2009) analysis of the emergence of the American 'penal state', which ties developments in penality to an analysis of the predatory logic of neo-liberalism and new forms of regulating of the poor striving to compel them into the post-Fordist labour market. The neo-liberal drive to economic deregulation, and welfare state retraction, has been accompanied by an expanding, repressive penal apparatus and the individualizing of responsibility through cultural tropes. Wacquant's key move is to identify the double regulation of the lower strata through the yoking of social and penal policy for those at the bottom of an increasingly polarized class structure, which aims to keep the increasingly precarious '(sub) proletariat' (2009:297) under control and contained in a 'carceral-assistential lattice' (2009:304). The state has reconfigured welfare entitlements under a 'workfare' system in which benefits operate under a contractual system, which is itself punitive towards those unable or unwilling to work, and 'prisonfare' is now the dominant way of governing social marginality (2009:312). In effect, workfare and prisonfare operate in tandem and draw the dividing line between the deserving and the undeserving poor, between 'wholesome "working families" and the corrupt and fearsome "underclass"' (2009:293).

Although Wacquant is at pains to distance himself from the 'narrowly materialist vision of the political economy of punishment' (2009:xviii), critics argue that his approach does not so much overcome the 'materialist/symbolic divide' as reproduce it through concluding that 'the neoliberal penal state reveals its *instrumental* side against the new poor, while projecting is purely *symbolic* hold on the rest of society – specifically, on the middle classes it struggles to reassure by allowing them to witness the punitive excess unleashed against the new dangerous classes' (De Giorgi, 2013:49, emphasis in original). In other words, the symbolic power of the penal state is largely understood in terms of ideological legitimation and the main role of it is to govern social insecurity in a deregulated labour market, which recalls some earlier Marxist explanations discussed above. Others have complained that his work is too 'heavily structuralist' and lacks a serious 'analysis of politics' (Campbell, 2010:62), a point echoed by Frances Fox Piven (2010:114) who maintains that much of 'the drive for tough drug laws, mandatory sentencing, and prison construction was generated by electoral politics, and particularly by the so-called Republican "southern strategy" of demonizing African Americans in order to draw white voters away from the Democratic party with which blacks had come to be associated'.

There is an extensive body of scholarship that has explicitly addressed the racialized dynamics of mass incarceration. Some see it as the latest stage in a process that begins with slavery and moves on to convict leasing, through Jim Crow laws, and right up to the ghetto to subjugate African-Americans. While there are continuities between these racial caste systems of social control, it is important not to treat them as one and the same, not least since that underplays the enormous extent of prison expansion since the 1970s (Gottschalk, 2006). Nevertheless, a convicted African-American man today has barely 'more rights, and arguably less respect, than a black man living in Alabama at the height of Jim Crow' and once 'labeled a felon, the old forms of discrimination – employment discrimination, housing discrimination, denial of food stamps and other public benefits, and exclusion for jury service – are suddenly legal' (M. Alexander, 2010:2). This perspective explains how racial hierarchies are maintained through a supposedly 'colour-blind' criminal justice system, in which the 'War on Drugs' plays a prominent role in shaping penal expansion (Lynch, 2012).

A third approach situates mass incarceration alongside other developments in crime control – from policing and crime prevention to sentencing and electronic surveillance – where the rise of risk-management techniques has come to particular prominence. An especially influential statement of this position is Malcolm Feeley and Jonathan Simon's (1992, 1994) discussion of what they term 'the new penology' in relation to a then largely unremarked set of transformations in criminal justice occurring in the United States. As they put it:

> the new penology is markedly less concerned with responsibility, fault, moral sensibility, diagnosis, or intervention and treatment of the individual offender. Rather it is concerned with techniques to identify, classify and manage groupings sorted by dangerousness. The task is managerial, not transformative.
>
> (Feeley and Simon, 1992:452)

The new penology is based on actuarial techniques, probability calculations, and statistical distributions to measure risk. For Feeley and Simon, the 'old penology' was preoccupied with such matters as guilt, responsibility, and obligation, as well as diagnosis, intervention, and treatment of the individual offender, whereas, they claim the 'new penology' is radically different and actuarial in orientation as it is concerned with techniques for identifying, classifying, and managing groups assorted by levels of dangerousness. The aim is not to intervene in offenders' lives for the purposes of ascertaining responsibility or rehabilitating them. It is instead a strategy of managing dangerousness, and the shift is from individualized discipline and rehabilitation to the control of entire populations. Feeley and Simon (1992) give the example of how at one extreme the prison provides maximum security at a high cost for those who pose the greatest risk, and at the other, probation provides low-cost surveillance for low-risk offenders. They coin the phrase 'actuarial justice' to express some of the internal tensions posed by the new penology.

The importance of Feeley and Smith's work lies not simply in highlighting how the use of imprisonment, probation, parole, and community punishments has in each case accelerated in recent times, but in that 'the new penology is in part the product of a societal accommodation to routinely high volumes of crime, as well as of the refinement of professional practices for monitoring, surveillance and aggregate management' (Sparks, 2000:131). In other words, the causes of crime are no longer seen as important. Instead, probabilities are central, for actuarial justice 'does not see a world free of crime but rather one where the best practices of damage limitation have been put in place' (Young, 1999b:391). The focus of 'new penology' scholarship chimed with a set of authors developing Foucault's later work on governmentality (O'Malley, 1992; Garland, 1997; Rose, 1996; Simon, 2007). Here, risk is seen as a particular way of thinking born in the nineteenth century and is especially concerned with the historical development of the statistical and human sciences and their use of techniques to manage populations through health, welfare, and social security. According to this view, government during the twentieth century has become increasingly preoccupied with the management of risks through applying actuarial techniques developed in the insurance industries. It is important to note that actuarial understandings of risk in insurance are associated with chance, probability, and randomness as opposed to notions of danger and peril.

This approach developed at the same time, though at some remove, from sociological understandings of the 'risk society' (Beck, 1986; Giddens, 1990). This perspective originated in the sociology of modernity and is primarily concerned with the emergence of an entirely new set of 'risky' social circumstances. Anthony Giddens (1990) in his book *The Consequences of Modernity* argues that one of the defining features of late modernity is the development of a 'calculative attitude' in individuals and institutions to deal with the issues of risk, trust, and security in these troubling times. He maintains that risk is both globalized (something that exists on a global scale rather than at a local level) yet also personalized, built into people's subjective concerns about their identity. His argument echoes Ulrich Beck's (1986) discussion of the 'risk society'. For Beck, the 'risk society' is a distinct stage of modernity that has replaced the 'class society' of the industrial era. He argues that politics in class society is concerned not with risk, but with the 'attainment and retention of social wealth' (Taylor, 1999:207). New technologies are generating global 'modernization risks' that are of a quite different order from those found throughout earlier human history. Of course, past societies were risky and dangerous places too – whole populations could be wiped out by major earthquakes, floods, or plagues, for example. But Beck argues that new kinds of risks appear with the industrial world which are not 'in nature' but 'manufactured'.

These 'manufactured risks' are taking us to the edge of catastrophe. They include environmental disaster, nuclear war, genetic modification, computer viruses, stock market meltdown, and international terrorism. The risk society is a society of 'fate' as class divisions have been overridden by the similarity of destinies that we all share. For Beck, those of us who live in risk societies are no longer concerned with such matters as justice and equality. Instead, we try to prevent the worst, and consequently a 'risk society is one obsessed with security' (Johnston, 2000:24) and is characterized by a '*defensive* individualism that has replaced traditional solidarity as the dominant trait in late-modern identity' (Hudson, 2003:53, emphasis in original). It is important to recognize that Giddens and Beck are concerned with the sociological preconditions of risk in late modernity, and neither explicitly addresses crime or punishment; their insights have been developed by criminologists (Ericson and Haggerty, 1998; Taylor, 1999) to understand contemporary patterns of social control. Yet it remains the case that analyses of risk and criminal justice have kept more modest theoretical ambitions (O'Malley, 2010) and it is the governmentality approach that is still the prevailing form of explanation.

The United States is clearly at the vanguard of building the carceral state, while the United Kingdom (largely England and Wales) has also witnessed one of the most significant rises in imprisonment in Europe (Newburn, 2007; Sim, 2009). For instance, in 2012, 153 persons were incarcerated per 100,000 population in England and Wales, compared to 102 in France and 71 in Norway (Carrabine et al., 2014:363). Yet England and Wales lie some way behind the global leaders in imprisonment – Russia, the United States, China, and South Africa – as well as most of the countries in Eastern Europe. There are important geographical variations at work in this 'punitive turn':

> In many of these developments, the United States has been a net exporter of ideas and technologies, such as broken windows policing and mandatory minimum sentencing. But not in all. The United Kingdom has been a leader in the use of CCTV video surveillance and the collection of DNA; France was an early innovator in the field of paramilitary anti-riot security forces; and Italy has been at the forefront of bunker-style judicial proceedings. The leading actuarial instrument used in the United States – the 'Level of Services Inventory' (LSI-R) – was actually invented and developed by Canadian researchers, and the same is true of the Hare Psychopathy Checklist-Revised (PCL-R).
>
> (Harcourt, 2010:75)

Even in the United States the pattern is uneven at state level: some have sought to moderate penal expansion, while others have enthusiastically pursued punitive excess (Barker, 2009; Lynch, 2009). In Europe punitiveness varies considerably between countries (Snacken, 2010), while Pratt (2008) has turned his attention to explain why Scandinavian countries have retained low rates of imprisonment and remained largely immune from the decivilizing forces operating in the anglophone world. The implication is that the 'neoliberal political economy' which those countries have embraced accounts 'for their concentration in the top ranks of imprisonment growth, while the more social democratic and corporatist countries of continental Europe have thus far resisted it' (Simon, 2013:77).

Conclusion

In this chapter I have reviewed the main theoretical axes in 'punishment and society' scholarship in an effort to understand contemporary patterns of social control. By no means is it a comprehensive discussion, but what should be clear is that this is a diverse body of work, with the main traditions in social theory used in creative ways and giving shape to a distinctive field of study. It is hard to escape the conclusion that a more comparative focus is long overdue in a field rich with historical insight, and it is worth emphasizing that there are more than 10.1 million people held in prisons throughout the world. Yet almost half are found in just three countries – the United States (2.29 million), China (1.65 million plus an unknown number of pre-trial detainees and prisoners in 'administrative detention'), and Russia (0.81 million), while the numbers are growing across all five continents (Walmsley, 2011:1). As commentators have noted it is truly striking how three countries at the extreme ends of Cold War politics, with 'such dramatically different histories, cultures and patterns of crime, should hold, as it were, gold, silver and bronze positions in the world league table of numbers of prisoners' (King, 2007:98). In the next chapter the importance of geography is discussed in more depth in an effort to assess the difference that place makes to social practice.

6

Geography

The relationships that obtain between crime and place have long animated the criminological imagination. From Victorian explorations of urban squalor in London, through the moral mapping of modernity in Chicago, to recent excavations of postmodernity in fortress Los Angeles, it is clear that the city has preoccupied thinking about crime. Going further back in time the idea of an 'underworld' has been a persistent trope in popular culture and is often depicted as shadowy, deviant spaces of criminal collaboration where sophisticated outlaw networks extend over many localities. Then, as now, mobility was key, with migration and immigration being crucial factors. Indeed, it was the nomadic rootlessness of vagabonds and rogues that enabled some to prosper amid the growing social complexities of London in the sixteenth century: 'Criminal areas came to possess an elaborate yet unofficial social world with its own criminal vocabulary, criminal technology, division of labour, apprenticeship system, criminal haunts, and style of collective life' (McMullan, 1984:157). Also crucial was the role of the marketplace, which was at the centre of most towns and cities, and the pivotal point around which trade and commerce grew – both legal and illegal. According to Weber (1921/1958:77) all European cities, as they evolved from ancient Greece to the medieval world, are a distinctive 'fusion of the fortress and the market'.

It was the economic function of the great trading towns that fuelled their growing power and led to political freedom – using their wealth to buy from barons the right to self-government and emancipation from the ties of feudal obligation (Pirenne, 1925). The defensive walls protected citizens, encouraging individual and collective liberation, but also spoke to the inherently authoritarian character of the urban condition. The contemporary revival of the medieval idea of the 'city as a fortress constructed *against* outsiders' should not lead us to ignore how 'the rise of the modern industrial city in the nineteenth century very much coincided with the knowing and determined attempt to "tear down" (or rethink the use of) the perimeter walls of the city, in order to create a body of shared public space even among the unequal citizens of early capitalist

society' (Taylor, 1999:98, emphasis in original). During this time two contrasting views on the industrial city take shape, both hinging on biblical imagery
and the idea that a golden age of community had been lost or destroyed. One
likens the city to Babylon and an apocalyptic place from which to escape, the
other compares it to Jerusalem as a place to be rebuilt and transformed into an
urban utopia (Girouard, 1986; Hunt, 2005; Nead, 2005). These remain powerful imaginaries and they highlight how the city is an ambiguous place – both
fascinating and dangerous at the same time. There is an important sense in
which these polarizing tendencies are built into the social and spatial divisions
that define diverse urban forms.

The chapter begins by exploring how geographies of difference and exclusion
are crucial to understanding how problem places are constructed. In his *The
Country and the City* the literary critic Raymond Williams (1975) argues that
the popular view that a causal relationship exists between different settlement
types and the quality of life in them can be traced back to antiquity, but took
on a compelling mythologizing force during the industrial revolution. Here an
idealized, pastoral sense of rural community and solidarity is contrasted with
the city, represented as bleak, alienating, and degrading.[1] But he is careful to
acknowledge that the city also offers a dynamic 'sense of possibility, of meeting
and of movement' (Williams, 1975:6), echoing Simmel's (1903/1950) earlier
more ambivalent understanding of metropolitan life. The chapter then turns
to a discussion of how dystopian images of the city have concentrated on the
demonization of social housing, before a consideration of crimes of the powerful and the harms generated by globalization.

Criminal Areas and Divided Cities

Alongside population size and density the main defining feature of a city is,
as Louis Wirth (1938) argued, heterogeneity. Such diversity is manifest in all
manner of ways, but every city is composed of a 'motley of peoples and cultures, of highly differentiated modes of life between which there is only the
faintest communication, the greatest indifference and the broadest tolerance,
occasionally bitter strife, but always the sharpest contrast' (Wirth, 1938:20).
Divisions have always existed in cities, where extremes of wealth and poverty
are concentrated in certain parts, and the very notion of the dual city is deeply
engrained in the Western idea of the city itself (Sennett, 1990). In the ancient
Greek polis, which roughly translates as 'self-governing community', social life
was certainly more democratic than many other forms of urban civilization,
but not all were granted citizenship. Women, children, and slaves were excluded
from civic life, foreigners were barred from many institutions, while education
and class strongly influenced who participated in public affairs (Hall, 1999).
Cities have always been spaces of difference and complexity, and a good many
non-European cities have been characterized by cultural and racial diversity,

long before multiculturalism became a defining feature of such 'global' cities as London, Paris, and New York (King, 2003). The vivid and vibrant contrasts of urban life have inspired a considerable body of writing on the city as a site of desire, fantasy, and pleasure, as well as a space of anxiety, fear, and violence.

The idea of a subterranean 'otherworld' that mirrored and mimicked the more respectable 'upperworld' is a persistent theme appearing in a range of texts from Western Europe and North America, and in the colonial cities of empire (Shore, 2015). The concept of a criminal underworld belongs to this tradition of understanding the city. It is difficult to know just how organized, or disorganized, these formations actually were, yet it is nevertheless possible to chart the emergence of a whole literature dedicated to chronicling the dangers of metropolitan life. Gamini Salgādo's (1977) *The Elizabethan Underworld* provides a rich source of the alternative deviant worlds of London during the sixteenth and early seventeenth centuries and relishes in depicting the city as teeming with 'underworld folk' each 'inhabiting their own zones' yet 'also flowing freely through the city: segregated in some respects, all too proximate in others' (Gelder, 2007:7). The book uses material from a genre of writing that became known as 'rogue literature' and while we need to be wary of reading these narratives as faithful and authentic accounts of early subcultural life, it is clear that they do articulate how the illicit and outlaw were being imaginatively positioned in the metropolis. The fears and fantasies driving these elite interpretations of how the poor and outcast lived helped furnish the idea of 'a vast criminal underground of organised guilds, complete with their own internally coherent barter economy, master-apprentice relations, secret languages, and patrons' (Dionne, 2004:33).

Not only did the 'craft thieves' of Tudor London have their own slang (cant), neighbourhoods (sanctuaries), and meeting places, there were in fact two 'distinct criminal underworlds at this period: that of the wayfaring rogues and vagabonds who lived by stealing and begging – often under false pretences; and that of the London-based thieves and tricksters' (McIntosh, 1971:101). The first group were defined by their rootlessness and lived on the road, wandering from place to place, while the latter were more professional criminals plying their own distinctive craft in highly competent ways. They could draw on an extensive network of enablers and supporters, where dealers in stolen goods were central to the emergent forms of criminal collaboration that would later became a more familiar feature of the urban landscape (Sharpe, 1999). Some historians have been careful to argue that 'these criminal communities are rarely fixed in their identities', rather the 'networks often overlap and communities might come together in a fragile and often short-lived way'; yet on other occasions the ties can be strong where the 'alliances are deep-seated, based on family and on deep connections to community' (Shore, 2015:15). The figures of the rogue and vagabond also persist into the seventeenth and eighteenth centuries, chiming with images of prostitution, where each is understood to migrate to particular parts of the city and are innately drawn to a dissolute life of vice (Gelder, 2007:8–10).

Industrialization and urbanization brought about fundamental changes in social relations, producing unprecedented inequalities and spatial divisions based on the economic geography of class. One of the earliest and most influential accounts of the devastating consequences of industrial urbanism is to be found in Engels' (1845/1993) study of the horrors endured in Manchester's working-class districts. In particular, he notes how the wealthy 'can take the shortest road through the middle of all the labouring districts to their place of business, without ever seeing that they are in the midst of the grimy misery that lurks to the right and the left', going on to write that he has 'never seen so systematic a shutting out of the working class from the thoroughfares, so tender a concealment of everything which might affront the eyes and the nerves of the bourgeoisie, as in Manchester' (Engels, 1845/1993:59–9). The wretched conditions described by Engels anticipates the fictional worlds drawn by Charles Dickens and Elizabeth Gaskell, and the social commentary of Henry Mayhew and Thomas Beames, which sought to identify the relationships between the dangerous classes and the underworld. Beames (1850/1970:4) also observes how the facades of the main thoroughfares masked the misery behind them, where it was only when New Oxford Street was constructed in London that certain parts of the 'rookeries' (cheap lodging houses in multiple occupation) became accessible, describing them as criminal sanctuaries and 'pauper colonies' where 'human masses' are 'pent up, crowded, crammed into courts and alleys'.

It was around this time that the word 'warren' also came to prominence as a depiction of a 'tangled nest of poor dwellings'; in earlier usage it had meant brothel, so that the word 'rookery' implied 'a crammed, non-conjugal gathering of birds' while the term 'warren' conveyed 'a sense of sleazy, indiscriminate breeding' (Pearson, 1975:155). This would become a persistent theme in nineteenth-century writing on the city – how it prolifically *bred* the poor and the criminal. Henry Mayhew (1861–2) further documented urban street life, vividly drawing attention to the myriad 'wandering tribes' of London and depicting the dangerous and criminal classes as a barbaric, nomadic *race* apart from civilized metropolitan society. Victorian London was a city divided in strict class terms, with its wealth, prosperity, and respectability concentrated in the west, while its poverty, deprivation, and pollution were largely confined to the east, with a narrow strip of 'rookeries' circling the central core of the capital itself. As a result:

> the propertied middle class making its way into work in the City had to walk through a threatening and crowded corridor of street markets and narrow alleys, populated, at least according to the ethnographic observation (and fertile imagination) of Henry Mayhew, by a kaleidoscopic mass of 'costermongers', as well as women working the street market in sex (prostitutes), beggars, pickpockets, and others.
>
> (Taylor, 1999:99)

The physical separation of the rich and poor in cities took more complex forms later in the nineteenth century, when the 'flight to the suburbs' initially took hold and was made possible by new modes of consumption and transportation enabling the affluent to withdraw from the world of industrial-commercial production.

Distance drew a distinction between home and work, so that suburbs came to be understood as a 'rural substitute' where 'families, secure friendships, community and tranquillity' could flourish (Stevenson, 2003:124). The dynamics of residential segregation were famously mapped by the Chicago School sociologist Ernest Burgess (1925) in his 'zonal theory of urban development', which maintained that cities typically grew outwards from a central core in a series of concentric rings where different ethnic groups and classes were spatially concentrated. Drawing on biological metaphors this ecological approach emphasized how different human species competed over space, where the suggestion was that the 'keener, the more energetic, and the more ambitious' immigrants would swiftly move out of their 'ghettoes and immigrant colonies' into the outer zones of city and assimilate into the upward mobility of the American class structure (Park, 1926:9). At the hub of Burgess's model was the central business district (CBD), which was enveloped by a transitional zone, containing rows of deteriorating tenements, often built in the shadow of ageing factories. As the least desirable area, the zone was the first port of call for newly arrived immigrants and the only place to live for those too poor to live anywhere else. Three further residential zones of increasing wealth and status circled the low-rent zone in transition, where an array of social problems was concentrated.

In line with the evolutionary logic informing zonal theory, ethnic affiliation 'was seen to retard Americanization' and immigrant communities were seen as synonymous with 'syndicate crime, vice' and other pathologies (Lin, 2005:101). Jan Lin highlights how anti-ethnic assumptions informed Chicago School sociologists and their understanding of immigrant enclaves. To take one example, Walter Reckless (1971:246) wrote:

> The relationship of Chinatown to the commercialized vice areas of American cities is too well known to need elaboration. It is only fair to say, however, that the assumption of the usual parasitic activities by the Chinese in the Western World is probably to be explained by their natural segregation at the center of cities, as well as by their uncertain economic and social status.
>
> (cited in Lin, 2005:101)

Although Chinatowns have long been a feature of North American cities they have recently been transformed by changes in the global economy and Lin provides a perceptive overview of how ethnic neighbourhoods have been understood by sociologists, noting how a new international division of labour has produced a dual-city process of urban development.

Today, New York's Chinatown is a community sharply divided between wealthy entrepreneurs and destitute illegal immigrants working in the precarious informal sector. Rather than extreme diversity, there is a striking polarity in the enclave economy and a vivid example of the contrast in 'New York's Chinatown is the sight of sidewalk peddlers plying their wares and produce from tables or canvas sheets on Canal Street in front of the guarded glass offices of transnational banks such as the Bank of East Asia and the Hong Kong and Shanghai Banking Corporation' (Lin, 2005:107). The dual-city approach is one that grew out of Marxist urban studies, which marked a decisive break with the Chicago School paradigm and its biological analogies, viewing the struggle for urban space not in evolutionary terms but as a form of class struggle. In books such as David Harvey's (1973) *Social Justice and the City* and Manuel Castells' (1972) *The Urban Question* it was maintained that social divisions in the city are shaped by labour market position and it is economic forces that sustain structural urban inequality. The rise of a political economy approach in the United States is often associated with Harvey Molotch (1976) and his argument that the city is a 'growth machine', which he later developed with John Logan (1987) in *Urban Fortunes*, to explain how powerful groups act in concert to promote such growth.

The dual-city approach has been criticized for depicting divisions in ways that are too homogenizing and for failing to grasp the complexities within social classes and ethnic groups. These problems have been addressed by Peter Marcuse (1989, 1995, 2000) who insists that cities are now 'quartered', suggesting that while they have always been divided the origins of contemporary urban divisions are different and more destructive than those of the past. In his view cities are increasingly fragmented and chaotic, yet underlying the disarray there are patterns. Quartered cities are intricately linked and differentiated by walls or fortification. Marcuse identifies several types of city: the residential, gentrified, suburban, tenement, and abandoned city, while the economic city is further divided into the controlling city, advanced services, direct production, unskilled work and informal, and the residual city. Consequently, 'we may almost describe many of our contemporary cities as entirely fragmented, composed only of a collection of separate areas of concentration of different people all desiring to stay apart from all others' (Marcuse, 2000:272). These ideas are taken further in Mike Davis's (1992, 1998) extraordinary analyses of the emergence of the 'fortress city' in Los Angeles.

The key theme that runs through his work is the increasing militarization of urban space and the defence of luxury lifestyles through private policing, state-of-the-art electronic surveillance, and the destruction of public space. The driving force behind this militarization and segregation is fear in the imaginations of the middle classes. Although there have been dramatic increases in street violence, these are contained in ethnic and class enclaves, which serve to justify and reinforce urban apartheid in the ghettoes and barrios of North American cities, and Los Angeles is at the cutting edge of these transformations.

The physical form of the city is divided into fortified cells of affluence and places of terror where the police wage war on the criminalized poor. Others too have found in Los Angeles a paradigm of the postmodern metropolis and one to be contrasted with Chicago as the epitome of the modern city organized around a single centre. Whereas Los Angeles is disorganized around a collage of many suburban nuclei,

> [t]he consequent urban aggregate is characterized by acute fragmentation and specialization – a partitioned gaming board subject to perverse laws and peculiarly discrete, disjointed urban outcomes. Given the pervasive presence of crime, corruption, and violence in the global city (not to mention geo-political transitions, as nation-states gave way to micro-nationalisms and transnational criminal organizations), the city as gaming board seems an especially appropriate twenty-first century successor to the concentrically ringed city of the early twentieth.
>
> (Dear, 2005:67)

This trend of fortification and sequestration is most pronounced in the United States, but it is a process that can be found in more or less brutal forms in cities around the world.

In the United Kingdom dystopian images of the city have tended to con-centrate on the demonization of social housing. Council estates perform an ideologically important role as a signifier and marker of 'problem' people and places (Johnston and Mooney, 2007; McKenzie, 2014). In many of these estates across the United Kingdom, and also more broadly in Europe, there were and are heavy concentrations of unemployment and poverty that are 'without historical precedent in any "developed" society' and parallel pro-cesses of 'pauperization, evacuation and dereliction have been in full flow in the United States' since the early 1980s (Taylor, 1999:115). This is not to imply that forms of marginality in Europe are exactly following the black American ghetto experience, rather that social and spatial exclusion on either side of the Atlantic shares some significant features. In a series of influential publications Wacquant (2007, 2008, 2009) has coined the term 'territorial stigmatisation' to describe the symbolic and material assaults on the most disadvantaged and outcast. As he put it, in 'every metropolis of the First World, one or more towns, districts or concentrations of public housing are publicly known and recognized as those urban hellholes in which violence, vice, and dereliction are the order of things' (Wacquant, 2007:67). These widely despised, blemished places are largely the product of state policies and are bound up with the con-dition of 'advanced marginality' resulting from uneven development in capital-ist economies and neo-liberal governance, where the formation of an enduring 'precariat' is one of the defining features of the post-industrial landscape.

The logic of collective defamation is accompanied by the relegation of the poorest to decomposing neighbourhoods starved of public and private resources, in which the sources of such stigma are 'diffuse, rather than mono-lithic' (Garbin and Millington, 2012:2068). We will see in the next chapter how 'scum semiotics' (Tyler, 2013:1.2) thrives on class hostility and antagonism, but here we need to acknowledge how the distinctions drawn between 'problem' places and populations and supposedly 'normal' ones are inflected with classed assumptions about poor communities. For instance, social housing tenants are often criticized for lacking 'aspiration and enterprise', yet they are also defined 'as "victims" of the Keynesian welfare state in general and of social housing in particular' as the tenancies themselves are held 'responsible for tenants' lack of mobility, tying residents into the bounded space of the "welfare ghetto", una-ble to leave' (Hancock and Mooney, 2013:54). Of course, life in council estates is considerably more complex and textured than these accounts allow, where networks of 'being and belonging' generate important ways of 'getting by' in disadvantaged neighbourhoods, which have been subjected to economic hard-ship, poor housing, and territorial stigma for generations (McKenzie, 2014).

Excluded from regular, paid work survival in the post-industrial milieu is found in 'individual strategies of "self-provisioning", "shadow work" and unreported employment, underground commerce, criminal activities and quasi-institutionalized "hustling"', each of 'which do little to alleviate precari-ousness' since the informal economy reinforces, rather than reduces, structural inequalities (Wacquant, 2007:71). As Hobbs (1988:8) noted in his ethnogra-phy of London's East End the population were constantly switching between legal and illegal entrepreneurial activities: 'everyone was "at it" and some were "at it" more than most.' The region is a distinct one in the capital, with its own inimitable and individualistic culture built up over centuries, to the extent that it had long been defined as a 'deviant area'. Yet as Hobbs (1988:108) maintains it was market forces that 'created the East End, and its culture is a cumulative response to the problems created by those forces'. Throughout his work Hobbs emphasizes how crime is an integral, everyday feature of urban life and in this it serves as an invaluable entry point into a consideration of how organized crime has been conceptualized and moves away from an exclusive preoccupa-tion with working-class crime to crimes of the powerful.

Organized Crime

The concept of 'organized crime' is a much contested one, emerging initially in the United States as a somewhat vague alien conspiracy theory to explain how vice districts were able to flourish in major cities. In many respects the American understanding of ethnically homogeneous 'crime syndicates' – that is associations of business people, criminals, law enforcement, and politi-cians – formed to conduct illegal enterprises and make a profit still sets the terms of debate. To meet the growing demand for alcohol (whatever time of day or night), drugs, gambling, prostitution, and other associated illegal activities – such as loan sharking, money laundering, and labour – racketeering thrived in the various vice districts of expanding urban centres. Each of the great waves of nineteenth- and early-twentieth-century migrations from Europe to America helped shape illegal markets, where Irish criminal entrepreneurs initially operated in the urban North East in the mid to late nineteenth century, to be subsequently followed by Jewish and then Italian crime families, who only really emerged after corrupt relations had become firmly entrenched in American cities (Haller, 1990). The vice districts and crime syndicates prospered because of corrupt city government and all benefited: citizens could indulge in alcohol, drugs, gambling and sex; ethnic groups had a means of achieving social mobility; police and city officials gained financially (Walker, 1980:107). It has been estimated that from the Civil War onward, perhaps even earlier, the provision of illegal goods and services was syndicated through carefully coordinated partnerships between police, politicians, and racketeers. To the extent that by the early twentieth century 'it would not be possible to understand the structure of local politics without a knowledge of the structure of gambling syndicates' (Haller, 1976:106).

The first sociological study on organized crime was Frederic Thrasher's (1927:409–451), which included a chapter on 'The Gang and Organized Crime', drew on the concept of organized crime as it had been developed by a civic association, the Chicago Crime Commission, which had coined it in 1919, to describe 'the orderly fashion in which the so-called "criminal class" of Chicago's estimated "10,000 professional criminals" allegedly pursued "crime as a business"' (von Lampe, 2002:190). This was at the same time that the Volstead Act came into force, which made it illegal to produce, distribute, and sell alcohol, thus launching the prohibition era (1920–1933) and inspiring the rapid development of new illegal enterprises. Criminal syndicates grew larger and more complex, involving a variety of different ethnic groups (Haller, 1976:109). According to one influential account it was near the end of prohibition that a national crime syndicate emerged, which was extremely centralized and tightly controlled by a small, stratified group and was the outcome of 'a series of "gangland wars" in which an alliance of Italians and Sicilians first conquered other groups and then fought each other' (Cressey, 1969:9).

In his book *Theft of the Nation* Donald Cressey (1969) establishes a distinctive Mafia paradigm, as the academic consultant on the 1967 US President's Commission on Organized Crime, he became convinced of a nationwide conspiracy and popularised the official view of it resembling a corporate hierarchy, vertically integrated and horizontally coordinated. Ever since the 1950s the Mafia as an alien conspiracy has been integral to the understanding of organized crime in the United States and the imagery has been reinforced in popular culture through such fictional representations as *The Godfather, Goodfellas,* and *The Sopranos.* Much of Cressey's (1969) account relies on the testimony of one gangster, Joseph Valachi, known as the 'canary that sang' and detailed his view of the structure of a centrally controlled criminal organization, governed by an Italian-American 'Commission' made up of the leaders of the most pow-erful 'families', while the 'boss' of each family manages the activities of 'under-bosses' and 'soldiers'.

By targeting Italians as the prime movers in the chaotic free-for-all of pro-hibition, while ignoring the crooked involvement of established politicians and law enforcement in the bootlegging operations, the state created 'an endur-ing template for the essentially alien nature of organized criminality' (Hobbs, 2012:257). It is a vision of an 'octopus of crime' (Sterling, 1990, 1994) with a controlling head and tentacles spreading out around the world, which has informed American foreign policy and the policies of the United Nations, espe-cially since the end of the Cold War and the identification of organized crime as a major internal threat to European states that was now both imminent and transnational. On this reckoning a 'New Evil Empire' has emerged that is taking advantage of globalization through building international alliances and establishing colonies around the world. Manuel Castells (2000:166) insists that a new phenomenon of 'global crime' is now in place, resulting from the 'networking of powerful criminal organizations, and their associates, in shared activities throughout the planet'. Alongside the traditional criminal groups like the American Cosa Nostra and Sicilian Mafia, the Japanese Yakuza and the Chinese Triads, more recent phenomenon like the Columbian and Mexican drug 'cartels', Nigerian criminal networks, Jamaican Posses, and such sinister-sounding entities as the Russian Mafiya alongside many others, 'have come together in a global, diversified network' (Castells, 2000:167).

International alliances, joint ventures, and 'subcontracting' are said to be among the shared features of international criminal cooperation as illicit enter-prises expand into new territories (Castells, 2000; Shelley, 2006; Williams, 2001). In doing so they have moved away from what is considered to be the traditional, centralized, organizational structure of a 'mafia' and adopted a more dispersed, flexible, looser and 'liquid' structure (Varese, 2013). Moreover, comparisons with terrorism are also emphasized:

> Both criminals and terrorists have developed transnational networks, dis-persing their activities, their planning, and their logistics across several con-tinents, and thereby confounding the state-based legal systems that are used to combat transnational crime in all its permutations. Transnational crimi-nals are major beneficiaries of globalization. Terrorists and criminals move people, money, and commodities through a world where the increasing flows of people, money, and commodities provide excellent cover for their activities. Both terrorists and transnational crime groups have globalized to reach their markets, to perpetuate their acts, and to evade detection.
>
> (Shelley, 2006:43)

Such arguments have been enthusiastically picked up by policy makers and law enforcement officials to the extent that 'transnational organized crime' has been constructed as a major problem since the 1990s. The collapse of the Soviet Union also saw secretive state intelligence agencies and military forces reorient themselves to 'new' security threats, energetically presenting them as foreign conspiracies and gain further resources to combat the 'exotic big brands of global organised crime: Triads, Yardies, Russians, Colombians, Italians and Turks' (Hobbs, 2012:259). The threat is clearly presented as alien and offers a narrative of a global underworld alliance that is unencumbered by empirical evidence. This is not to suggest that organized criminal groups do not exist, even in a city like New York where attempts to document the activities of 'La Cosa Nostra' (Jacobs et al., 1994) have been extensive, they have notably failed to find convincing evidence of such a gang *dominating* a 'broad range of criminal activity, even in the North-Eastern US' (Levi, 2012:601) let alone commanding a shadow international network of criminality. Furthermore, the alien conspiracy thesis ignores the subtle ties between the organization of crime and the organization of everyday social relations, which offers an important alternative account of how to understand the diverse communities of practice that make up criminal enterprises.

The origins of this competing view are to be found in critics of Cressey's (1969) account of a nationwide conspiracy, where organized crime is depicted as a centralized, hierarchical entity run along military lines by Italians. One of the most influential critics was Dwight Smith (1975, 1980) who argued that criminals should not be understood as a class or a race apart, but rather as entrepreneurs who operated under conditions of illegality and opened up a new focus on the economic principles structuring activities. In a series of publications Alan Block (1983, 1991, 1994) has insisted that the attribution of rational organization and predictable rules in the underworld, which depicts a monolithic, corporate hierarchy, rests too heavily on evidence drawn from a legal apparatus that is prone to seeing their targets along the same institutional lines as they themselves are organized. Likewise, Peter Reuter (1983) further disputed the conventional wisdom that criminal networks are large enterprises controlling illicit markets, and instead suggested a more disjointed, flexible and fluid set of relationships. His characterization of 'dis-organized' crime is intended to convey their fragmented, unruly nature and challenge the mono-lithic image presented by American law enforcement personnel. In his research on illegal markets in New York he found they are populated by numerous, relatively small and mostly ephemeral enterprises competing with one another. Here the defining feature is patron-client relationships, which exhibit no rigid formal structure, but make use of whatever resources are at hand and offer protection services to those trading in illicit commodities. Consequently, it is 'because of their reputation for violence and discipline, *Mafiosi* and other "gangsters" play a key role in criminal dispute-settlement in the US and Italy' (Levi, 1998:337).

In the *Sicilian Mafia* Diego Gambetta maintains that it evolved due to the lack of trust in underworld relationships and 'it has remained there to this very day', as he suggests it 'is a difficult industry to export. Not unlike mining, it is heavily dependent on the local environment' (Gambetta, 1993:249, 251). This is a crucial point and it highlights the importance of place, as well as the significance of social networks in securing loyal collaborations in situations of endemic uncertainty. In the UK context, as we have seen above, elements of criminal organization have long been features of urban life and Hobbs (2001) has demonstrated how the traditional criminal family 'firm' was deeply rooted in working-class neighbourhoods, but has since adapted to new opportunities in the post-industrial landscape. It is changes in the political economy of the locality that provide the dynamic for innovations in criminal collaboration. The example he gives of the drug trade is one which offers 'innovative engage-ments with the market', while it has 'created disintegrated criminal firms typi-fied by flexibility and unpredictability, operating within multi-layered networks of pecuniary opportunity constituted by both criminal networks and specific activity networks' (Hobbs, 2001:555). Both Hobbs (1997) and Ruggiero (1995) argue that the organization of criminal labour closely mirrors the organization of legitimate labour, and it is clear that the routine business of criminal col-laboration requires an entrepreneurial structure. These insights into the eco-nomic principles at work in organized crime emphasize the close ties between 'underworld' culture and 'upperworld' institutions.

Returning to the United States and a study of organized crime in Seattle also found that the vice district was flourishing and controlled not by a separate, hermetically sealed 'Cosa Nostra', but by:

> A loose affiliation of businessmen, politicians, union leaders, and law-enforcement official who cooperate to coordinate the production and distri-bution of illegal goods and services, for which there is substantial demand.
>
> (Chambliss, 1988:151)

The most successful criminal enterprises are loosely structured networks, which also involve 'upright' business people and public officials, and are multifaceted, mutating and flexible enough to respond to the fast-changing market place of illicit goods. There are many examples of alliances between underworld and corporate world and these go far beyond the 'occasional hiring of mob-sters to break strikes' as was typical in the past, now 'there would be no mob control of much of the toxic waste business, for example, if some eminently respectable chemical companies were not so keen to cut their disposal costs' (Naylor, 1996:81). Unlike previous eras contemporary organized crime, which is focused on drugs, fraud, and counterfeiting, is at once both global and local. Today we must consider some, though not all, forms of organized criminal collaboration as involving both local dimensions and international connec-tions and resources. In this context the concept of 'glocalization' (Robertson, 1995) is significant not least since 'current research indicates that even the classic "international" criminal organizations function as interdependent local units' (Hobbs, 1998:419). This view was confirmed in Federico Varese's (2012) account of how a Russian criminal organization sought to operate in a new territory, in this instance Italy, and found that the migration was the result of conflicts among crime leaders in Moscow. The core activity of the group, running a protection racket and described by the FBI as the most powerful Eurasian organized crime group in the world, remained in the territory of origin. At the same time, the new cell established a money laundering service for the main group while building a basic organizational structure that established extensive links with local criminals and entrepreneurs in order to identify economic investment opportunities.

The business deals included buying sparkling wine, food products, wood, furniture, wheat, steel, pharmaceutical goods, Olivetti computers, Armani suits, works of art, gold, helicopters, and antennas. In this nuanced analysis the idea of a global alliance of transnational criminals is found wanting and instead a more complex picture emerges:

> a mafioso is in a new territory because he escapes to it. Once there, he explores local opportunities. He does not receive a salary from back home; thus, the analogy with a firm opening a branch abroad is misleading. The homeland may do no more than bestow a seal of approval on the existence of the outpost, which has a great deal of autonomy. The outpost abroad is not a branch of a corporation, but rather a semiautonomous unit allied to the homeland.
>
> (Varese, 2012:249)

The key implication is that contemporary crime groups do not need to acquire territorial dominance in a new locale, and in this example the transition from the raw muscle of protection to predatory entrepreneur relied on the legal economy and a vast network of contacts in it. Similarly, Paddy Rawlinson's (2010) research on the relationship between organized crime and the legitimate business structures in the former Soviet Union goes some way to dispelling the popular, media myth that Russia's crime problem is due to Slavic mobster gangs. Instead she maintains that the 'pathologies present in so called "gangster" capitalism are also present in Western economies and cannot be ring-fenced as Russia's failure to embrace capitalism properly' (Rawlinson, 2010:4).

More generally it is claimed that the success of organized crime in Italy, Russia, and many parts of Latin America is due to a profound lack of trust in society between citizens and government (Gambetta, 2009). This systemic feature also imposes limits on the kind of expansion opportunities available, and as we have seen 'mafioisi' tend to find themselves abroad due to pressure of events, rather than a strategic plan to conquer new territories. Where they are successful, in the longer term, is often a result of a sudden market expansion that is neither exploited by local rivals nor blocked by authorities. In the final analysis it is the inability of the state to govern economic transformations that gives criminal groups the opportunity to thrive (Varese, 2011). Of some significance here is the growth of e-crime which has accompanied technological innovations in the field of electronic information and communications technology (ICT) over the last two decades. Much recent attention has focused on the phenomenon of illicit e-markets operating on the 'dark web', such as 'BlackMarket Reloaded, where AK47s are on sale alongside Afghan heroin, or CC Paradise, selling stolen credit-card data' (Franklin-Wallis, 2013:1). Silk Road is the most well-known and was set up in 2011 along similar lines as Amazon and eBay, where users could sign up to buy and sell an extensive range of illicit goods, all delivered through the post. The FBI shut down the site in 2013, but with the result that:

> the libertarian free-trade zone that the Silk Road once stood for has devolved into a more fragmented, less ethical, and far less trusted collection of scam-ridden black market bazaars. Instead of the Silk Road's principled—if still very illegal—alternative to the violence and unpredictable products of street dealers, the dark web's economy has become nearly as shady as the Internet back alley politicians and moralizing TV pundits have long compared it to.
> (Greenberg, 2016:1)

The new ICTs not only make it much easier for criminals to bypass national boundaries but also offer 'more sophisticated techniques to support and develop networks for drugs trafficking, money laundering, illegal arms trafficking, smuggling and the like' (Thomas and Loader, 2000:3).

Yvonne Jewkes (2003:20–21) suggests that cybercrimes can be classified into two categories: 'new crimes using new tools', these are crimes such as hacking and sabotage through viruses; and 'conventional crimes' using ICTs, which include fraud, stalking, and identity theft. She acknowledges that there a number of additional activities that are not strictly illegal but would be considered harmful to some users, including certain forms of pornography and unsolicited email in the form of 'spam'. It is important to note that criminal activity on the Internet is not an 'all engulfing "cyber-tsunami", but, like the terrestrial world, a large range of frequently occurring small-impact crimes' (Wall, 2001:xi). Moreover, the arrival of modern ICTs does not eliminate existing patterns of criminality. It is unlikely that illicit e-markets will ever replace buying stolen goods or drugs from friends or neighbourhood dealers, which themselves rely on order, stability, and trust across the network of drug-brokerage activities (Pearson and Hobbs, 2003). Doubts have also been raised on the likely effects ICTs will have on 'illicit migration, which requires clandestine services that are difficult to formalise, and are greatly influenced by trust and interpersonal relationships that cannot be taken for granted' (Levi, 2014:7). The creeping criminalization of migration, which has been termed 'crimmigration' (Stumpf, 2006) and has largely escaped criminological attention (exceptions include Aliverti, 2013; Bosworth, 2012; Cecchi, 2011; De Giorgi, 2010; Welch and Schuster, 2005).

The very term 'illegal immigrant' is a derogatory one, implying that migrants are criminal, when in fact they have 'usually only committed an administrative infraction' (Andersson, 2014:17). The considerable movements of people crossing borders in recent decades has hastened since the collapse of the Soviet Union, the expansion of the EU, and wars in the Middle East and elsewhere, each of which have 'created more diasporas with greater cross-border networks of trust and extended family "pressure", making the idea of "national" organised crime rather outmoded, though traffickers and fraudsters still have to borrow others' identities' (Levi, 2014:7). In his ethnography of clandestine migration routes from Africa to Europe, Ruben Andersson (2014:14) makes it clear there is an extensive industry built on subterranean movement, where the 'people smugglers', widely dubbed 'mafias', are 'nowhere near as organized as such a term implies – yet their trade, which grows alongside tougher controls, generates revenues estimated in the billions'. The term industry is used to emphasize how migrant illegality is processed and produced in several distinct, geographically dispersed domains that ultimately renders the business profitable. At the same, a vast security industry has been created around their clandestine movements, tightening border controls and preventing illegal entry.

Similar developments were also well underway in the United States, where President Clinton launched Operation Gatekeeper in 1994 along the US–Mexico border, which doubled the number of patrols and fortified the controls using the latest military hardware and infrastructure. It forced migrants away from the relatively safe coastal areas into the mountains and deserts straddling San Diego, where an estimated 1,600 migrants died in the first four years of the initiative, perishing either in the cold of the mountains or in the heat of the desert (Webber, 2004:137). Fifteen years later the death count stood at well over 5,000 and humanitarian activists have highlighted the systematic human rights violations that directly result from this policy (Cubbison, 2010). In Europe the borderlands are today described as extremely conflicted, 'where the objectives of protecting state security clash with the needs of vulnerable groups in precarious life situations' (Aas and Gundhus, 2015:2). Here there is a fraught and unruly set of relationships between policing and human rights at these key sites of global inequality. As such the many serious harms generated in these spaces returns us to important conceptual questions on what is 'crime' and whether certain activities of states and corporations should be addressed in criminology. It is to such matters we now turn.

Crimes of the Powerful

Ever since Sutherland developed the concept of 'white-collar crime' in the 1940s, which he defined as a crime committed by 'a person of high status in the course of his occupation' (1949:9), it has been the subject of controversy.

By challenging the conventional view of the criminal as typically lower class he demonstrated how powerful business and professional elites also routinely commit crime, suggesting it was almost endemic in national and transnational corporations. He details a vast range of corporate corruption and individual malpractice, which include price-fixing, anti-trust violations, violations of workers' safety legislation, bank frauds, infringement of patents, trademarks and copyrights, financial manipulations, and war crimes, among many others, to indicate that 'white-collar crime' is *serious* crime. Moreover, its absence from discussion in conventional criminology is a scandal, a point he had first aired in his presidential address to the American Sociological Association (Sutherland, 1940). However, his definition is full of ambiguity and is no doubt a reflection of the mass of empirical material he had collected over a decade. A long-standing complaint is that it is not clear, for example, whether the crimes are committed by, for, or against corporations – and this has given rise to an intense debate over delineating an appropriate field of inquiry. Among the implications that flow from this definition is the need to enlarge the scope of criminology to take account of a broader range of conduct and the political processes that define it as criminal or not, where there is a clear accusation of unfairness in the making and enforcing of criminal law. In his reckoning any 'criminology which did not devote considerable effort explaining and publicizing corporate crime would ... have failed in its scientific duty' (Box, 1983:18).

An early and perceptive critic, Paul Tappan (1947:99) argued that extending the label 'crime' to cover acts that do not violate the criminal law is to enter into a problematic sphere of moralistic reasoning and would end up including many acts that are 'within the framework of normal business practice'. Instead he defended a 'rigorous' legal definition against Sutherland's broader sociological position, maintaining that without a strict adherence to it the concept of crime would become so open-ended as to be meaningless. Tappan also insisted that 'those offences typically committed by business people are inherently different from criminal offences; and this view, that there are qualitative differences between criminal offences on the one hand and regulatory offences on the other, is one which is still widely held' (Slapper and Tombs, 1999:6). If one of the aims of Sutherland was to shift the focus of academic criminology, then his efforts have largely failed. With one or two notable exceptions the study of corporate crime remained largely neglected until the 1970s and only really until the advent of a critical criminology which sought to reckon with the crimes of the powerful (Pearce, 1976). Here the question of who are the *real* criminals was posed with considerable force.

In the North American strand some wanted to expand the definition of crime to include not only the legal harms resulting from economic exploitation in capitalist society, but also the crimes of governments and their agencies of social control (Quinney, 1977). The offences that can be regarded as state crime range from bribe-taking by officials to genocidal mass murder. One of the difficulties is that such categories encompass quite disparate activities so that conceptual objections and obstacles soon arise, where the 'analytic value' of using the term 'crime' to 'designate morally abhorrent state practices' can 'appear questionable' (Green and Ward, 2000:102–3). In this context it is worth quoting Stan Cohen's (1979/1988) assessment of the desire to enlarge the definition of crime:

> To me, this has always seemed little more than a muckraking and moralistic exercise, in the best senses. This position attacks the state definition of crime and tries to redefine and extend criminology's subject matter in terms of violations of politically defined human rights (such as food, shelter, dignity). Thus, imperialism, racism, sexism, colonialism, capitalism, and exploitation are all to fall within the rubric of criminology. This is, if course, no mere plea for demarcating new academic subject lines, drawing up new book lists, and asking different exam questions (though, curiously from such a group of radicals, it usually looks to be just this). It announces a moral stance: not just that we should "study" (and certainly not "appreciate") all these evils but that we should *condemn* them, condemn them as if they were like or worse than the crimes that fill our current textbooks and our criminal justice system. It is not always too clear whether we are being asked to condemn these evils *instead of* conventionally defined crimes or *in addition* to these crimes, but in either case the moral element is right in the open. Indeed, this element appears with such naïve and evangelical fervour in some American adherents of radical criminology that one wonders what they were doing in the sixties and what sort of sociology they have ever read.
>
> (Cohen, 1979/1988:120)

I have quoted Cohen's assessment at length as it gives a strong sense of the contradictions that still remain unresolved, though it is significant that in his later work he did attempt to criminologically justify an approach to state crimes 'without our object of study becoming simply everything we might not like at the time' (Cohen, 1993:98). In doing so he offered an alternative to legalistic definitions of crime through some fundamental human rights principles.

A further reason to question legally based conceptualizations of state crimes arises from the view that because states have the authority to make laws and 'the ability to criminalize certain actions, they also have the power to avoid the criminalization of their own activities' (Carrabine et al., 2014:476). Consequently, some have argued for a 'social harms' perspective (Hillyard et al., 2004) as many practices that cause serious harm are either not part of criminal law or, if they could be dealt with it, are either ignored or handled without using it. Take the example of 'safety crimes', which Steve Tombs (2000, 2004) has highlighted in his studies of work-related harm. He found that a focus on recorded occupational injury involves over 1 million workplace injuries per year in the United Kingdom, but once restricted to 'crimes' this shrinks to just over 1,000 successfully prosecuted health and safety offences.

These are enormous differences, and as he emphasizes they have profound implications in terms of what sense can be made of the data conceptually, theoretically, and politically. State crime can be defined as a form of 'organisational deviance involving human rights violations by state agencies', but as Tony Ward (2004:84) goes on to point out 'states also cause harm in ways that are not deviant but, on the contrary, are central to their normal functioning'. These are important insights and suggest a continuity between legality and illegality that is essential to understanding crimes of the powerful. The study of environmental harm, for example, involves analysing the harm produced both by criminal conduct and completely lawful activities (Ruggiero, 2013). Green criminology ranges in scope from the local to the global, but also finds itself in the same theoretical predicament and has tended to focus more on the study of 'harms' than legally defined crimes (South, 2015).

Others have worked with the conceptual slippage itself and explored the connections between legal, semi-legal, and illegal activities in different countries as the relationships vary considerably. Indeed, many of the crimes have an international dimension as white-collar criminals exploit differences between national legal systems. As David Nelken (2012:641) explains, this inevitably involves paying close 'attention to the comparative dimension'. Bribery, for example, is said to be especially important in the international arms trade in the newly liberalized global market. It is an inherently dirty business. Even when the weapons are manufactured in major Western countries for legitimate 'sale strictly to their own military forces, business-as-usual means commercial espionage, bid-rigging, phony invoicing, and a revolving door relationship between producer, purchaser and public overseer that, a century earlier, would have made an American railroad baron blush' (Naylor, 1994:3). More recently the tax affairs of transnational corporations, which include Apple, Google, Microsoft, Amazon, and Starbucks, have come under scrutiny, as some of the largest global businesses now pay little or no tax. That they have been able to do so is partly due to the increasingly sophisticated methods corporations use to minimize their tax bill. Some do so illegally through tax evasion, but others use innocuous-sounding strategies of 'tax efficiency' by creatively interpreting tax rules. Few will be surprised to learn that large corporations take such steps to reduce the tax they pay; yet what is alarming is not just the extent of tax evasion but the active collusion of governments in the process. The key site of conflict in corporate taxation is no longer between corporations and governments, but between governments and governments, each one competing to attract new private sector investment and deliberately creating environments where big businesses can avoid paying tax with impunity (Farnsworth and Fooks, 2015).

The crisis in global financial markets that began to unfold in Autumn 2007 has largely passed criminology by. As has been recently pointed out, this should shock no one: 'with its overwhelming emphasis on crimes of the relatively powerless, criminology generally failed the challenge of the Great

Economic Meltdown' (Pontell et al., 2014:8). Yet there is much that the discipline can offer to an understanding of the crisis. It was not just caused by an appetite for risk-taking among major financial institutions across the world; the regulatory regimes at both national and international levels 'either allowed or encouraged such activities' and as such the crisis involved not just forms of 'corporate crime and harm, but state complicity in these' (Tombs, 2015:57). Those criminologists who have studied what happened in any depth acknowledge that it is difficult to give an accessible outline of the 'financial horse-trading' that went on as their operational success depended on 'complexity and lack of transparency' (Nelken, 2012:651). In addition, various kinds of fraudulent enterprise permeated the markets to such an extent 'that rather shady practices became almost normalized amongst companies from the 1990s onwards' (Dorn, 2010:28). Consequently, it was frequently hard to tell the difference between white-collar crime and ordinary business transactions (Hagan, 2010).

Empire, Harm, and Globalization

In an important contribution to the social harm perspective David Friedrichs and Jessica Friedrichs (2002) have coined the term 'crimes of globalization' to describe the immensely damaging consequences of international financial institutions on the developing nations of the Global South. Their argument is that the ideologies, policies, and practices of the World Bank, the World Trade Organization, and the International Monetary Fund (IMF) privilege transnational corporate interests and those of advanced industrialized states, which combined with the arrogance with which they enforce a 'top-down' form of globalization serves to enable rather than curtail criminal activities. They build their argument from a case study of a World Bank-financed dam in Thailand, where they note that dam building is one of the favoured projects of the Bank. However, the forced resettlement of people has given rise to accusations that the World Bank is 'complicit in policies with genocidal consequences, with exacerbating ethnic conflict, with increasing the gap between rich and poor, with fostering immense ecological and environmental damage, and with the callous displacement of vast numbers of indigenous people in developing countries from their original homes and communities' (Friedrichs and Friedrichs, 2002:23). As later noted by Dawn Rothe and David Friedrichs (2006), international financial institutions impose 'structural adjustment policies' on borrowing states, supposedly to create socio-economic conditions more conducive to growth, which often results in privatizing state assets, opening up economies to cheap imports, accepting currency devaluations, and reducing government spending in ways set by the lenders. It is a political economy of development that 'builds a process in which poverty is, in a counterintuitive sense, not reduced but embedded and reproduced' (Bracking, 2009:xiii).

In a further study of crimes of globalization, Rothe and colleagues (2009) describe how structural adjustment policies helped to create the conditions that led to the genocide in Rwanda in the early 1990s. For instance, money from international financial institutions allocated for commodity imports were diverted by the government to buy military hardware. From October 1990 Rwandan armed forces grew from 5,000 to 40,000 men, requiring a considerable influx of international money to pay the new recruits and finance massive arms purchases, which would later be used to organize and equip the militias in preparation for the genocide. They do not argue that the IMF or World Bank deliberately set out to cause an economic collapse through the forced currency devaluation, rapid inflation, and mass unemployment, but rather their systematic inattention to the deteriorating conditions and use of their funds to buy unprecedented weaponry helped set the scene for the disaster. In their more recent account of the concept they provide analyses of further case studies to underline the criminogenic consequences of globalization, though the focus remains firmly on crimes of the powerful (Rothe and Friedrichs, 2015). There are important links to be made here to what has been called a 'criminology of empire' (Iadicola, 2010:31) and although this argument is made to discuss the contemporary United States as an 'empire in denial' it can clearly help explain the historical centrality of violence in the Western conquest of those populations decimated by colonial rule and the slave trade that accompanied European expansion.

The revival of terms such as empire and imperialism to describe current international affairs is partly explained by geopolitical events, namely the neo-conservative-led invasions of Afghanistan and Iraq, but also the publication of Antonio Negri and Michael Hardt's (2000) influential book *Empire*, which anticipated some of the malign consequences of this colonial adventure. Yet these ideas were not just revived by the radical left. As David Hesmondhalgh (2008:95) demonstrates, liberal and conservative thinkers have also been drawn to imperialism – as in 2002 when the *New York Times* 'famously gave up its front page to the words "The American empire. Get used to it"' – and other commentators have since proclaimed the virtues of 'enlightened' empire in an effort to grasp this new world order. But some caution is needed here, because 'imperialism' is being used in different ways and David Harvey's (2003:26) concept of 'capitalist imperialism' is especially helpful, defined as a 'a contradictory fusion of "the politics of state and empire" ... and the molecular processes of capital accumulation in space and time'. Far from being new, the imperialism of the American century is in fact much more like the British imperialism of old, which rediscovered the 'original sin of simple robbery' that Harvey goes on to describe as 'accumulation by dispossession' (itself a revision of Marx's concept of primitive accumulation). The significance of Harvey's work is that it provides an understanding of a political economy that situates the global commodification of culture in a context of capitalist accumulation, where efforts to secure market dominance are paramount.

In order to grasp how the colonial legacy continues to shape contemporary patterns of violence around the world it is important to begin with the harms of empire. These have been put in the following way:

> The story of empire is the story of crime and violence. Empires are, crimi-nologically speaking, criminal organizations. They are organized to con-quer and control the resources and markets of other territories and people. From the perspective of the conquered, all empires are criminal. On the other hand, from the perspective of the conquerors, empires are civilizers, liberators, and in the most recent justification, democratizers of the world's peoples, at least that part of the world they can dominate. However, the process of domination begins with conquest or wars of aggression, which in most cases also involves genocide or ethnic cleansing. After conquest there are the crimes of empire of theft of acquisition of the valued resources, and then crimes of empire to maintain control of the vanquished such as assassinations, torture and illegal imprisonment.
>
> (Iadicola, 2010:33–4)

Business and violence are linked in many ways. Among the most important are those discussed in Ruggiero's (2010:107–8) account of the 'bellicose cor-poration' which describes how international developments agencies and world financial organizations are the vehicles funnelling money into 'the coffers of large corporations' that is then 'turned into debt for the "aided" country' along the lines described above. Yet war itself can be regarded as among the crimes of the powerful, not least since it opens up ungovernable, lawless spaces in which state-corporate crime can flourish, and Ruggiero shows how the privatization of the post-invasion Iraqi economy secured huge profits for large US and UK companies such as Aegis and Halliburton. The financial scandal in Iraq is one of the greatest in history, where money that was meant to benefit the people of Iraq has instead been 'appropriated by private foreign companies' or has 'just disappeared' (Ruggiero, 2010:115).

Conclusion

It is also important to recognize that the social sciences themselves were shaped within a culture of imperialism, and they each have long taken the contrast between metropolitan and colonized societies for granted. The impact of these global divisions of knowledge production has been the target of Raewyn Connell's (2007) *Southern Theory* and related post-colonial critiques of the Eurocentrism underpinning intellectual work (see also Bhambra, 2007; Chen, 2010 and Santos, 2014). This scholarship reveals how mainstream institu-tions perpetuate a highly skewed and ultimately provincial understanding of the world. Social science is largely based, she argues, on the experience of a handful of societies in 'the North', yet has successfully presented itself as universal, timeless, and placeless where the tendency is to only see from the centre. She is highly critical, for example, of the literature on globalization, suggesting it arises 'from the project of constructing a model of the world from the perspective of the metropole, while imagining one is taking a global perspective' (Connell, 2007:59). Most thinkers simply do not refer to scholarship from the periphery when presenting theories of globalization, assuming that the work of the likes of Ulrich Beck, Anthony Giddens, and Zygmunt Bauman are applicable anywhere. Tellingly Connell's project is not just aimed at deconstructing 'Northern Theory'; it is an attempt to show how subaltern societies produce a good deal of social thought about the modern world, which the Global North has much to learn from. It has much intellectual power, if not more political relevance, so that the problem is certainly not a lack of ideas from the periphery, but 'a deficit of recognition and circulation' (Connell, 2015:215).

Although her arguments were largely focused on sociology (see McLennan, 2013 for a nuanced response from the discipline) they apply with considerable force to criminology. Several of them have been recently developed by Kerry Carrington and colleagues (2016) in a wide-ranging account of how it is at once a theoretical, empirical, and political project aimed at bridging global divisions and democratizing knowledge production. Their purpose is to decolonize criminology and they offer three distinct examples of how this could be achieved. Firstly, they describe the many different worlds of violence to be found in the North and South, and the interconnections between them. Secondly, the distinctive patterns of gendered crime and victimization in the global periphery are examined, to highlight how they have been shaped by diverse cultural, social, religious, and political factors. Thirdly, the historical dynamics and contemporary patterns of penal practice are in need of rethinking, not least since empire is the 'connecting thread' and 'punishment was itself an instrument for projecting imperial power and culture across the globe' (Carrington et al., 2016:12), which continues to inform existing forms of rule. Clearly this summary can only gesture towards the significance of these arguments, but they do pose fundamental questions and open up the possibility of making social science truly global. It is significant that Carrington and colleagues see this project as not just another instance of the ever-increasing fragmentation of the field, a point I will return to in the conclusion of the book.

7

Representation

In criminology there is now a rich tradition of research on 'crime and the media', which owes much to the pioneering work of figures such as Stanley Cohen, Stuart Hall, and Jock Young, not least since they each were associated with developing the concept of moral panic – one of the very few terms from the social sciences to have entered into popular vocabulary. From its initial formulation in the early 1970s the concept has been adapted, criticized, and dismissed in equal measure by criminologists, sociologists, and other commentators. Yet, at the same time, the social processes described by moral panic theory are now so well known to journalists, politicians, and the public generally that certain reactions are entirely predictable and greeted with cynical weariness, or even ridicule, when the scaremongering becomes all too transparent. There is now an extensive literature on the topic and the chapter begins by discussing some of the most significant criticisms of it, but will insist that contemporary media spectacles do still foster distinctive moral relations in quite fundamental ways.

According to some commentators not only is it becoming increasingly impossible to distinguish between media image and social reality, but it is the case that contemporary forms of sociality are multiply mediated (Brown, 2011). The blurring of boundaries is captured well in the following passage:

> Today, as criminals videotape their crimes and post them on YouTube, as security agents scrutinize the image-making of criminals on millions of surveillance monitors, as insurrectionist groups upload video compilations (filmed from several angles) of 'successful' suicide bomb attacks and roadside IED (Improvized Explosive Device) detonations, as images of brutality and victimization pop up on office computer screens and children's mobile phones, as 'reality TV' shows take the viewer ever deeper inside the world of the beat cop and prison setting, there can be no other option but the development of a thoroughgoing *visual* criminology.
>
> (Hayward, 2010:2, emphasis in original)

119

It is significant that Keith Hayward highlights the power of images in shaping the social imaginary and this theme will be developed in the chapter. Of course, the 2011 protests and revolutions in the Middle East were also characterized by distinctive forms of cyber-organizing through social media such as Facebook, Twitter, and YouTube, which helped shape grass-roots political activism while also enabling new forms of surveillance dedicated to countering dissent. More recently the Islamic State's use of social media to post videos of their warriors beheading hostages has attracted widespread shock and condemnation, and has been understood as a form of 'terror marketing' (Mosendz, 2014).

These developments reveal how the very reach of global media networks is now unparalleled. Of course, it is not simply that there are many more media technologies consumed all over the world, but that these developments are breaking down conventional understandings of time and space through making events instantly available to us wherever we are. The 'speed' of modern communication is not a politically neutral occurrence (Virilio, 1986), as the acceleration of perception does not necessarily bring us closer together but can reinforce the distance between neighbours and strangers. In a classic essay on television news Michael Ignatieff (1999:25) has described how this tendency has prompted 'one of the dangerous cultural moods of our time', the belief that the world is so out of control and so dreadful that all we can do is disengage from it.

This experience of dislocation and fatalism is far removed from the optimism of the earliest media theorists, who saw the growth in electronic communications in positive terms. Marshall McLuhan (1964), for example, coined the term 'global village' to describe how modern media could transcend the divisive nationalisms of the past, increasing mutual responsibility and uniting us all. The rise of digital media and techno-culture has certainly seen a vast expansion of global cultural flows, but a key question remains over the kinds of connectivity encouraged in increasingly networked societies. It is significant that the dominant preoccupations of criminologists in this area over the last 40 years or so have been with the distinctive moral force of the media, in that much used and abused concept of moral panic, which can be understood as a particularly dramatic form of symbolic othering and public condemnation of deviance.

Moral Panics

Moral panics can be analysed from a range of theoretical perspectives. These include the symbolic interactionism of the original definitions, later Marxist revisions, various postmodern challenges, and more orthodox attempts to tame the concept in American sociology through the study of collective behaviour. Yet what is lost in this migration is any sense of the urgent politics of anxiety that is crucial to the development of the concept in Britain. Indeed, here all of the recent attempts to update the concept are drawn to the risk society thesis, while across the Atlantic North American scholarship has focused on social problem construction in ways that have often required the analyst to suspend any 'particular political or ideological assumptions' (Best, 2008:ix).

However, I will argue that the concept remains a crucial one and needs to more thoroughly reconnect with the sociology of modernity to make sense of the fears haunting our social worlds. I begin by outlining the sociological origins of moral panics, before describing the criticisms the concept has received and then insisting that contemporary media spectacles do still foster distinctive moral relations in quite fundamental ways. From the outset the concept of moral panic has been concerned with societal reaction and their symptomatic character – how they are rooted in major underlying structural changes and the impassioned outrage they can provoke reveal much about the contours of normality, tolerance, and repression endured in a society. The founding texts are Jock Young's (1971) *The Drugtakers* and Stanley Cohen's (1972) *Folk Devils and Moral Panics*. They both innovatively built on developments American sociology of deviance tradition. These developments, combined with the British statistician Lesley Wilkins' (1964) understanding of 'deviancy amplification', were crucial to how the concept evolved in Britain. Both acknowledge the influence of Marshall McLuhan's (1964) celebrated account of the consequences of the shift from print to electronic media, captured in his iconic phrase that the 'medium is the message'.

McLuhan (1964) argued that the world initially expanded through urbanization and transport developments, but has now 'imploded' as the mass media bring the world closer together again. It is this 'implosive factor' that Cohen and Young (1973:340) find essential, for the 'media are the major and at times the sole source of information about a whole range of phenomena' and thereby 'points to continual bombardment by images of phenomena that otherwise could be conveniently forgotten'. The model used to explain how moral panics occur is deviancy amplification and versions of it are to be found in all the classic studies. Cohen (1972/2002) uses the notion to show how the petty delinquencies of rival groups of mods and rockers at seaside resorts were blown up into serious threats to law and order, and he goes to some lengths to situate the moral panic in the context of post-war social change.

Young (1971) also used the idea of deviancy amplification in his study of drug use in bohemian London, describing how the mass media transformed marijuana use into a social problem through sensationalist and lurid accounts of hippie lifestyles.

There is a strong Durkheimian theme here, in that the boundaries of normality and order are reinforced through the condemnation of the deviant and thereby generate powerful feelings of 'collective effervescence'. But what Cohen (1972) and Young (1971) both were emphasizing was that this process only occurred in modernity through a considerable distortion of reality. This emphasis on how the media distort the reality of social problems was developed by Stuart Hall and his colleagues in their *Policing the Crisis: Mugging, the State, and Law and Order* (1978). In this book an explicitly Marxist account of crime is developed that stands in some contrast to this Durkheimian sociology of deviance tradition. The book ostensibly explores the moral panic that developed in Britain in the early 1970s over the phenomenon of mugging. They demonstrate how the police, media, and judiciary interact to produce ideological closure around the issue through a signification spiral. Black youth are cast as the folk devil in police and media portrayals of the archetypal mugger – a scapegoat for all social anxieties produced by the changes to an affluent but destabilized society.

In criminology the concept has received extensive criticism. Some took issue with the empirical evidence presented by Hall and his colleagues (Waddington, 1986) and for overstating the extent to which the criminality crisis was contrived by elites for dominant interests (Goode and Ben-Yehuda, 1994). Sympathetic critics have applauded the theoretical sophistication of the analysis, but worry about the consequences this has had for the study of street crime (Hallsworth, 2008). By the 1990s the complaint had become that the concept of moral panic is used indiscriminately and 'applied to anything from single mothers to working mothers, from guns to Ecstasy, and from pornography on the Internet to the dangers of state censorship' (Miller and Kitzinger, 1998:221). Meanwhile, others warned against eliding all anxieties under a single heading 'of some (hypothetically universal, endlessly cyclical) feature of social life, namely panickyness' (Sparks, 1992:65).

In his wide-ranging review of the concept Cohen (2002:xxvii) acknowledged that the term 'panic' has caused much trouble, but remains 'convinced that the analogy works'. The term does still convey well the drama, urgency, and energy of certain media narratives, but problems persist in the contrast between an 'irrational' panic and the supposedly 'rational' analysis of it. It is this last difficulty that lies at the centre of Simon Watney's (1987/1997) perceptive critique. He argued that the gradual and staged creation of folk devils as described in classic moral panic theory was incapable of grasping how the entire field of sexuality is saturated with 'monstrous' representations. Nor can it distinguish between different degrees of anxiety or explain how sexuality is regulated through a multiplicity of overlapping and competing institutions.

Critical Updates

These ideas were developed by Angela McRobbie and Sarah Thornton (1995) in their influential attempt to update moral panic theory in the light of multimediated social worlds. Aside from increasing in frequency, moral panics are also far more likely to be contested, while the 'hard and fast boundaries between "normal" and "deviant" would seem to be less common' (McRobbie and Thornton, 1995:572–3). On their reckoning these changes result from the vast expansion and diversification of the mass media, which for Garland (2008:17, emphasis in original) heralds a significant 'shift *away* from moral panics as traditionally conceived (involving a vertical relation between society and a deviant group) towards something more closely resembling American-style "culture wars" (which involve a more horizontal conflict between social groups)'.

The extent of pluralism should not be overstated here. While it is clear that there has been a proliferation of communication technologies, encouraging new spaces for diverse niche interests, there has also been a broader tendency towards the merging of news and entertainment. Arguably it is conflict rather than consensus that is the decisive change. This is due to the bitterness of contemporary identity politics, which not only provokes deeply polarized reactions to most social issues but also suggests a significant normative shift in the status of many deviant groups has taken place – though clearly not all, as the pariah figures of the paedophile and terrorist continue to testify in very different ways. Likewise, Young (2009:13) has described how indignant moral outrage is still stoked by powerful feelings of *ressentiment*: 'the alarm about pit-bulls may well be vested in the fears of an underclass, of "chavs", the pronouncement on the dangers of binge drinking may well relate to a moral dislike of the hedonism of modern youth, and the "dissolute" nature of the night-time economy.' It is highly significant that much of the earlier commentary on the underclass relied on characterizing certain groups in the working class as suffering from a pathological relationship to *production* (the world of socially useful labour), whereas 'chavs' are defined through a pathological relationship with *consumption* – as manifest in dire forms of taste poverty (Hayward and Yar, 2006). A recent analysis of the mediation of the August 2011 riots has revealed how 'scum semiotics' was mobilized through using 'the same stigmatising language which had systematically mocked, humiliated and shamed disenfranchised young people as "chav scum" for the preceding decade' (Tyler, 2013:3.1).

At the same time there have arisen new sites of social anxiety generated by the pace and scale of industrial advances in Western societies. These have built up around nuclear, chemical, biological, environmental, genetic, and medical hazards. Some well-known examples include global warming, nuclear fallout, toxic pollution, bovine spongiform encephalopathy (BSE), bird flu, and other food scares that have made us acutely aware of the catastrophic potential of scientific and technological developments. Many have turned to the concept of 'risk society' (Beck, 1986) to understand the anxieties provoked by these transitions to late modernity. According to Beck the pace of technological innovation generates global risks, such as nuclear war and environmental catastrophe, which outstrip our ability to control them, creating new hazards and uncertainties that previous generations did not have to face. Yet accompanying these global risks is a more pervasive 'ambient fear' that 'saturates the social spaces of everyday life' and penetrates deep into 'the banal minutiae of our lives' (Hubbard, 2003:52). Urban fortress living, manifest in the protection of privileged consumption places (private homes, retail parks, heritage centres, leisure complexes) distinguishes between those who belong and those who threaten. Each of these defensive responses to insecurity only serves to heighten our awareness of unforeseen danger lurking around every corner.

The increased frequency of dramatic moral narratives in the mass media is partly a response to increased market competition, but is also a key means by which the risky character of contemporary society is communicated and takes the form of moral panic in modern Britain 'due to factors such as the loss of authority of traditional elites, anxieties about national identity in the face of increasing external influences and internal diversity' (Thompson, 1998:141). Moral panics are today an integral dimension of modern media culture. They have become an institutionalized aspect of social life and are a routine part of governing through crime – encouraging a new kind of political subjectivity that sees danger and menace everywhere. Malcolm Feeley and Jonathan Simon (2007:51) contend that 'moral panics are now part of the manufactured background, a feature of the larger order of knowledge and power that never goes away or recedes, and that must be constantly guarded against' (Feeley and Simon, 2007:51). In this they share the diagnosis that the 'problem of uncertainty' (Ericson, 2007:204) has become the dominant principle organizing political authority and social relations in neo-liberal societies.

Much of this literature can be situated in broader concerns with the culture of fear so prevalent in contemporary life and one important development has been to subject this writing to critical scrutiny by arguing that moral panics should be understood in a political economy of moral regulation (Critcher, 2009, 2011). The concept of moral regulation was initially formulated in a history of English state formation. It was deployed to explore the processes of legitimation enabling the state to successfully challenge the authority of church and monarchy to become the central power broker in society (Corrigan and Sayer, 1985). Sean Hier (2002, 2008) has been at the forefront of efforts to rethink moral panic research in terms of a volatile politics of moralization. He insists that 'the convulsive power of the "panic", combined with the long-term reserve of regulatory projects, is where the real thrust of moral governance (of the self as well as others) is to be located' (Hier, 2002:332). The approach still conveys the implosive character of contemporary media spectacles and the distinctive moral relationships that the media impose upon audiences. These are crucial points, as indignant denunciation is only one way of responding to what is seen and read. Indeed, one of the fundamental requirements of viewing is that we are obliged to take sides. The act of not looking or changing channels if a story is too disturbing is to ignore the pain experienced by others. To turn away, feel pity, get angry, or become overwhelmed by the horror of it all are each dispositions that a culture of spectatorship encourages. In what follows I develop these arguments through a consideration of the different moral relations the modern mass media cultivate and their place in public life.

Both Jock Young and Stanley Cohen made clear their indebtedness to the famous Canadian media theorist Marshall McLuhan. Although McLuhan remains a somewhat controversial figure, his overall contribution is one that emphasizes how different media fundamentally change social life. Throughout his career McLuhan remained convinced that developments in media technologies brought many benefits, especially with 'cool' media – such as television, hi-fi systems, and telephones – that require high levels of audience participation to complete meaning. In doing so these media reconnect our senses, encourage intense involvement, and bring us together to produce social bonds enabling the 'human family' to become 'tribal once more' (McLuhan, 1964/1994:172). One of the examples he uses is how televised events such as President Kennedy's funeral illustrate the 'unrivalled power of TV' to unite 'an entire population in a ritual process' (McLuhan, 1964/1994:337). The key significance then of the 'implosion' of electric media is that they do not just bring us physically closer together, but emotionally move us to communally participate in human solidarity. This is an understanding of the media that sees the possibilities of a global conscience united in emotional empathy towards the suffering of distant strangers. Had McLuhan lived to see the public responses to the Ethiopia famine in 1984, the Asian tsunami in 2004, and the Haiti earthquake in 2010 then he may well have found encouraging evidence for this internationalization of responsibility that media coverage makes possible.

Of course, the early moral panic theorists shared this Durkheimian understanding of the power of the mass media to ritually unite communities in emotionally charged ways, but the shared indignation generated in response to certain kinds of deviance was regarded as not only unhealthy but intensely neurotic. The roots of this social attitude have been traced by Svend Ranulf (1938), where he describes how communities restore their unity by condemning and persecuting suitable foreign, or marginal, groups in a discussion of the rise of Nazism in Germany and Protestant puritanism in England. Here moral indignation is understood as a transhistorical phenomenon of '*ressentiment*', which reinforces group cohesion by scapegoating foreign, polluting bodies (Jews in 1930s Germany, idle vagabonds in Calvinist asceticism). In highlighting the collective hostility moral panics unleash the new deviancy theorists were also echoing other critics of McLuhan's optimistic understanding of the media. Even those who are clearly influenced by McLuhan reverse his central claims:

> Much of the time we are witnesses to what is rightly called a "pseudo" public sphere, where politicians and docile politicians act out a travesty of democratic debate. No wonder, as Jean Baudrillard (1983) suggests, the masses are generally turned off from 'serious' politics and turned on to something else that is much more entertaining.
>
> (McGuigan, 2005:429)

Ever since Baudrillard's 1967 review of *Understanding Media*, he has been regarded as a postmodern proponent of McLuhan's vision. Yet he utterly rejects neo-tribal optimism, while taking the idea that the 'medium is the message' beyond anything envisaged by McLuhan.

Baudrillard follows McLuhan by seeing the message of television as lying not in its content, but in the new, destructive modes of perception it imposes. Too much is seen obscenely fast. As he puts it, we 'are no longer a part of the drama of alienation; we live in the ecstasy of communication' and 'this ecstasy is obscene' (Baudrillard, 1985:130). Baudrillard's is clearly a hyperbolic voice, but his overall point is that the contemporary media transform social experiences in quite damaging ways – where the banal becomes serious, democracy turns into show business and incoherence is privileged over meaningful debate. In developing his media theory Baudrillard draws on the work of an American historian Daniel Boorstin and his 1961 book *The Image*. Now largely neglected the book is full of contemporary resonance. For instance, he is the source of one of the most widely quoted aphorisms about celebrity: '*the celebrity is a person who is well-known for their well-knownness* ... fabricated on purpose to satisfy our exaggerated expectations of human greatness' (Boorstin, 1961:57–8, emphasis in original). Boorstin also coined the term 'pseudo-event' to describe events which are created for the sole purpose of being reported or reproduced, like press conferences and presidential debates, which are then judged for their success on how widely they are reported. Writing over 50 years ago he claimed that the torrent of 'pseudo-events' has flushed away the distinction between 'hard' and 'soft' news (Boorstin, 1961:23) to the extent that one of the few exceptions remains the reporting of crime.

Both Baudrillard and Boorstin rework an earlier Frankfurt School-style critique of mass society, where the culture industries operate as a totalitarian force suppressing social solidarities. It is clear that both share 'the belief that something is lost in the social and technical advance of the contemporary media, and that the latter do not merely transform experience but *kill* it' (Merrin, 2005:55, emphasis in original). The destructive power of contemporary media lies in the way audiences are rendered almost helpless before the endless flow of mediated misery encountered in their daily lives. Ultimately, the most profound moral demand television makes on spectators is to place us as witnesses of human suffering, without giving us the option to act directly on it (Ellis, 2000:1). However, there are many ways spectators respond to and actively involve themselves with what they see on screen, read in newspapers, or browse online.

Ethics, Rhetoric, and Performativity

A central claim of this chapter is that the discourses produced by mediated moral panics should be understood as rhetorics of indignant denunciation – these are typically directed at the scapegoats, but the persecutors could also find themselves angrily accused of prejudice. In his account of how modern media use images and language to render distant suffering not only intelligible but also morally acceptable to the spectator, Luc Boltanski (1999) identifies three rhetorical 'topics' in which audiences engage with mediated misfortune. The distinctive argument is that ever since the end of the eighteenth century, when pity became central to politics, the topics of 'denunciation', 'sentiment', and 'aesthetics' have become the ethically proper ways of responding to the disturbing spectacles of distant suffering. In doing so they provide an invaluable starting point for understanding how mediatized events can, at times, unleash great social change, while at others produce little more than banal indifference among media audiences. Each involve competing ways of organizing emotions and, by extension, the norms that govern the ethics of cosmopolitan citizenship.

Although indignant denunciation is motivated by anger it 'can be criticised as an empty substitute for action' (Boltanski, 1999:70) and is often discredited for the ways it appeals to vindictive desires such as revenge, envy, and resentment. A second way spectators can sympathize with the unfortunate is through 'sentiment', which provokes a 'tender-heartedness' that recognizes the suffering of another, so as to be moved to compassion. However, it is this very sentimentalism itself that has been condemned and disqualified as an indulgence. To take an example that exemplifies some of these issues, ever since the 1960s the image of a starving African child, with pleading eyes, had become a powerful symbol of human suffering and was used by agencies such as Oxfam and Save the Children in appeals to Western adults for charitable donations.

By the 1980s the images had become more shocking – pictures of emaciated bodies of starving young children, only hours from death, featured in a number of campaigns, accompanied by text explaining that 'While you're eating between meals, he's dying between meals' and 'You're not the only one with weight problems' (Holland, 2006:153–5). Neo-colonial critics attacked this kind of imagery for stressing helplessness and dependence, which sustains 'a patronizing, offensive and misleading view of the developing world as a spectacle of tragedy, disaster, disease and cruelty' (Cohen, 2001:178). From the 1990s onward such imagery was denounced as 'aid pornography' while hiding the close relationships between Western affluence and the increasing poverty in the rest of the world. New codes of practice were drafted in response and most agencies pursued a strategy of 'positive images' where recipients are not seen as feeble beneficiaries of charitable donations.

Problems remain though about the reality behind, and the rhetoric of, the image – too much 'information can confuse the power of the image, and an understanding of political complexities deflects emotional response' (Holland, 2006:155). Of course, these humanitarian organizations are acutely aware of 'compassion fatigue' and have developed sophisticated ways of renewing campaigns in response to criticism and apathy. One recent policy, favoured among several international development charities, has been to use celebrities in an effort to attract popular media coverage and personalize complex situations, so that foreign affairs are made accessible to the ordinary public. This trend towards a 'theatricality' of humanitarianism has been criticized for encouraging viewing publics to relate to the symbolic portrayal of human misery more in terms of their feelings for celebrities like Angelina Jolie than the actual situation of those enduring the suffering (Chouliaraki, 2012). The clear worry is that by transforming politics into entertainment the difficulties surrounding development issues are submerged beneath the banalities of celebrity lifestyle, brand identity, and show business.

The third possibility of engaged spectatorship arises from criticism of the first two. It consists of being moved by neither indignation nor sentimentalism, but instead through an aesthetics of the sublime, where 'suffering is looked at in the face and confronted in its truth, that is to say as pure *evil*' (Boltanski, 1999:119, emphasis in original). The complaint here though is that to aestheticize tragedy will ultimately anaesthetize the feelings of those who witness suffering. Indeed, Boltanski's book concludes with a discussion of the contemporary 'crisis of pity' rendered by the mass media and the 'spectacle' effects they produce. Susan Sontag has made a similar point:

> Imagery that would have had an audience cringing and recoiling in disgust forty years ago is watched without so much as a blink by every teenager in the multiplex. Indeed, mayhem is entertaining rather than shocking to many people in most cultures.
>
> (Sontag, 2003:90)

It is significant that Cohen (2002:xxxv) has himself moved from an early interest in overreaction (panic) to underreaction (denial) in his later work – the 'ways we are manipulated into taking some things too seriously and other things not seriously enough'. Elsewhere I have developed these arguments in relation to the sexual torture scenes so apparent in the notorious Abu Ghraib photographs, which did not provoke shock so much as recognition among many commentators (Carrabine, 2011). A long-standing complaint surrounding war photography, as we will see in the next section, is that it transforms the horror and violence of armed conflict into an attractive, aesthetic experience. To take one example, David Shields (2015) has collected 64 glossy war photos which were published on the front page of the *New York Times* from the invasions of Afghanistan in 2001 and Iraq in 2003 up to 2013. By arranging them thematically the intention is to underline how they reproduce and reinforce certain visual tropes that glamourize war. The accusation is that the newspaper does all it can to transform violence into beauty, which ultimately serves to imply that 'a chaotic world is under control' (Shields, 2015:9).

The crucial point though is that mediated communication fundamentally shapes our experience of reality. Yet the unexpected and the exceptional still happen and it remains the job of the media to translate these spontaneous anomalies into neat and tidy stories. Occasionally though these events can produce an electrifying force that unleashes cultural change and quite profound social transformations. An influential theorization of such 'mediatized public crises' lies in Jeffrey Alexander and Ronald Jacobs' (1998) account of the contested and disruptive dynamics of exceptional news stories. Here they emphasize the importance of ritual, symbolism, and emotional appeals as well as narrative, drama, and performance to the unfolding sense of crisis. It is an optimistic vision, for when these 'mediatized public crises' occur they suggest that:

> the media create public narratives that emphasize not only the tragic distance between is and ought but the possibility of heroically overcoming it. Such narratives prescribe struggles to make 'real' institutional relationships more consistent with the normative standards of the utopian civil society discourse.
>
> (Alexander and Jacobs, 1998:28)

Their analysis demonstrates how the Watergate crisis of 1972 and the Rodney King beating of 1991 both disturbed the moral order and became catalysts for social change, largely through the communicative power of the media.

These elements are picked up in in Simon Cottle's (2005, 2006) attempts to extend these insights. Drawing on Victor Turner's (1974) anthropology, this framework shows how 'social dramas can generate emotional intensity, mobilize moral solidarity and encourage social reflexivity in precipitous moments that reside, on occasion, outside of "normal" space and time' (Cottle, 2005:53). The case he initially uses to build his argument is the racist murder of Stephen Lawrence and its gradual transformation into a 'mediatized public crisis' that challenged the normative contours of British society. There have been many racist murders in Britain, yet the killing of Stephen Lawrence in south-east London in April 1993 became an exceptional case and eventually prompted widespread criticism of powerful state institutions. More recently Cottle (2012) has used the framework to explore the ritualization of catastrophe in press coverage to highlight how disasters, once mediated, are often narrated through established cultural codes and scripts full of emotion, but with different political ramifications. As he puts it, to fully grasp 'the complexities of empathy and engagement, politics and pity that are variously summoned through mediatized disasters, we need to better understand how some disasters become performatively enacted in the world's news media' (Cottle, 2012:278).

The understanding of media performativity here is a dynamic one and while it deploys a sequential structure along the lines of Turner's depiction of 'social dramas', this is conceptualized in such a way that seeks to avoid deterministic thinking, not least since the spontaneity of liminality opens up the 'realm of pure possibility' (Turner, 1967:97) and makes it difficult to predict how stories will unfold. Mass mediated rituals are volatile precisely because they offer an opportunity for both 'waging' and 'narrating politics' (Ettema, 1990:478).

Take the example of media scandals, which like moral panics have been theorized as summoning up collective boundaries 'to police perceived transgressions', and are also 'highly symbolic "affairs" (figuratively or literally) that involve public performances designed to salvage institutional and/or personal reputations, trust, and legitimacy' (Cottle, 2012:265). Alexander (2004) has also used a performative framework for understanding the September 11 terrorist attacks, situating the event in terms of actors, audiences, props, scripts, and plots, an approach further refined in case studies of Obama's election (J.Alexander, 2010) and the Arab Spring (Alexander, 2011).

Cultural Sociology

It is important to situate this work in the context of the 'strong program' in cultural sociology, which has emerged as a 'significant and confident intervention, designed to re-orientate sociology and cultural studies alike in quite fundamental ways' (McLennan, 2005:1). Since the 1990s it has established an academic base (Yale Center for Cultural Sociology), book series (Palgrave), handbook (*Oxford Handbook of Cultural Sociology*), and since 2013 also a journal (*American Journal of Cultural Sociology*). Alexander is the leading light in this new American cultural sociology, which he and his students sharply differentiate from other competing approaches such as Bourdieu's sociological analysis, Birmingham cultural studies, and Foucauldian governmentality perspectives – all examples of which are condemned for treating culture as a 'feeble and ambivalent variable' (Alexander, 2003:6–7). These are formidable targets and the clear implication is they are 'weak' approaches that reduce culture to a product of social structure or materialist elements such as class, interests, and power. In contrast, the 'strong program' is committed to an autonomous conception of culture and is dedicated to revealing the pivotal role culture plays in shaping social life. The approach was spelled out in 1988 in his introduction to the edited collection *Durkheimian Sociology: Cultural Studies*, which is premised on an argument that the later writings of Durkheim provide a vital resource for contemporary sociology and its focus on symbolic process. This later scholarship culminated in *The Elementary Forms of Religious Life* (1912) and the move to the study of religion in Durkheim was 'because he wanted to give cultural processes more theoretical autonomy' (Alexander, 1988:2). In this account Durkheim is seen as providing an important, if largely unacknowledged, legacy for the development of semiotic and ritual analysis.

Over the years, this neo-Durkheimian framework has been deployed in a variety of empirical contexts, including race (Jacobs, 2000), punishment (Smith, 2008), and politics (Ku, 1999), where the theoretical drive emphasizes the collective conscience at work in civil society. One strand has been to focus on 'cultural trauma' in Alexander's (2002:5) own study of the Holocaust to demonstrate 'that even the most calamitous and biological of social facts – the prototypical evil of genocidal mass murder – can be understood only inside of symbolic codes and narratives'. For some critics the 'strong program' is a project 'persistently dogged by an ultimately one-sided preference for *idealist* formulations and valuations' and reveals the limits of the critical purchase of this specific brand of cultural theory (McLennan, 2005:1–2, emphasis in original). Others have sought to defend neo-Marxist and materialist perspectives against this brand of cultural sociology, but I have no wish to replace a one-sided idealist argument, with another equally one-sided materialist position. As Vic Gatrell (1994:25) put it, only 'rash historians would privilege material or political or cultural causes without interrelating all three' and this injunction is one that needs to be kept firmly in sight as the field is theoretically reconfigured.

More recently an 'iconic turn' has been announced by proponents of the 'strong program' in cultural sociology (Bartmański and Alexander, 2012). Building on Durkheim's classic analysis of totemism, where he explained how the power of sacred symbols derived from their ability to represent collective identity, the iconic turn is geared towards grasping the very materiality of an image. In this understanding an image is more than simply a 'projection of social meanings: it is a complex sensory experience' (Sonnevend, 2012:219). Iconicity is concerned with 'experiencing material objects, not only understanding them cognitively or evaluating them morally but also feeling their sensual, aesthetic force' (Bartmański and Alexander, 2012:1). The cultural sociology of iconic power highlights the interactions between aesthetic surface and discursive depth. In doing so, this work can be read as an attempt to take a position in the rapidly expanding field of interest in visual culture across the humanities and social sciences, and which will be explored in more detail in the next section. They note, for example, how:

> The logocentrism of modern Western culture (Jay 1993) has downplayed the visual surface, maintaining that it is preceded by depth and, therefore, merely reflects it. Postmodern theory inverts this thesis, downplaying discursive meaning and giving priority to the physicality of surface ... If logocentrism unduly represses the surface, postmodern thinkers go too far the other way. Their stance runs the risk of being iconoclastic *á rebours*. Identifying meaning with discourse and reason, and presence with image and emotion, postmodern theory reproduces the old dualisms instead of reconfiguring them.
>
> (Bartmański and Alexander, 2012:4)

Critics have pointed out how this 'iconic turn' has largely ignored already existing work in the social sciences, which has not only addressed the social production and consumption of culture, but has also analysed the objectifying power of material objects (Santoro and Solaroli, 2016). A major absence is the sociology of Bourdieu, who from his early work on photography through to his later writing on art and culture, offers rich interpretive insights that are neglected in this reframing of iconic power.

One significant omission is Bourdieu's relationship to the art historian Erwin Panofsky, who is widely regarded as founding the modern study of iconology in the 1920s and 1930s (and thus anticipating the iconic turn by several decades). Panofsky further refined the method in his *Gothic Architecture and Scholasticism* (1951). The book was later translated by Bourdieu (1967) and published with a postface where he discusses the sociological significance of Panofsky's study, especially in the concept of 'habitus' for describing the relationship between predispositions acquired through educational institutions and the aesthetic rules of composition deployed in medieval architecture. In a subsequent essay Bourdieu (1968/2003) draws on Panofsky's layered levels of signification to demonstrate how art connoisseurship marks out status distinctions and lends itself to a charismatic ideology of taste, which functions as an important form of cultural capital. Although the 'strong program' has largely ignored Bourdieu's work, for the reasons outlined above (and which I do not share), their ambition to broaden 'sociological epistemology in an aesthetic way' (Bartmański and Alexander, 2012:5) is important, and one I develop in what follows, not least since there remains hardly any consensus over how 'the visual' should be analysed or explained (Wilkinson, 2013:262).

These tensions are very much to the fore in Bourdieu's own work. During his extensive fieldwork in Algeria in the late 1950s and early 1960s he took thousands of photographs documenting the suffering experienced in a colonial war; yet only a few were ever published in his writing about the period. Most would remain unknown until 2000 when they were exhibited and subsequently published in his *Picturing Algeria* (Bourdieu, 2012). The relationship between his photographic record and issues of politics, ethics, and aesthetics has been discussed by Les Back (2009:473), where he makes the telling remark that 'as a profession we are just not very good at looking at photographs for their sociological value'. In order to do so we can draw on two fundamental points. These can be summarized as follows:

> The first is that images do not simply have a representational power in depicting an external reality but that they possess a *performative* power upon this reality, simultaneously constituting it in meaning ... The second ... is that our moral and political response to images of vulnerability and violence is not only a question of personal convictions or intimate emotions, but primarily a product of the *collective imaginations of the world*, of self and other, that such imagery disseminates and legitimises in our (Western) societies.
>
> (Chouliaraki and Blaagard, 2013:254, emphasis in original)

As these authors go on to argue, images of other people's suffering not only depict the world as it is, but also prompt emotions and ideas about how the world might be.

To understand how these processes operate necessitates examining how media organizations and institutionalized practice produce news stories, the textual conventions and meanings embedded in them, and the diverse ways in which audiences respond. Moreover, it requires a normative commitment to not simply exposing the socially constructed nature of reality but rather reopening important epistemological questions over the sociology of knowledge and rival ways of knowing the world. The distinction between what *is* and what *ought to be* is also integral to news reporting. The 'new journalism' of the late nineteenth century sought to expose hidden realities, by revealing the secrets of the rich and prompting sympathy for the poor through 'human interest' stories. This was as true for crusading editors like W. T. Stead in Britain and Joseph Pulitzer in the United States as it was for the 'muckraking' journalism of Lincoln Steffens and Ida Tarbell, and has informed much of the subsequent investigative reporting that flourished in the 1960s and 1970s, while more contemporary 'citizen journalism' has the capacity to present alternative truths and challenge official assertions of fact. Indeed, it has been argued that 'scandal hunting' is now the 'default position across the UK national press, and any number of online news and social media sites' (Greer and McLaughlin, 2016:8).

In a series of publications Chris Greer and Eugene McLaughlin (2011, 2012a, 2012b, 2013, 2015) have tracked how 'trial by media' has become a market-driven form of populist justice, where news consumers are actively recruited to participate in the hunt for scandal, and has given rise to distinctive forms of regulatory governance by the state. Yet what should now be abundantly clear from this chapter is that the contemporary world is very much a 'seen' experience. In many instances we encounter 'a sort of frenzy of the visible' prompting radical transformations 'in our capacity for self and social understanding' (Wilkinson, 2013:261). The final section of this chapter concentrates on the 'visual turn' in criminology and discusses some of the ways in which the field can be reconfigured in light of these developments.

Visual Criminology

Across the social sciences there has been a resurgence of interest in visual methods, which has been accompanied by a rise in scholarship on visual culture that has now established itself as an exciting and expanding intellectual field. In criminology while there is a rich tradition of research on 'crime and the media', described above, specific attention to the *visual*, or indeed on the role and place of the *image* in crime, in crime control and in criminal justice, has long been lacking. This omission is particularly surprising given just how deepseated the cultural fascination with the spectacle of crime and punishment is in the popular imagination. Of course, there have been some significant interventions in recent years, which would include Katherine Biber's (2007) *Captive*

Images, Judith Resnick and Dennis Curtis's (2011) *Representing Justice*, Jonathan Finn's (2009) *Capturing the Criminal Image*, and Alison Young's (2005) *Judging the Image*. They have each made ambitious attempts to understand the power of representation and bring new ways of thinking to bear in the discipline. Today images are everywhere, and they have a profound impact on our sense of ourselves as 'modern' (Jervis, 1998). Indeed, the term 'ocular-centralism' was coined to describe a world saturated by visual experiences and the privileging of vision in Western philosophy and social theory (Jay, 1993).

The challenge then is to construct an approach that can do justice to both the power of images in social life and their place in social research. There are now several accounts of how to conduct research with visual materials and they each survey the different ways images have been used to understand the world (some recent examples include Harper, 2012; Rose, 2012; Pink, 2013). Anthropologists and sociologists, for example, have used photographs from the beginning as both disciplines began to explore societies near and afar, but they gradually fell out of favour as they were deemed too subjective, unsystematic, and eccentric. As Howard Becker explains:

> Sociologists lost interest in reformist uses of photography as they shifted their attention from reform to scientific generalization … and very few photographs accompanied sociological articles and books. Anthropologists complained that their colleagues made photographs that were no different from ones tourists made of exotic places and that served no better purpose than those amateur works.

> (Becker, 2004:193–4)

To take the example of sociology, the ties with photography were established very early on, and practitioners sought to promote social reform by exposing the injustices associated with the modern age. Crusading journalists such as Jacob Riis photographed the crushing slum poverty in New York in the 1880s (an undertaking pioneered several decades earlier in British cities by a number of different urban explorers), while Lewis Hine's involvement with the sustained campaign against child labour is often said to have led to the passage of laws ending child slavery. Between 1907 and 1918 he travelled around the United States taking over 5,000 photographs of children at work, often tricking the managers, to create what he termed a 'photo story', where words and pictures combine to produce a powerful, non-linear narrative (Marien, 2010:207). At around the same time early editions of the *American Journal of Sociology* routinely included photographs to accompany the 'muckraking' reformist articles it published during the first 15 years of its existence. This tradition was much later reclaimed and reworked by Howard Becker (1974, 1995, 1982/2008) across a series of influential publications that argued for a more ambitious use of visual material to explore society.

Consequently, it is helpful to identify three distinctive, but overlapping, genres that can help sharpen the discussion. Documentary photography, photojournalism, and visual sociology each see it as 'their main business to describe what has not yet been described' and 'to tell the big news' in their respective explorations of society (Becker, 1974:3). Each have different uses and diverse histories, but the boundaries between them are occasionally blurred, so considering them as distinctive genres will help shed light on what they are trying to achieve in particular contexts. One immediate difficulty facing any attempt at defining 'documentary photography' is that practically every photograph is a document of something, and from the beginning the medium itself has largely been understood through its capacity to record an objective and faithful image of events with an unprecedented authority. Although all photos are documentary in the sense that they have an indexical relationship with whatever was in front of the lens when the image was made, we can make some broad distinctions between photographs intended for 'public' or 'private' viewing, and those which are 'caught' in 'candid' moments as opposed to those which are 'arranged' in some 'covertly contrived' ways (Goffman, 1979:14).

A further way out of the definitional difficulties is to situate documentary in relation to a distinctive kind of social investigation and it was this practice that John Grierson had in mind when he coined the term 'documentary' in 1926. Indeed, the documentary movement would flourish in the 1930s and combined both physical activity (constructing a text, object, or image) and ethical task (explaining the truth of the world), which are tied together in his formulation of documentary as 'the creative treatment of actuality' (Grierson, 1966:147). The juxtaposition between the creative (artistic license) and the actual (reality as it is) lies at the heart of the tradition and has been the cause of much controversy. Despite being a 'genre of actuality' the main purpose of documentary, as it developed in the 1930s, was to 'educate one's feelings' as practitioners concluded that while we 'understand a historical document intellectually' we also 'understand a human document emotionally' (Stott, 1973:8) and so the affective came to be prioritized in the movement.

The movement also anticipates the 'golden age' of photojournalism (1930s–1950s) when 'reportage' became a staple of newspaper and magazine coverage. Indeed, the rapid expansion of the market during this period, with magazines such as *Look* and *Life* in the United States, *Illustrated* and *Picture Post* in Britain, and *Vu* in France, gave outlets for influential photographers, such as W. Eugene Smith, Robert Capa, and Henri Cartier-Bresson, to have their work commissioned and published. These mass-circulation picture magazines emerged between the wars, initially in Germany, and then quickly spread to other countries. Using innovative juxtapositions of image and text the term 'photojournalism' came to describe the new practice. Yet photography has a long and troubled history in Western journalism and Karin Becker (1990/2003) has charted some of these dynamics across distinct types of publication. She highlights how it was in the tabloid newspapers of the 1920s that large, eye-catching photographs of crime, violence, disaster, and society scandals came to prominence – telling stories quickly, through sensational pictures and short captions. Press historians see this as a nadir for journalism and the 'abundant use of pictorial material' was regarded 'as conclusive proof both of declining literary standards and a nefarious plan to exploit hopelessly naïve and illiterate people' (Carlebach, 1997:145). If the tabloid press undermined the credibility of the photograph as a medium for serious news, then it was the simultaneous rise of picture magazines that established the genre of the photo essay – where images and text could be spread out as running narratives across several pages.

Assignments from these publications were especially coveted and the magazines became a global phenomenon. With their distinctive styles and expert photography they underlined the importance of the 'camera as witness', where the photojournalist takes pictures to fulfil an editorial requirement and 'answer the essential journalistic questions: who, what, where, when, and why' (Gefter, 2009:123). By the 1970s their popularity had fallen, with the likes of *Life* and *Look* closing, partly as a result of the rise of television and changes in press ownership, while new kinds of colour newspaper supplements appeared, which were mainly led by advertising and lifestyle features. As the business of journalism has changed so photojournalists have had to adapt to new constraints and find fresh outlets to pursue their practice. Indeed, a case can be made that socially conscious photojournalism has flourished independently of the print media for decades now, where the pictures are more likely to be seen on the walls of galleries and museum exhibitions, and in elegant books than in newspapers and magazines.

War is a major subject for photographers and World War II effaced the distinction between civilian and combatant to the extent that ever since then those caught up in the conflict have received as much attention as the soldiers themselves. Indeed, it is often said that the stream of horrific images from Vietnam provided normative criticism of the war. The 1972 photograph of a naked Vietnamese girl running away from a village just napalmed by US planes is one of the most distressing images of the era and brought home the terror of the indiscriminate killing. Robert Capa's statement that 'if your pictures aren't good enough, you're not close enough' (cited in Marien, 2003:303) has long been the credo of the war photographer rushing off to battle to capture the death and destruction. It was the Spanish Civil War (1936–39) that was the first to be covered by corps of professional photographers from the frontline and Capa's photograph of a Republican soldier 'shot' by his camera at the same time as bullets rip through his crumpling body is one of the defining images of the war. As Sontag (2003:20) explains – it 'is a shocking image, and that is the point'. Or as Peter Howe, a former picture editor at *Life,* put it, 'the job of the photojournalist is to witness those things that people don't want to think about. When they're doing the job right, they are taking photographs that people don't want to publish by their very nature' (cited in Lowe, 2014:211).

Alongside this socially concerned photography, which is dedicated to bearing witness and political critique, there remained a mass market for sensationalized images of working-class life and the urban condition. Indeed, the picturing of 'news' was absolutely central to the development of a global visual economy and one that shows no sign of diminishing in today's digital age.

Among the most infamous photographers exploiting this appetite was Arthur Fellig, more well known by his nickname Weegee, who in graphic black-and-white photography captured the gruesome detail of gang executions, car crashes, and tenement fires that he then sold to the New York City tabloid editors. Such brutal pictures became the staple images of the mass circulation press in the 1930s and effectively changed journalistic practices overnight (Lee and Meyer, 2008). Phil Carney (2010:26) has placed Weegee in a discussion of the relationships between spectacle, predation, and paparazzi, suggesting he was 'the first photographer to stalk and ensnare his prey with stealth and speed', establishing practices that would become increasingly popular as a market devoted to publishing candid images of celebrities' unguarded moments came to prominence. These 'stolen images' undermined what a 'good' photograph should look like, with their 'awkward composition, harsh contrasts and uncertain focus' (Becker, 1990/2003:301) and are now an integral feature of tabloid, celebrity culture.

Weegee provides an important bridge from the conventional topics of documentary photography into the new directions taken in the post-war period, when the 'new' documentarists began exploring more 'subjective' approaches to image making, which reopened important questions about photography's complex relationship with reality (Carrabine, 2012b). Yet it is important to note that crime photographers are rarely able to capture the criminal act itself and represent the act by focusing on its 'after-effects and constituent parts' so that 'weapons, suspects, victims, locations, accomplices, and bloody crime sites are usually photographed separately, often at some remove in time and space from the crime itself' (Straw, 2015:139). The resulting visual coverage then is fragmented, and overlaps to an extent with official forensic photography, but tends to draw from a fairly stable repertoire of images with varying degrees of documentary credibility and journalistic value.

For much of the twentieth century sociology has shown little interest in the use of images, and remains dominated by words and figures. Although the use of visual material has remained a marginal activity in the discipline, there have been some significant interventions. One important example is Bourdieu's (1965/1990) collaborative work on photography which he sees as an ordinary, 'middlebrow art form' through which class taste is pictured in family snapshots, holiday souvenirs, and wedding portraits. In Bourdieu it is a practice that is sociologically important because it both *portrays* the social world and *betrays* the choices made by the photographer. The book demonstrated how a cultural practice such as photography, which in principle was open to almost everyone and had not yet acquired an elaborate set of aesthetic judgement criteria, could still sustain social hierarchies and class divisions. The work opened up the questions of what could be learned from analysing the photographs people take and what is it that people do with them – revealing how taste is far from being an inimitable personal faculty, but is instead an essentially social phenomenon structuring perceptions of the world. Recent research has focused on how class, gender, place, and identity shape amateur photographic practice (Rose, 2004), while the conventions informing the 'digital turn' in distinctive communities and their legitimation have become the focus of attention as photography has become ever more ubiquitous in everyday life (Murray, 2008; Hand, 2012).

Few sociologists have done more than Howard Becker to rework and reclaim the importance of the visual in the discipline. His essay on 'Photography and Sociology' (Becker, 1974) highlights how both are interested in social problems and exotic subcultures, while many photographers have been drawn to capturing the ambience of urban life in ways that parallel the sociological thinking of Simmel and his subsequent followers. These arguments are enlarged in his edited collection *Exploring Society Photographically* (Becker, 1981), which originally accompanied an exhibition of 12 distinctive projects exploring social worlds. It begins with Gregory Bateson and Margaret Mead's (1942) study of *Balinese Character: A Photographic Analysis,* which is now regarded as a key intervention in anthropology, as it moved well beyond what were the conventional ethnographic uses of visual material. Also included is a selection of images from Bruce Jackson's (1977) *Killing Time* taken from Cummins Prison Farm in Arkansas. A Professor of English, he has been documenting prison life across various media since the early 1960s, and his other work includes *A Thief's Primer* (1969), *Portraits from a Drawer* (2009), and most recently *In This Timeless Time: Living and Dying on Death Row in America* (with Diane Christian, 2012), which clearly speaks to criminological issues in compelling and provocative ways. Indeed, imprisonment has proved to be a particularly important site for photographers and the website and blog at www.prisonphotography.org lists some 120 professional practitioners who have sought to convey the pains of confinement in visually striking ways (see also Carrabine, 2016).

The last foundational text I want to discuss is Erving Goffman's (1979) *Gender Advertisements,* which reproduces a large number of commercial advertisements and uses them as visual data. As the title suggests the book addresses how gender relations are displayed in them and draws on his previous work deploying dramaturgical metaphors to examine social interaction. He maintains that advertisements can be productively compared to stage scenes, where the ritual displays in them tell us much about gendered social relations in society at large. Much of the book is organized to indicate the various ways gender inequalities are enacted through the sheer attention to detail. The section on the 'ritualization of subordination', for example, has an account of how 'Women frequently, men very infrequently, are posed in a display of the "bashful knee bend"' (Goffman, 1979:45), and the accompanying array of visual evidence featuring this form of deferent gesture gives a social scientific understanding of how gender differences are expressed.

Some of these issues have been imaginatively taken up by the photographer and documentary filmmaker Lauren Greenfield (2002), who has explored the various 'body projects' young women pursue in light of the exhibitionist tendencies of contemporary American femininity and the difficulties of living up to the expectations posed by popular culture in their daily grooming rituals. In some respects, this is indicative of a post-feminist sensibility based on sexual confidence and autonomy, where 'raunch culture' is understood as a shift 'from an external, male judging gaze to a self-policing narcissistic gaze' in a highly sexualized culture that is changing the boundaries between public and private spheres (Gill, 2010:103). Here new forms of 'public intimacy' are developing in a 'striptease culture', which is preoccupied with self-revelation and confessional exposure in ever louder and more mediatized ways (McNair, 2002). Indeed, the phrase 'oversharing' has come to describe the phenomenon where 'too' much is revealed about ourselves on social media through the constant documenting and displaying of our private lives to others (Agger, 2015). Of course, much of this is taking place in 'acts of visual communication on a scale that is unprecedented' (Hand, 2012:194) and the full implications of this transformation have yet to be addressed. However, I want to conclude this chapter with some examples exploring similar avenues as Greenfield, which uses a photographic project to dissect society, but focuses on explicitly criminological themes and topics.

Conclusion

There is a long and influential line of critique on photographic representation that is deeply suspicious of how the camera aestheticizes all that it pictures. It features in the writing of Allan Sekula, Martha Rosler, and Susan Sontag and can be traced back to Walter Benjamin's (1934/1982) dire warnings on photography's ability to beautify suffering. What each thinker shares is the conviction that 'aestheticizing suffering is inherently both artistically and politically reactionary, a way of mistreating the subject and inviting passive consumption, narcissistic appropriation, condescension, or even sadism on the part of viewers' (Reinhardt, 2007:14). Elsewhere I have described how some contemporary practitioners have responded to the complaint that much photojournalism and social documentary exploits the other and reinforces the differences between the superior and the inferior (Carrabine, 2012a, 2014, 2015). During the 1970s and 1980s the very practice of documentary critique came under sustained critique, when the movement was charged with exploiting the other and the 'truth claims' debunked as stage-managed fictions. Under these, and other criticisms, documentary fell out of fashion, but more recently there has been a resurgence of interest in the genre. Contemporary practitioners seem to be less troubled by terms such as 'truth', 'evidence', and 'reality', which is not to say they are blind to the way photographs are constructed, but they are more attuned to them as 'carefully fabricated cultural objects' (Price, 2009:107).

One recent development has been the turn to making documentary-style pictures that appear devoid of 'any significant or identifiable subject matter' (Batchen, 2012:233). An example of such an approach is the work of the French photographer Sophie Ristelhueber who has paid particular attention to the ruins and traces left by war and the scars it leaves on the landscape. In her series *WB* (*West Bank*) she 'refused to photograph the great separation wall that embodies the policy of a state and the media icon of the "Middle Eastern problem"'; rather, she took photographs of the small roadblocks the Israelis had built on 'country roads with whatever means available' and from such an elevated 'viewpoint that transforms the blocks of the barriers into elements of the landscape' (Rancière, 2011:104). This more allusive approach is also exemplified in the Chilean artist Alfredo Jaar, who has produced several works on the Rwandan genocide of 1994, none of which depict a single instant of the carnage. Across a series of pieces he has explored the limits of representation, exposing media culture's inability to see and stop the slaughter. Likewise, the failure of Western governments to intervene in the conflict in the former Yugoslavia is a theme explored in Simon Norfolk's (2005) *Bleed*. It revisits the frozen landscapes of eastern Bosnia where thousands were massacred and the almost abstract images become powerful allegories for the secrets buried beneath the ice. For Norfolk it was crucial to know the exact location of the gravesites, to give the work a forensic credibility and visual power. As he explains, 'it's even more important when the picture uses metaphors; if the detective work was poor then the whole project would unravel quickly. The only way you can come at it in such a symbolic way is if you are one hundred percent sure that here are the locations – otherwise it's a weak, feeble approach' (cited in Lowe, 2014:225). The tension between the arresting beauty of the images and the fact that something terrible is contained in them enables him to make a strong moral argument about the nature of guilt.

A rather different exponent of the method is Bruno Serralongue who in his *Fait Divers* series traced crime and accident scenes as they were described in the regional newspaper *Nice-Matin*. Working between late 1993 and April 1995 he would take pictures of the deserted scene in and around Nice, France, where only very recently something terrible had happened. Although the photos 'look too suspiciously banal' on their own, once they are accompanied by text below the image, the effect is disconcerting and is an ironic comment on the 'role of the photographer-as-detective' albeit 'one who always arrives at the scene too late' (Van Gelder and West, 2011:159). Others too have become preoccupied with conveying traumatic events that for various reasons have left hardly any visual traces. This is especially the case in Antonio Olmos's (2013) efforts to photograph all the sites where murders occurred in London, England, between

1 January 2011 and 31 December 2012, which are collected in his profoundly moving book *Landscape of Murder*. The sites were visited within a few days of the crime, and the images not only capture fleeting moments of grief (huddled friends, wilting flowers, messages of condolence) and remnants of forensic investigation (fluttering police tape, scattered traffic cones), but occasionally nothing at all remains to indicate that a life has ended violently at the site. The book is not so much about violence and death, but rather a way of seeing place and giving memory to mostly forgotten events, and in doing so it presents a very different portrait of the city. In this it shares much with the genre of 'aftermath photography' and the 'forensic turn' where there is an acknowledgement that the camera is a 'secondary witness' that does not depict the trauma itself, but rather the spaces in which it occurred and the traces left behind, so that the 'act of secondary witnessing takes on an overly moral character as the witness is actively choosing to make their statement about the past rather than passively being there at the time of the occurrence' (Lowe, 2014:217).

The question of photography's roles as a credible eyewitness is explore by Taryn Simon (2003) in her work with the Innocence Project in the United States, which was established in 1992 and primarily uses DNA testing to overturn wrongful convictions. As she explains:

> The primary cause of wrongful conviction was mistaken identification. A victim or eyewitness identifies a suspect perpetrator through law enforcement's use of photographs and lineups. These identifications rely on the assumption of precise visual memory. But through exposure to composite sketches, mugshots, Polaroids, and lineups, eyewitness memory can change. Police officers and prosecutors influence memory both unintentionally and intentionally – through the ways in which they conduct the identification process. They can shape, and even generate, what comes to be known as eyewitness testimony.
>
> (Simon, Neufeld and Scheck, 2003:7)

Images in these cases were deeply implicated in transforming innocent citizens into violent criminals and securing their convictions. In 2002 Simon photographed several of these men at locations that had profound significance in their wrongful imprisonment, often the scene of crime. This particular place is both arbitrary and crucial – it is somewhere they had never been, yet changed their lives forever. The haunting narrative portraits Simon produced highlights photography's ability to blur truth and fiction and the devastating consequences this can have. Each photograph is accompanied by commentary from the two lawyers who co-founded the Innocence Project, Peter Neufeld and Barry Scheck (who both also worked on the O. J. Simpson defence team in 1995), and it quickly becomes apparent that there remain many still falsely imprisoned because of failings in the legal system. Simon's images directly confront the contradiction between truth and justice, and in them we see a 'mixture of anger, resignation, and fear in the photographed images of the innocents forged by the unimaginable horror of spending a decade or more in prison because they happened to be a person of the wrong color or class, in the wrong place, at the wrong time' (Courtney and Lyng, 2007:189).

These are only a handful of recent examples and what should be clear from this brief discussion of the documentary tradition is that it is not only flourishing, but has much to offer a visually informed criminology. Although the genre can be condemned and dismissed for its morbid fascination with human suffering, it also offers new ways of seeing social practices. Despite all the contradictions running through the tradition, the desire to bear witness to the suffering and violence of the age remains paramount, and requires of us to learn new ways of seeing, especially in those places where seeing is not simple and is often hidden from view. Indeed, it is also clear that accompanying this resurgence of interest in using images to tell stories about social worlds there has also been an emergence of a rich body of theoretical writing focusing on the ethical and political implications of the visual, working within, around, and against the traditions described in this chapter.

8

Conclusion

The opening chapters of the book began by discussing the relationship between criminology and sociology as they have developed over time. In this closing chapter I want to revisit these arguments in an effort to place the work I have described across the four substantive themes that have taken up the bulk of the book. The metaphor of 'rendezvous subject' is a well-used one, and it is the traffic in multidisciplinary approaches that has sustained post-war British criminology, but which have also left it prone to a bewildering eclecticism and disorganized fragmentation. Under these circumstances the growing separation of criminology from sociology is to be resisted; instead a renewed focus on how dialogues across many disciplines can be facilitated is the way forward. For some, contemporary criminology has all the organizational trappings of an academic discipline, but has no intellectual core around which the diverse approaches and speciality areas can cohere. The worry is that an 'independent criminology' will further 'fragment into distinct specialisms' with an increasingly inward focus resulting in 'negative consequences for collective learning' (Garland, 2011:312).

The dangers of an ever narrowing specialization is highlighted by the current 'tendency of criminologists to Balkanise themselves, often preaching to the converted via specialist outlets and citation clubs' in turn this 'has drastically reduced the potential impact of their scholarship, exacerbating the retreat from sociology, and severely restricting criminology's range' (Hobbs, 2012:262). Equally this is a major problem for sociology, where whole subfields of the discipline migrate and establish themselves as new areas or applied subjects, as health studies, social policy, media studies, and others have done in Britain – at some cost to the overall coherence, institutional reputation, and well-being of the discipline (Holmwood, 2010). Likewise, much of the sociology of work is now to be found in business and management schools and will lead to a dilution of the 'sociological imagination' in these environments (Halford and Strangleman, 2009:819).

In the US context Andrew Abbott (2001:134) has noted how 'status differences' work to keep certain hierarchies in place: 'Criminology departments hire from sociology departments, but seldom vice versa.' Here conventional disciplines have been able to maintain their dominance, despite a plethora of applied subject areas growing around them. Abbott explains how a fairly long historical process has shaped a structure of flexibly stable core of disciplines, surrounded by a heady blur of interdisciplinarity, where the conventional disciplines stand in superiority. As it is here that the original, transformative work takes place and where reputations are forged through a process of 'settlement', by which he means the 'link between a discipline and what it knows' (Abbott, 2001:136), academics compete with one another through redefining each other's work. Abbott offers the example of how professors of English claim superiority over anthropologists and sociologists in the interpretation of modern cultural artefacts, like advertisements, as they are textual phenomena and ultimately subject to the 'master' discipline of English. This movement is rarely a two-way exchange of ideas; developments in the applied field are seldom translated back into the primary field. Crucially, the applied areas are not self-reproducing, but rely on the 'continued importation, and, in consequence on the health of the exporter disciplines' (Holmwood, 2010:646). The strong departmental structure of the US university system has helped to sustain the disciplinary status of sociology, but the prospects in the United Kingdom are bleaker in Holmwood's reckoning, due to the twin threats of interdisciplinarity and the audit culture regulating higher education in the country (though see Savage, 2010 for a nuanced critique of this view).

The expansion of criminology has 'marginalised critical writing and reduced theory from a live contested quality that ran like a thread through all aspects of scholarship to a niche or specialism' (Hobbs, 2012:262). This tendency was identified over 15 years ago in the United States, where Currie (1998:18) distinguished between three divisions in American criminology: a large, technocratic, 'mainstream' that rarely ventures into the public arena; a small, but extremely vocal and influential right-wing set of commentators; and a slightly larger radical ghetto, which is content to go 'along with the definition of itself as a fringe, or as a kind of sub-specialization within the larger field'. For Abbot (2001) this fragmenting is part of the normal 'chaos of disciplines' and a healthy sign of well-being, as disciplines cycle through a pattern of core principles. In discussing this argument Holmwood (2010:649–50) maintains there is rarely any agreement on what constitutes the organizing core of sociology, meaning that it constantly 'has to be achieved against an internal tendency to self-subversion' and this might be best seen as 'a particular kind of "dissensus"'.

Sociology has diversified and fragmented to such an extent that it is now far less possible to claim a clear centre to the discipline (Urry, 2005), but important questions remain over the kind of relationships sociology should be cultivating with other disciplines in the social sciences and humanities (Scott, 2005).

Few would insist on 'any kind of isolationism for sociology' nor argue against 'multidisciplinarity', but in a context where there is 'a strong sense of what different disciplines can bring to debate, not the collapse of disciplines into indistinctiveness' (Halford and Strangleman, 2009:821). Scott (2005) builds his argument from some questions initially posed by Urry (1981) over two opposing conceptualizations of sociology: one sees it as the Queen of the Sciences, in a Comtean sense, standing at the head of a hierarchy of disciplines, while the other views it as a parasite – scavenging off the discarded remnants from more autonomous disciplines, resulting in a disparate mix of 'sociologies of' one thing or another. Such an approach might be called 'promiscuous' but a more generous reading would be to describe it as a 'cosmopolitan' vision, which is an orientation Outhwaite (2015:121–2) commends in his recent overview of social theory and stands in contrast to the 'soft imperialism' of sociology. Both frames of reference carry risks, but the cosmopolitan is a broader approach, spanning the social sciences and bridging the divide with the humanities, but 'feeling not quite at home anywhere' (ibid.).

Although Urry (2005:1) maintains there must be 'strong and coherent disciplines', as there is 'nothing worse than lower common denominator interdisciplinarity', he does point out the opportunities fragmentation provides, helping to enliven and transform mainstream concerns. But the problem, once we consider sociological criminology, is that some of its central concepts – deviance, moral panic, social control, subculture, to name just a few – no longer command the attention they once did and sound like ideas that have run their course. As topics they remain popular on undergraduate modules and dissertations, but not many would say they are at the cutting edge of contemporary thinking. Of course, this waxing and waning of interest in particular concepts is an endemic feature of scholarship; paradigm-shifting eruptions are inevitably followed by patterns of 'normal science' and then a winding down and eventual exhaustion, once there is little new to say, remaining dormant until revived by a fresh intervention restarting the cycle. But this is not to say that the processes they describe or the questions they pose disappear; rather, they are reworked in different settings and it is this dynamic I have explored in the preceding chapters.

In the last few years important new ideas from radical philosophy and theoretical psychoanalysis have been introduced to criminology by Steve Hall and Simon Winlow (2015) in their efforts to develop an 'ultra-realist' approach. Written in a deliberately provocative style they attempt nothing less than the deconstruction of the dominant paradigms of criminological thought. But it is a bleak and often one-dimensional take on social relationships, while the relentless drive to demolish left-liberal scholarship has the unfortunate tendency to overshadow the originality of their own insights. Nevertheless, I share their desire to revitalize criminology and could not agree more with their contention that we:

no longer live in the 1960s, and whilst we should respect some of the major theoretical accomplishments of the past, we should not slavishly regard this particular period as the pinnacle of human thought and attempt to make its theories fit into a very different political, economic, cultural and ideological climate. Instead, we should, in an exercise shorn of sentimental attachment and vested interests, take from those theories what remains vital and pertinent before redoubling our efforts to make sense of the world as it is and as it could be.

(Hall and Winlow, 2012:9)

This motif of recognizing the new without losing sight of what is still valuable in the old serves as an invaluable blueprint for how theoretical work in the social sciences should proceed. Social theory itself is home to a much broader family than those who formally describe themselves as sociologists and would include such thinkers as Hegel, Nietzsche, Freud, and Fanon alongside the holy trinity of Marx, Durkheim, and Weber in the 'classics', while the 'contemporary' pantheon is full of imaginative possibilities and it is to Hall and Winlow's credit that they have urged an encounter with ideas that exist well outside the mainstream of what now passes for theoretical criminology.

One of the consequences of the striking expansion of criminology over the last 25 years or so has been the development of distinct specialisms and the invention of an entire criminological tradition. But somewhere along the way it lost 'its sociological soul' and nowhere is this more apparent than in the 'false dichotomy that has been created in British criminology between the economic and the cultural' (Hobbs, 2012:262–3). Earlier in this book I discussed how the new criminology project was dedicated to developing a 'fully social theory of deviance'. Famously it never delivered on this promise, and the work that is often said to have come the closest is Hall and colleagues' (1978) *Policing the Crisis*, but there are others – not least Taylor's (1999) own *Crime in Context*, which combines a nuanced understanding of the political economy of crime with a thorough handle on its cultural dynamics in competitive, market societies. A different kind of example would be Garland's (1990) *Punishment and Modern Society*, which was a wide-ranging survey of the classic social theorists who have explored the institutional complexity of punishment, to reveal the broader structural forces, cultural sensibilities, political conflicts, and social relations sustaining penal systems. More recently Hobbs' (2013) *Lush Life* is the culmination of decades of ethnographic research highlighting the flexible nature of criminal markets, the constructed and contested notion of organized crime, which interacts with upper and underworlds, and is increasingly normalized in the evolving complexities of urban living.

These are only a handful of examples and readers will no doubt be able to call on others, but my more general point is that criminology needs to renew its relationship with the sociological imagination. It is worth spending a little more time on an exemplar, and Nicole Rafter's (2016) last book *The Crime of all Crimes* is a powerful indication of what criminology can bring to the study of genocide, making it no longer possible for the discipline to shy away from understanding organized mass murder. As she acknowledges, genocide studies is today a crowded, multidisciplinary field, but it rarely deals with genocide as a crime. It is this absence the book tackles and it does so through a rigorous comparative criminology, which combines historical and sociological methods, in a systematic analysis of eight diverse genocides unfolding in the twentieth century. She challenges existing explanations, while offering a new framework drawing together macro (structural), meso (group), and micro (individual) levels of interaction and specifying their interrelationships. Much of the book is spent answering the question she poses at the outset: 'What do genocides look like? Do most or all of them in fact resemble the Holocaust? If not, what – if anything – do genocides have in common?' (Rafter, 2016:2). The approach enables her to draw convincing conclusions on the causes of genocide through detailed comparison that strikes a balance been the idiosyncratic and general, the incidental and significant.

The order in which they are discussed is thematic rather than chronological, so that her initial example is the Katyn Forest genocide of 1940, in which 22,000 Polish civilians were systematically executed by Stalin's secret police. Yet it differs in so many ways from the Holocaust that even genocide scholars seldom discuss it. Rafter's substantive analysis begins by focusing on macro factors and provides a detailed account of the Herero genocide of 1904 in South West Africa, where an indigenous tribe was exterminated by the German army in an uneven colonial power struggle. There then follows a shift in focus to the group level as one of the first stages in the process of genocide is the reframing of identities, which is illustrated through the Indonesian genocide of 1965–1966, where Randall Collins' (2008) theory of violence is used to understand the shifting dynamics of 'hot' and 'cold' emotions involved in slaughter. Attention next turns to the micro level, for when 'we come down to it, it is *individuals* who open the canister of poison gas, deliver the neck shot, and smash infants against walls' (Rafter, 2016:106, emphasis in original). Here she tackles the 'How could they do it?' question by developing a three-stage sequence she terms 'splitting', which involves the psychological processes of 'moral disengagement', 'empathy dimming', and 'objectification'. This analysis is applied to the Cambodian genocide of 1975–1979, during which time over 2 million died at the hands of Pol Pot's regime.

Crucially, Rafter examines those gangs or militias mobilized to carry out the slaughter, which she calls 'genocidal organizations'. Here she compares and contrasts those involved in the Armenian genocide of 1915–1923 and the Nazi genocide of the disabled, 1939–1945. In the former, perpetrated against an ethnic group in the newly forming nation of Turkey, a shadowy Special Organization (the unit's literal name in translation) was established to carry out the extermination and claimed over 1 million lives. By concentrating on the Nazi genocide of the disabled Rafter describes how the 'euthanasia' programme began and was organized by a secret group of well-respected physicians who designed, ran, and professionally profited from murdering helpless children. Their methods 'worked so well that six "euthanasia" killing centers were established throughout Germany and Austria; their mock "shower rooms," where victims were gassed, and crematoria became models for those later built at the infamous death camps' (Rafter, 2016:139). Their victims remain largely unnoticed and unremarked, even by specialists in Nazi history like Zygmunt Bauman (1989). Although his modernity thesis has been challenged by more recent work emphasizing the savage and chaotic character of the Holocaust, it does apply to the genocide of the disabled, which was carefully planned, extremely rationalized, and elaborately bureaucratic, in the initial stages at the least. But by developing her long-standing interest in the history of eugenics and the treatment of mentally disabled people, Rafter sheds fresh light on Hitler's genocidal policies.

Likewise, Rafter's work on gender and crime informs her analysis of genocidal rape. Previously, rape was often regarded as a spoil of war, but now mass rape is used as a form of genocide itself – where the gendered violence is an instrument of terror and used to secure social control. These effects are demonstrated through the Rwandan genocide of 1994, where the highly public nature of the mass rapes worked to torment not only Tutsi women but also Tutsi men, forced to watch the suffering of family members which they were unable to prevent. But as Rafter goes on to point out genocide 'intersects with three types of crime – political, organized, and white collar – that criminologists have been studying for decades but seldom in terms of mass violence' (Rafter, 2016:225). The book is a landmark achievement, not least since it makes the topic of genocide absolutely fundamental to criminology, but it demonstrates the importance of weaving together different levels of analysis to produce work that unsettles orthodoxies.

Although I am urging criminology to renew its relationship with the sociological imagination, this should not be a one-way street, especially since social theory itself is understood to be in a state of crisis. At the moment there are two directions in which academic social theory can go. One will further contribute to disciplinary fragmentation, where academic social theory establishes itself as 'a kind of sub-discipline, distinct from the main fields of philosophy, sociology, politics and so on', the other is a more 'cosmopolitan' approach spanning divisions between social science and the humanities, and 'including the social thought generated by social movements and others outside the academy' (Outhwaite, 2015:121). It seems to me that the latter is a welcome move away from the Comtean 'imperial' vision of sociology towards 'an intellectual space in which sociology and its "others" coexist and hybridically operate in a variety of settings, of which universities are only one element' (Stanley, 2005:1.9). Criminology is just one of the 'others' that have grown out of a sociological specialism, but the challenges it presents to the intellectual jurisdiction of the discipline are serious and demand extended consideration. This point can be put another way:

> doing good social science is a better objective than doing good criminology because sometimes thinking too much like a criminologist can cause us to do bad social science. Criminology becomes a break on good analysis when members of the discipline feel that criminal justice institutions are the important things to study in pursuit of objectives that range from reducing rape to reducing environmental destruction.
>
> (Braithwaite, 2013:8)

John Braithwaite is also cautioning against the narrowing of criminology's range and the dangers this presents to social science.

In Mills (1959) the sociological imagination is conceived as occupying the intersection of biography, history, and social structure. It is well worth recalling that Mills drew the important distinction between 'the personal troubles of milieu' and 'the public issues of social structure' and then advocated a perspective weaving human travails with the bigger political picture:

> Do not allow public issues as they are officially formulated, or troubles as they are privately felt, to determine the problems that you take up for study ... Know that many personal troubles cannot be solved merely as troubles, but must be understood in terms of public issues – and in terms of the problems of history-making. Know that the human meaning of public issues must be revealed by relating them to personal troubles – and to the problems of the individual life. Know that the problems of social science, when adequately formulated, must include both troubles and issues, both biography and history, and the range of their intricate relations. Within that range the life of the individual and the making of societies occur; and within that range the sociological imagination has its chance to make a difference in the quality of human life in our time.
>
> (Mills, 1959:226)

The clear message we can take from this passage is that the problems generated by crime, deviance, and punishment should not just be situated at an individual level of motivation or whim, but in wider social structures and historical processes.

It is an approach that is not just restricted to those who 'work in Departments of Sociology or to card-carrying sociologists' (Scott, 2005:3.2), but all three dimensions (of biography, history, and structure) are indispensable if the sociological imagination is to flourish as a unifying force. What is clear is that much sociology, 'core' and otherwise, has proceeded as 'though history and biography are optional extras' (Stanley, 2005:5.5). For Liz Stanley the sociological imagination has the potential to be an organizing principle around which UK sociology can cohere, while remaining open to the different ways in which the term might be developed. By distilling a sense of crisis in mid-twentieth-century sociology, Mills' ambition was to help change it by rescuing it from the combined perils of grand theory and abstracted empiricism, which were thwarting sociology from its real, liberating promise. In this regard criminology should be seen as a province of sociology and some of its main concerns lie at the very centre of sociological thinking. It is this core that is in urgent need of rediscovery if criminology is to regain intellectual energy and vitality.

The importance of *The Sociological Imagination* today is that it offers a particular sensibility that is inevitably bound up with critique. Of course, the great irony, as I explained at the beginning of this book, is that the force of Mills' scathing assessment of sociology has itself been lost over the years, domesticated and tamed. Few today practice the sociological imagination in the way that Mills had intended (Goode, 2008:251), which is fundamentally a critique of the discipline itself and its relationship to others. The way contemporary commentators on the current state of sociology mourn its decline and fragmentation has been challenged by Michael Burawoy (2005), where he points out that what has happened instead is that sociology has been enlivened by new voices. A similar point has also been made by Stanley (2005), writing on the United Kingdom, where she argues that the 'declinists' are really bemoaning their loss of prestige and authority as the discipline has become home to new and radical voices from the margins. Evidently there are dangers, but it is also worth reminding ourselves of the opportunities such fragmentation provides, helping to enrich and transform mainstream concerns, while potentially becoming home to new and radical voices from the margins. It is perhaps no accident that Mills has also been rediscovered by criminologists (Young, 2011; Frauley, 2015) as they try to produce creative, boundary-challenging work, and in this the margins can help revive the sociological soul of criminology.

Endnotes

Chapter 1   Introduction

1 Goode (2008:245) gives the example of how Robert Merton had written to a colleague in December 1946 claiming that Mills is 'the outstanding sociologist of his age in the country', yet within a year Merton declined to support Mills' promotion in the sociology department, while much later Zygmunt Bauman claimed that Mills' death was thought to have been caused by 'the merciless campaign of defamation to which he was subjected throughout the whole of his academic career' (cited in Goode, 2008:250). In Becker's (1994) view he 'was a difficult smart ass' who ended up marginalizing himself and was driven by the desire to become a Professional Big Thinker, while to 'many staid professionals Mills always seemed too big, too political, too productive and too famous' (Jacoby, 2000:155). At root Mills was intent on becoming a major public intellectual, with a distinctive moral vision, that clearly strove for a critically minded 'public sociology' to contest post-war American culture and politics.

2 Brown has defined mediatization as a powerful force eroding divisions between 'fact and fiction, nature and culture, global and local, science and art, technology and humanity' to the extent that 'the media in the twenty-first century have so undermined the ability to construct an *apparent* distinction between reality and representation that the modernist episteme has begun to seem somewhat shaky' (Brown, 2003:22, emphasis in original).

Chapter 2   Formative Positions

1 Intellectuals in the fourteenth and fifteenth centuries saw themselves as participating in the 'renaissance' or rebirth of ancient classical thought after the European 'Dark Ages', which led to the great scientific discoveries associated with the likes of Copernicus, Galileo, Kepler, and Newton from the fifteenth to the seventeenth centuries. Although Renaissance thought posed a radical questioning of the word of God, it was a radicalism that the Church could in principle accommodate, and scientists themselves strove to reconcile. For example, Galileo sought to situate his findings in a 'framework acceptable to the post-medieval Church' and as Geoffrey Hawthorn (1987:9) points out 'there seems no good theological reason why this should have been impossible or even difficult'. That he was found guilty of heresy in 1615 and spent the remainder of his life under house arrest suggests that the Church was well aware of the power of science to undermine ecclesiastical authority.

2 Wild was already a notorious London figure and his career as a 'thief-taker' was well known to be a cover for his activities as a fence for stolen goods and he presided over the city's criminals by playing them off against one another in a web of intrigue

and influence until his execution in 1725. In his account Fielding drew the barbed comparison between Wild's criminal organization and Robert Walpole's manipulative control of government. Walpole had just resigned as prime minister in 1742 following a long period of ruling through a mix of bribery, patronage, and plotting that made him the perfect metaphor of larger political corruption. Despite defeat in the House of Commons the King elevated him to the House of Lords as a peer, from where Walpole maintained considerable influence over government. It is this clear parallel, where one villain ends up hanged and the other runs the country, which Fielding subjects to fierce critique in his account of the 'Great Man'.

3 Utilitarian philosophy establishes what is good to do on the grounds of social usefulness and it judges actions by their consequences. It stipulates that 'the good' is human happiness, not some abstract metaphysical property, like the idea of 'natural rights', which Bentham famously dismissed as 'nonsense on stilts' or an empirically unknowable object, as in the will of God. Bentham's objective was to establish the law on a rational basis, which for him meant the facts of pleasure and pain rather than the vague fictions of natural rights. For Bentham the only rights were legal rights: 'legitimate, enforceable rights come not from nature but from laws duly passed by the supreme authority of the state' (Feldman, 2002:25) and justified by arguments of social utility. Utilitarianism thereby inspired a 'positive rights' tradition grounded in the legal positivism that continues to be influential many areas of the law today.

4 The book received substantial acclaim on publication in Germany in 1845, where the writing style and detailed observation were especially praised, but the book had to wait until 1887 for an English translation to appear and it is largely in the context of the Marxist socialist tradition that the text has been understood. Of course, this is not surprising as the book did provide the empirical base for Marx's subsequent theories and while there remains controversy over the revolutionary predictions forcefully depicted and the charge of social murder levelled against the English bourgeoisie in the text, these should not overshadow the pioneering achievements of the work as a systematic account of urban poverty and the corrosive effects of industrial capitalism.

5 Valiér (1995:6) notes that the courts made little use of child guidance clinics during the interwar years, citing as an example that the clients of Whitechapel and Islington clinics were more likely to be bedwetters than delinquents (Thom, 1992). Although the extent to which they used psychoanalytical ideas varied from clinic to clinic, it is clear that by the late 1930s the child guidance movement had become a key site for the elaboration of psychoanalytical approaches to juvenile delinquency.

6 Burt's work has since been embroiled in controversy, not least since he has been accused of falsifying his research findings, but up until the 1950s he would have been regarded as 'a giant, head and shoulders above most others' (Morris, 1988:28).

7 A year later the Howard League for Penal Reform established the *Howard Journal of Criminal Justice* in 1961, and for the next four decades these two journals were the main sites of publication for British criminologists, until the remarkable proliferation of journals from the 1990s onwards.

Chapter 3   Sociological Traditions

1 The spelling 'preverts' is an allusion to Stanley Kubrick's film *Dr Strangelove* and is meant to suggest sexual perversion. Liazos (1972:103) explains that it is derived from two sources: 'a. A Yale Undergraduate once told me that the deviance course

was known among Yale students as "nuts and sluts." b. A former colleague of mine at Quinnipiac College, John Bancroft, often told me that the deviance course was "all about those preverts"'.

Chapter 4 Transgression

1 There are important parallels here with recent attempts to understand the 'motif of ecstatic transgression as fundamental to the act of serial killing' (King, 2006:113), and the rise of this very particular form of violence (multiple murder, sexual mutilation, and defilement) has been equated with the constitution of the postmodern self.

2 The concept of intersectionality was initially coined by US legal scholar Kimberlé Crenshaw (1991) to interrogate how the various dimensions of social location and identity interact for different groups of women and men. It emerged from long-standing black feminist concerns over how women of colour occupied a 'distinct space of Otherness' (Henne and Troshynski, 2013:4) and has its origins in political activism as well as social theory. Marginalized by both white feminists and male black critical race activists attention was drawn to the ways that both sexism and racism feature in the lives of black women, who often do not conform to the generalized depictions of 'womanhood' prevailing in the feminist movement at the time, which largely spoke to women who are 'white, middle class, and of Anglo-Saxon-Protestant extract' (Smart, 1995:163). Overall, the critique undermined simplistic ideas of a 'woman's perspective' and any unified feminist politics for change organized around a 'sisterhood' began to unravel as other significant sites and sources of difference came to the fore – especially around sexuality, disability, and nationality, among others.

3 There are some similarities here with Judith Butler (1990) and her suggestion that gender is something one 'does', which must be repeatedly 'performed' and worn somewhat theatrically. Her work is one of the founding texts of queer theory, not least since she maintained that such performances are shaped by a powerful 'heterosexual matrix' constructing subjectivity and prescribing ways to act. She has since cautioned against overly simplistic appropriations of her 'performative' approach, not least since they tend to ignore the phenomenological and semiotic traditions from which it emerged and her insistence that social agents perform gender often without realizing they are doing so, through language, gestures, and body positions.

4 The Race and Politics Group at the CCCS was formed by Paul Gilroy alongside fellow postgraduate students Valerie Amos, Hazel Carby, Simon Jones, Errol Lawrence, and John Solomos and the publication of the *Empire Strikes Back* by the group provoked intense debate and drew criticism from, among others, John Rex (1983) and Jock Young (1983:135), who accused the writers of committing 'an act of propaganda, not of scholarship'. Today it is regarded as one of the most important books written on racism in late-twentieth-century Britain and eventually opened up a 'paradigm shift in the sociology of race and ethnicity' (Virdee, 2014:1823), not least since it charged sociology with contributing to the problem of racism by producing pathological accounts of black family life and culture, while profoundly criticizing the theory and practice of socialist politics in Britain.

5 The three books are Mitchell Duneier's (1999) *Sidewalk*, which tracks the trade in second-hand books and magazines among homeless vendors in Manhattan; Elijah Anderson's (1999) *Code of the Street*, which documents the set of informal rules

governing interactions between 'street' and 'decent' families in Philadelphia; and Katherine Newman's (1999) *No Shame in My Game*, which examines how the 'working poor' cope with life in Harlem's low-wage, service economy.

Chapter 5　Control

1　Ironically, Clifford Shearing and Philip Stenning (1985) took issue with Cohen's 'dispersal of discipline' thesis and explained how the forms of consumer control developed in theme parks such as Disney World provide a compelling exemplar of contemporary disciplinary projects. They highlight how social control becomes a commodity that can be bought and sold, anticipating the remarkable growth in the private security sector, while revealing the ways modern consumers are seduced into conformity in these sites.

2　Sentencing is often used as an example to illustrate how the two elements are combined as there is a formal element which involves dealing with offenders in a procedurally consistent fashion to ensure fairness and a substantive element of doing what is the most appropriate in the particular case. Not only can this result in an individualized and paternalistic form of justice for female offenders (Edwards, 1984), but the balance between the two shifts over time and has in recent decades moved in a logic of justice direction over the ethic of care (Hudson, 1993).

Chapter 6　Geography

1　The earliest sociological statement on this dichotomy was Ferdinand Tönnies' (1887/1957) discussion of two contrasting concepts of *gemeinschaft*, social relations of communal solidarity found in rural localities of the past, and *gesellschaft*, social relations of calculative and contractual association typical of the city. The argument that impersonal, urban market relations were corroding traditional solidarities based on intimate, harmonious ties between kin, neighbours, and village is further developed by the Chicagoan sociologist Louis Wirth (1938) in his famous essay 'Urbanism as a Way of Life'. The essay is a systematic attempt to grasp the differences between urban and rural people through their adaptations to the settlement patterns in which they lived, suggesting that the quality of life in them could be ranked on a continuum from simple rural societies through to complex urban environments. At work is a nostalgic vision, privileging a golden age of simplicity and harmony lost or destroyed by the ever-expanding modern city. As Williams (1975:94) puts it, 'the idea of an ordered and happier past set against the disturbances and disorder of the present' is an 'idealisation, based on a temporary situation and on a deep desire for stability' serving 'to cover and to evade the actual and bitter contradictions of the time'. These insights were subsequently developed by Geoff Pearson (1983) in his *Hooligan: A History of Respectable Fears*, which highlights how youth crime is often depicted as a threatening departure from the stable traditions of a 'golden age' of peace and tranquillity. Instead, he reveals how successive generations have repeatedly articulated the same anxieties about moral decline and social breakdown, concluding that there is a remarkable consistency and continuity in these 'respectable fears'.

References

Aas, F. and H. Grundhus (2015) 'Policing Humanitarian Borderlands: Frontex, Human Rights and the Precariousness of Life', *British Journal of Criminology*, 55(1):1–18.

Abbott, A. (2001) *Chaos of Disciplines*, Chicago: University of Chicago Press.

Agger, B. (2015) *Oversharing*, Oxon: Routledge.

Agnew, R. (1992) 'Foundation for a General Strain Theory of Crime and Delinquency', *Criminology*, 30:47–87.

Akers, R. and G. Jensen (2003) *Social Learning Theory and the Explanation of Crime: A Guide for the New Century*, Boston, MA: Northeastern University Press.

Alexander, J. (1988) 'Introduction: Durkheimian Sociology and Cultural Studies Today', in Alexander, J. (ed.) *Durkheimian Sociology: Cultural Studies*, Cambridge: Cambridge University Press, pp. 1–21.

Alexander, J. (1996) 'The Centrality of the Classics', in Turner, S. (ed.) *Social Theory and Sociology: The Classics and Beyond*, Oxford: Blackwell.

Alexander, J. (2003) *The Meanings of Social Life: A Cultural Sociology*, Oxford: Oxford University Press.

Alexander, J. (2004) 'From the Depths of Despair: Performance, Counterperformance, and "September 11"', *Sociological Theory*, 22(1):88–105.

Alexander, J. (2010) *The Performance of Politics: Obama's Victory and the Struggle for Democratic Power*, Oxford: Oxford University Press.

Alexander, J. (2011) *Performative Revolution in Egypt*, New York: Bloomsbury.

Alexander, J. and R. Jacobs (1998) 'Mass Communication, Ritual and Civil Society', in Liebes, T. and J. Curran (eds.) *Media, Ritual and Identity*, London: Routledge.

Alexander, M. (2010b) *The New Jim Crow: Mass Incarceration in the Age of Colorblindness*, New York: The New Press.

Aliverti, A. (2013) *Crimes of Mobility: Criminal Law and the Regulation of Immigration*, Abingdon: Routledge.

Anderson, E. (1999) The Code of the Streets: Decency, Violence and the Moral Life of the Inner City, New York: W.W. Norton.

Anderson, E. (2002) 'The Ideologically Driven Critique', *American Journal of Sociology*, 107(6):1533–1550.

Andersen, M. and P. Hill Collins (1992) 'Preface', in Andersen, M. and P. Hill Collins (eds.) *Race, Class and Gender*, Belmont, CA: Wadsworth.

Anderson, P. (1968) 'Components of the National Culture', *New Left Review*, 50:3–59.

Andersson, R. (2014) *Illegality, Inc: Clandestine Migration and the Business of Bordering Europe*, California: University of California Press.

Aronowitz, S. (2003) 'A Mills Revival?', *Logos*, 2(3):1–27.

Back, L. (2009) 'Portrayal and Betrayal: Bourdieu, Photography and Sociological Life', *The Sociological Review*, 57(3):471–490.

Bakhtin, M. (1984) *Rabelais and His World*, Bloomington: Indiana University Press.

Ball, K., K. Haggerty and D. Lyon (eds.) (2012) *Routledge Handbook of Surveillance Studies*, London: Routledge.

Barbalet, J. (2002) 'Moral Indignation, Class Inequality and Justice: An Exploration and Revision of Ranulf', *Theoretical Criminology*, 6(3):279–297.

Barker, V. (2009) *The Politics of Punishment: How the Democratic Process Shapes the Way America Punishes Offenders*, Oxford: Oxford University Press.

Bartmański, D. and J. Alexander (2012) 'Materiality and Meaning in Social Life: Toward an Iconic Turn in Cultural Sociology', in Alexander, J., D. Bartmański and B. Giesen (eds.) *Iconic Power: Materiality and Meaning in Social Life*, Basingstoke: Palgrave, pp. 1–12.

Batchen, G. (2012) 'Looking Askance', in Batchen, G., M. Gidley, N. Miller and J. Prosser (eds.) *Picturing Atrocity: Photography in Crisis*, London: Reaktion Books., pp. 227–239.

Baudrillard, J. (1983) *In the Shadow of Silent Majorities, or, the End of the Social*, New York: Semiotext(e).

Baudrillard, J. (1985) 'The Ecstasy of Communication', in Foster, H. (ed.) *Postmodern Culture*, London: Pluto Press.

Bauman, Z. (1989) *Modernity and the Holocaust*, Cambridge: Polity Press.

Beames, T. (1850) *The Rookeries of London*, London: Thomas Bosworth.

Beccaria, C. (1764/1986) *On Crimes and Punishment*, Indianapolis: Hackett.

Beck, U. (1986) *Risk Society*, London: Sage.

Becker, H. (1963) *Outsiders*, New York: Free Press.

Becker, H. (1974) 'Photography and Sociology', *Studies in the Anthropology of Visual Communication*, 1:3–26.

Becker, H. (1981) *Exploring Society Photographically*, Evanston, IL: Mary and Leigh Block Gallery, Northwestern University.

Becker, H. (1982/2008) *Art Worlds*, 2nd edn. Berkeley, CA: University of California Press.

Becker, H. (1994) 'Professional Sociology: The Case of C. Wright Mills', in Rist, R. (ed.) *The Democratic Imagination*, New Brunswick: Transaction Books.

Becker, H. (1995) 'Visual Sociology, Documentary Photography and Photojournalism: It's (Almost) All a Matter of Context', *Visual Sociology*, 10(1–2):5–14.

Becker, H. (2004) 'Afterword: Photography as Evidence, Photographs as Exposition', in Knowles, C. and P. Sweetman (eds.) *Picturing the Social Landscape: Visual Methods and the Sociological Imagination*, Oxon: Routledge, pp. 193–197.

Becker, K. (1990/2003) 'Photojournalism and the Tabloid Press', in Wells, L. (ed.) *The Photography Reader*, Oxon: Routledge, pp. 291–308.

Becker, P. and R. Wetzell (eds.) (2006) *Criminals and their Scientists: The History of Criminology in Historical Perspective*, Cambridge: Cambridge University Press.

Beirne, P. (1993) *Inventing Criminology: Essays on the Rise of 'Homo Criminalis'*, Albany: SUNY Press.

Benjamin, W. (1934/1982) 'The Author as Producer', in Burgin, V. (ed.) *Thinking Photography*, London: Macmillan, pp. 15–32.

Bennett, A. (2011) 'The Post-Subcultural Turn: Some Reflections Ten Years on', *Journal of Youth Studies*, 14(5):493–506.

Best, J. (2004) *Deviance: Career of a Concept*, Belmont, CA: Wadsworth.

Best, J. (2008) 'Foreword', in Waiton, S. (ed.) *The Politics of Antisocial Behaviour: Amoral Panics*, London: Routledge.

Bhambra, G. (2007) *Rethinking Modernity: Postcolonialism and the Sociological Imagination*, New York: Palgrave Macmillan.

Biber, K. (2007) *Captive Images*, Oxon: Routledge-Cavendish.

Binns, D. (1977) *Beyond the Sociology of Conflict*, London: Macmillan.

Blackman, S. (2014) 'Subculture Theory: An Historical and Contemporary Assessment of the Concept for Understanding Deviance', *Deviant Behavior*, 35:496–512.

Block, A. (1983) *East Side-West Side: Organizing Crime in New York, 1930–1950*, Newark, NJ: Transaction.

Block, A. (1991) *Masters of Paradise*, New Brunswick: Transaction.

Block, A. (1994) *Space, Time and Organized Crime*, New Brunswick: Transaction.

Boltanski, L. (1999) *Distant Suffering: Morality, Media and Politics*, Cambridge: Cambridge University Press.

Bonger, W. (1916/1969) *Criminality and Economic Conditions*, Bloomington: Indiana University Press.

Bonistall, E. and K. Ralston (2014) 'Deviant Career and Life-Course Criminology: Using Street Prostitution', in Anderson, T. (ed.) *Understanding Deviance: Connecting Classical and Contemporary Perspectives*, New York: Routledge.

Boorstin, D. (1961/1987) *The Image: A Guide to Pseudo-Events in America*, New York: Vintage Books.

Bosworth, M. (2000) 'Confining Femininity: A History of Gender, Power and Imprisonment', *Theoretical Criminology*, 4(3):265–284.

Bosworth, M. (2012) 'Subjectivity and Identity in Detention: Punishment and Society in a Global Age', *Theoretical Criminology*, 16(2):123–140.

Bosworth, M. and C. Hoyle (2011) 'What Is Criminology? An Introduction', in Bosworth, M. and C. Hoyle (eds.) *What Is Criminology?*, Oxford: Oxford University Press.

Bottoms, A. (1983) 'Neglected Features of Contemporary Penal Systems', in Garland, D. and P. Young (eds.) *The Power to Punish*, Aldershot: Ashgate.

Bourdieu, P. (1965/1990) *Photography: A Middlebrow Art*, Cambridge: Polity Press (with L. Boltanski, R. Castel, and J. Chamborendon).

Bourdieu, P. (1967) 'Postface', in Panofsky, E. (ed.) *Architecture gothique et pensée scholastique*, Paris, Éditions de Minuit.

Bourdieu, P. (1968/2003) 'Outline of a Sociological Theory of Art Perception', in Tanner, J. (ed.) *The Sociology of Art: A Reader*, London: Routledge.

Bourdieu, P. (1984) *Distinction: A Social Critique of the Judgement of Taste*, London: Routledge.

Bourdieu, P. (1988) 'Vive la Crise!', *Theory and Society*, 17(5):773–787.

Bourdieu, P. (2012) *Picturing Algeria*, New York: Columbia University Press.

Box, S. (1983) *Power, Crime and Mystification*, London: Routledge.

Bracking, S. (2009) *Money and Power*, London: Pluto Press.

Braithwaite, J. (2003) 'What's Wrong with the Sociology of Punishment', *Theoretical Criminology*, 7(1):5–28.

Braithwaite, J. (2013) 'One Retrospective of Pacific Criminology', *Australian & New Zealand Journal of Criminology*, 46(1):3–11.

Brewer, J. (2004) 'Imagining *The Sociological Imagination*', *The British Journal of Sociology*, 35(3):317–333.

Brookman, F., C. Mullins, T. Bennett and R. Wright (2007) 'Gender, Motivation and the Accomplishment of Street Robbery in the United Kingdom', *British Journal of Criminology*, 47(6):861–884.

Brown, S. (2003) *Crime and Law in Media Culture*, Buckingham: Open University Press.

Brown, S. (2011) 'Media/Crime/Millennium: Where Are We Now? A Reflective Review of Research and Theory Directions in the 21st Century', *Sociology Compass*, 5(6):413–425.

Burawoy, M. (2005) 'Provincializing the Social Sciences', in Steinmetz, G. (ed.) *The Politics of Method in the Human Sciences*, Durham, NC: Duke University Press.

Burgess, E. (1925) 'The Growth of the City', in Parke, R. and E. Burgess (eds.) *The City*, Chicago, IL: University of Chicago Press.

Burt, C. (1925) *The Young Delinquent*, London: University of London Press.

Butler, J. (1990) *Gender Trouble: Feminism and the Subversion of Identity*, London: Routledge.

Cain, M. (ed.) (1989) *Growing Up Good: Policing the Behaviour of Girls in Europe*, London: Sage.

Cain, M. (1990) 'Towards Transgression: New Directions in Feminist Criminology', *International Journal of the Sociology of Law*, 18:1–18.

Campbell, J. (2010) 'Neoliberalism's Penal and Debtor States: A Rejoinder to Löic Wacquant', *Theoretical Criminology*, 14(1):59–73.

Carlebach, M. (1997) *American Photojournalism Comes of Age*, Washington, DC: The Smithsonian Institution Press.

Carlen, P. (1976) *Magistrates' Justice*, London: Martin Robertson.

Carlen, P. (1983) *Women's Imprisonment*, London: Routledge and Kegan Paul.

Carlen, P. (1990) *Alternatives to Women's Imprisonment*, Buckingham: Open University Press.

Carlen, P. (2011) 'Against Evangelism in Academic Criminology: For Criminology as a Scientific Art', in Bosworth, M. and C. Hoyle (eds.) *What Is Criminology?*, Oxford: Oxford University Press.

Carney, P. (2010) 'Crime, Punishment and the Force of Photographic Spectacle', in Hayward, K. and M. Presdee (eds.) *Framing Crime: Cultural Criminology and the Image*, Oxon: Routledge, pp. 17–35.

Carney, P. and D. Dadusc (2014) 'Power and Servility: An Experiment in the Ethics of Security and Counter-Security', in Schuilenburg, M., R. van Steden and B. Oude Breuil (eds.) *Positive Criminology: Reflections on Care, Belonging and Security*, The Hague: Eleven International Publishing, pp. 71–83.

Carrabine, E. (2011) 'Images of Torture: Culture, Politics and Power', *Crime, Media, Culture*, 7(1):5–30.

Carrabine, E. (2012a) 'Just Images: Aesthetics, Ethics and Visual Criminology', *British Journal of Criminology*, 52(3):463–489.

Carrabine, E. (2012b) 'Telling Prison Stories: The Spectacle of Punishment and the Criminological Imagination', in Cheliotis, L. (ed.) *The Arts of Imprisonment*, Aldershot: Ashgate.

Carrabine, E. (2014) 'Seeing Things: Violence, Voyeurism and the Camera', *Theoretical Criminology*, 18(2):134–158.

Carrabine, E. (2015) 'Visual Criminology: History, Theory and Method', in Copes, H. and M. Miller (eds.) *The Routledge Handbook of Qualitative Criminology*, Oxon: Routledge, pp. 103–121.

Carrabine, E. (2016) 'Representing the Prison', in Jewkes, Y., B. Crewe and Jamie Bennett (eds.) *Prisons Handbook*, London: Routledge.

Carrabine, E., P. Cox, P. Fussey, R. Hobbs, N. South, D. Thiel and J. Turton (2014) *Criminology: A Sociological Introduction*, London: Routledge.

Carrington, K. R. Hogg and M. Sozzo (2016) 'Southern Criminology', *British Journal of Criminology*, 56(1):1–20.

Castells, M. (1972) *The Urban Question*, London: Edward Arnold.

Castells, M. (2000), *End of Millennium*, 2nd edn. Oxford: Blackwell Publishers.

Cecchi, D. (2011) 'The Criminalization of Immigration in Italy: Extent of the Phenomenon and Possible Interpretations', *Italian Sociological Review*, 1(1):34–42.

Centre for Contemporary Cultural Studies (1982) *The Empire Strikes Back: Race and Racism in Seventies Britain*, London: Hutchinson.

Chambliss, W. (1988) *On the Take*, Bloomington, IN: Indiana University Press.

Chan, W. and G. Rigakos (2002) 'Risk, Crime and Gender', *British Journal of Criminology*, 42(4):743–761.

Chen, K. (2010) *Asia as Method: Toward De-imperialization*, Durham, NC: Duke University Press.

Chernilo, D. (2006) 'Social Theory's Methodological Nationalism: Myth and Reality', *European Journal of Social Theory*, 9(1):5–22.

Chouliaraki, L. (2012) *The Ironic Spectator: Solidarity in the Age of Post-Humanism*, Cambridge: Polity Press.

Chouliaraki, L. and B. Blaagaard (2013) 'Special Issue: The Ethics of Images', *Visual Communication*, 12(3):253–259.

Clarke, G. (1981/1990) 'Defending Ski-jumpers' in Frith, S. and A. Goodwin (eds.) *On Record*, London: Routledge, pp. 81–96.

Clarke, J., S. Hall., T. Jefferson and B. Roberts (1976) 'Subcultures, Cultures and Class', in Hall, S. and T. Jefferson (eds.) *Resistance Through Rituals: Youth Subcultures in Post-War Britain*, London: Harper Collins.

Clarke, R. and M. Felson (eds.) (2008) *Routine Activity and Rational Choice*, New Brunswick, NJ: Transaction.

Clemmer, D. (1958) *The Prison Community,* New York: Rhinehart and Co.

Cloward, R. and L. Ohlin (1961) *Delinquency and Opportunity*, London: Routledge and Kegan Paul.

Cohen, A. (1955) *Delinquent Boys: The Culture of the Gang*, New York: Free Press.

Cohen, P. (1972) 'Subcultural Conflict and Working Class Community', *Working Papers in Cultural Studies*, 2:5–52.

Cohen, S. (1971/1988) 'Images of Deviance', in Cohen, S. (ed.) *Against Criminology*, Oxford: Transaction Books.

Cohen, S. (1972/2002) *Folk-Devils and Moral Panics: The Creation of the Mods and Rockers*, London: Routledge.

Cohen, S. (1979) 'The Punitive City: Notes on the Dispersal of Social Control', *Contemporary Crises*, 3(4):341–363.

Cohen, S. (1979/1988) 'Guilt, Justice and Tolerance: Some Old Concepts for a New Criminology', in Cohen, S. (ed.) *Against Criminology*, New Jersey: Transaction.

Cohen, S. (1980/1988) 'Symbols of Trouble', in Cohen, S. (ed.) *Against Criminology,* Oxford: Transaction, pp. 146–171.

Cohen, S. (1981/1988) 'Footprints in the Sand: A Further Report on Criminology and the Sociology of Deviance in Britain', in Cohen, S. (ed.) *Against Criminology,* Oxford: Transaction Books.

Cohen, S. (1985) *Visions of Social Control,* Cambridge: Polity Press.

Cohen, S. (1988) 'Against Criminology', in Cohen, S. (ed.) *Against Criminology,* Oxford: Transaction Books.

Cohen, S. (1992) *The Evolution of Women's Asylums Since 1500: From Refuges for Ex-Prostitutes to Shelters for Battered Women,* Oxford: Oxford University Press.

Cohen, S. (1993) 'Human Rights and Crimes of the State: The Culture of Denial', *Australian and New Zealand Journal of Criminology* 26(2):97–115.

Cohen, S. (2001) *States of Denial: Knowing About Atrocities and Suffering,* Cambridge: Polity Press.

Cohen, S. (2002) 'Moral Panics as Cultural Politics: Introduction to the Third Edition', in Cohen, S. (ed.) *Folk Devils and Moral Panics,* 3rd edn. London: Routledge.

Cohen, S. and J. Young (eds.) (1973) *The Manufacture of News,* London: Constable.

Coleman, R. and J. Sim (2000) '"You'll Never Walk Alone": CCTV Surveillance, Order and Neo-liberal Rule in Liverpool City Centre', *British Journal of Sociology,* 51(4):623–639.

Collier, R. (1998) *Masculinities, Crime and Criminology,* London: Sage.

Collins, R. (2008) *Violence,* Princeton, NJ: Princeton University Press.

Collison, M. (1996) 'In Search of the High Life: Drugs, Crime, Masculinities and Consumption', *British Journal of Criminology,* 36(3):428–443.

Connell, R. W. (1987) *Gender and Power,* Stanford, CA: Stanford University Press.

Connell, R. W. (1995) *Masculinities,* Oxford: Blackwell.

Connell, R. W. (2007) *Southern Theory: The Global Dynamics of Knowledge in the Social Science,* Cambridge: Polity Press.

Connell, R. W. (2015) 'Meeting at the Edge of Fear: Theory on a World Scale', *Feminist Theory,* 16:49–66.

Corrigan, P. and D. Sayer (1985) *The Great Arch: English State Formation as Cultural Revolution,* Oxford: Basil Blackwell.

Coser, L. (1978) 'American Trends', in Bottomore, T. and R. Nisbet (eds.) *A History of Sociological Analysis,* New York: Basic Books.

Cottle, S. (2005) 'Mediatized Public Crisis and Civil Society Renewal: The Racist Murder of Stephen Lawrence', *Crime, Media, Culture,* 1(1):49–71.

Cottle, S. (2006) *Mediatized Conflict,* Berkshire: Open University Press.

Cottle, S. (2012) 'Mediatized Disasters in the Global Age: On the Ritualization of Catastrophe', Chapter 10, pp. 259–283 in Alexander, J., R. Jacobs and P. Smith (eds.) *The Oxford Handbook of Cultural Sociology,* Oxford: Oxford University Press.

Courtney, D. and S. Lyng (2007) 'Taryn Simon and *The Innocents* Project', *Crime, Media, Culture,* 3(2):175–191.

Crenshaw, K. (1991) 'Mapping the Margins: Intersectionality, Identity Politics and Violence against Women of Color', *Stanford Law Review,* 43:1241–1299.

Cressey, D. (1969) *Theft of a Nation,* New York: Harper and Row.

Critcher, C. (2009) 'Widening the Focus: Moral Panics as Moral Regulation', *British Journal of Criminology,* 49(1):17–35.

Critcher, C. (2011) 'For a Political Economy of Moral Panics', *Crime, Media, Culture*, 7(3):259–275.

Cubbison, G. (2010) 'Operation Gatekeeper, 15 Years Later', in http://www.nbcsandiego.com/news/politics/Operation-Gatekeeper-at-15--62939412.html, Accessed 14 March 2016.

Currie, E. (1996) *Is America Winning the War on Crime and Should Britain Follow Its Example*, London: NACRO.

Currie, E. (1998) *Crime and Punishment in America*, New York: Metropolitan Books.

Daly, K. (1989) 'Criminal Justice Ideologies and Practices in Different Voices: Some Feminist Questions About Justice', *International Journal of the Sociology of Law*, 17:1–18.

Daly, K. (2002) 'Restorative Justice: The Real Story', *Punishment & Society*, 4(1):55–79.

Daly, K. (2013) 'Feminist Perspectives in Criminology: A Review with Gen Y in Mind', in McLaughlin, E. and T. Newburn (eds.) *The SAGE Handbook of Criminological Theory*, London: Sage.

Dandaneau, S. (2007) 'Mills, C. Wright (1916–1962)', in Ritzer, G. and M. Malden (eds.) *The Blackwell Encyclopaedia of Sociology*, Oxford: Blackwell.

Davis, M. (1992) *City of Quartz: Excavating the Future in Los Angeles*, London: Verso.

Davis, M. (1998) *Ecology of Fear: Los Angeles and the Imagination of Disaster*, New York: Metropolitan.

Davis, M. (1999) *The Ecology of Fear: Los Angeles and the Imagination of Disaster*, New York: Vintage.

De Beauvoir, S. (1949) *Le Deuxième Sexe*, Paris: Gallimard.

De Giorgi, A. (2006) *Re-thinking the Political Economy of Punishment: Perspectives on Post-Fordism and Penal Politics*, Aldershot: Ashgate.

De Giorgi, A. (2010) 'Immigration Control, Post-Fordism, and Less Eligibility: A Materialist Critique of Immigration Across Europe', *Punishment & Society*, 12(2):147–167.

De Giorgi, A. (2013) 'Punishment and Political Economy', in Simon, J. and R. Sparks (eds.) *The SAGE Handbook of Punishment and Society*, London: Sage, pp. 40–59.

Dear, M. (2005) 'Los Angeles and the Chicago School: An Invitation to a Debate', in Kleniewski, N. (ed.) *Cities and Society*, Oxford: Blackwell.

Deegan, M. (1988) *Jane Addams and the Men of the Chicago School, 1892–1918*, New Brunswick, NJ: Transaction Books.

Deleuze, G. (1992) 'Postscript on the Societies of Control', *October* 59(Winter):3–7.

Denzin, N. (1990) 'Presidential Address on "The Sociological Imagination" Revisited', *Sociological Quarterly*, 31(1):1–22.

Dionne, C. (2004) 'Fashioning Outlaws: The Early Modern Rogue and Urban Culture', in Dionne, C. and S. Mentz (eds.) *Rogues of Early Modern English Culture*, Ann Arbor: University of Michigan Press.

Dorn, N. (2010) 'The Governance of Securities: Ponzi Finance, Regulatory Convergence, Credit Crunch', *British Journal of Criminology*, 50(1):23–45.

Douglas, M. (1966) *Purity and Danger: An Analysis of Concepts of Pollution and Taboo*, London: Routledge and Kegan Paul.

Downes, D. (1966) *The Delinquent Solution*, London: Routledge and Kegan Paul.

Downes, D. (1986) 'Back to Basics: Reflections on Barbara Wootton's "Twelve Criminological Hypotheses"', in Bean, P. and D. Whytes (eds.) *Barbara Wootton: Social Sciences and Public Policy, Essays in Her Honour*, London: Tavistock.

Downes, D. (1988) 'The Sociology of Crime and Social Control in Britain, 1960–1987', in Rock, P. (ed.) *A History of British Criminology*, Oxford: Clarendon Press.

Duneier, M. (1999) *Sidewalk*, New York: Farrar, Straus and Giroux.

Durkheim, É. (1893/1960) *The Division of Labour in Modern Society*, Glencoe, IL: Free Press.

Durkheim, É. (1895/1966) *Rules of Sociological Method*, New York: Free Press.

Durkheim, É. (1897/1966) *Suicide: A Study in Sociology*, New York: Free Press.

Durkheim, É. (1901/1984) 'Two Laws of Penal Evolution', in Lukes, S. and A. Scull (eds.) *Durkheim and the Law*, Oxford: Basil Blackwell.

Durkheim, É. (1925/1961) *Moral Education*, New York: Free Press.

Edwards, S. (1984) *Women on Trial*, Manchester: Manchester University Press.

Elias, N. (1939/1984) *The Civilizing Process: Vol I, The History of Manners*, London: Blackwell.

Elias, N. (1966) *The Germans*, Cambridge: Polity Press.

Ellis, J. (2000) *Seeing Things: Television in an Age of Uncertainty*, London: I.B.Tauris.

Engels, F. (1845/1993) *The Condition of the Working Class in England*, Oxford: Oxford University Press.

Ericson, K. (1966) *Wayward Puritans*, New York: Wiley.

Ericson, R. (2007) *Crime in an Insecure World*, Cambridge: Polity Press.

Ericson, R. and K. Haggery (1998) *Policing the Risk Society*, Toronto: University of Toronto Press.

Ettema, J. (1990) 'Press Rites and Race Relations: A Study of Mass Mediated Ritual', *Critical Studies in Mass Communication*, 7:309–311.

Evans, R. (1982) *The Fabrication of Virtue: English Prison Architecture, 1750–1840*, Cambridge: Cambridge University Press.

Farnsworth, K. and G. Fooks (2015) 'Corporate Taxation, Corporate Power, and Corporate Harm', *Howard Journal of Criminal Justice*, 54(1):25–41.

Featherstone, M. (1992) 'Postmodernism and the Aestheticization of Everyday Life', in Lash, S. and J. Freedman (eds.) *Modernity and Identity*, Oxford: Blackwell.

Feeley, M. and J. Simon (1992) 'The New Penology: Notes on the Emerging Strategy of Corrections and its Implications', *Criminology*, 30(4):449–474.

Feeley, M. and J. Simon (1994) 'Actuarial Justice: The Emerging New Criminal Law', in Nelken, D. (ed.) *The Futures of Criminology*, London: Sage.

Feeley, M. and J. Simon (2007) '*Folk Devils and Moral Panics*: An Appreciation from North America', in Downes, D. et al (eds.) *Crime, Social Control and Human Rights: From Moral Panics to States of Denial, Essays in Honour of Stanley Cohen*, Devon: Willan.

Feldman, D. (2002) *Civil Liberties and Human Rights in England and Wales*, 2nd edn. Oxford: Oxford University Press.

Ferrell, J., K. Hayward, W. Morrison and M. Presdee (eds.) (2004) *Cultural Criminology Unleashed*, London: Glass House.

Ferrell, J., K. Hayward and J. Young (2008) *Cultural Criminology: An Invitation*, London: Sage.

Fine, R. (1985) *Democracy and the Rule of Law*, London: Pluto Press.

Finn, J. (2009) *Capturing the Criminal Image: From Mug Shot to Surveillance Society*, Minneapolis: University of Minnesota Press.

Fiske, J. (1998) 'Surveilling the City: Whiteness, the Black Man and Democratic Totalitarianism', *Theory, Culture and Society*, 15(2):67–88.

Fletcher, J. (1849) 'Moral and Educational Statistics of England and Wales', *Journal of the Statistical Society of London*, 12(3):189–335.

Fletcher, R. (1960) 'Book Review of the *Sociological Imagination*', *British Journal of Sociology*, 11(2):169–170.

Foucault, M. (1975/1991) *Discipline and Punish: The Birth of the Prison*, London: Penguin.

Foucault, M. (1980) (edited by Colin Gordon) *Power/Knowledge: Selected Interviews and Other Writings 1972–1977*, New York: Pantheon Books.

Foucault, M. (1982) 'The Subject and Power', in Dreyfus, H. and P. Rabinow (eds.) *Michel Foucault: Beyond Structuralism and Hermeneutics*, Chicago: University of Chicago Press.

Franklin-Wallis, O. (2013) 'Unravelling the Dark Web', in http://www.gq-magazine.co.uk/article/silk-road-online-drugs-guns-black-market, Accessed 27 Feb 2016.

Frauley, J. (2015) 'For a Refractive Criminology: Against Science Machines and Cheerful Robots', in Frauley, J. (ed.) *C. Wright Mills and the Criminological Imagination: Prospects for Creative Inquiry*, Farnham: Ashgate.

Friedrichs, D. and J. Friedrichs (2002) 'The World Bank and Crimes of Globalization: A Case Study', *Social Justice*, 29(1–2):13–36.

Gambetta, D. (1993) *The Sicilian Mafia*, London: Harvard University Press.

Gambetta, D. (2009) *Codes of the Underworld*, Princeton: Princeton University Press.

Garbin, D. and G. Millington (2012) 'Territorial Stigma and the Politics of Resistance in a Parisian *Banlieue*: La Courneuve and Beyond', *Urban Studies*, 49(10):2067–2083.

Garfinkel, H. (1956) 'Conditions of Successful Degradation Ceremonies', *American Journal of Sociology*, 61:420–424.

Garfinkel, S. (2000) *Database Nation: The Death of Privacy in the 21st Century*, Sebastopol, CA: O'Reilly.

Garland, D. (1985) *Punishment and Welfare*, Aldershot: Gower.

Garland, D. (1988) 'British Criminology Before 1935', in Rock, P. (ed.) *A History of British Criminology*, Oxford: Clarendon Press, pp. 1–17.

Garland, D. (1990) *Punishment and Modern Society: A Study in Social Theory*, Oxford: Oxford University Press.

Garland, D. (1996) 'The Limits of the Sovereign State: Strategies of Crime Control in Contemporary Society', *British Journal of Criminology*, 36(4):445–471.

Garland, D. (1997) "Governmentality' and the Problem of Crime', *Theoretical Criminology*, 1(2):173–214.

Garland, D. (2001) *The Culture of Control: Crime and Social Order in Contemporary Society*, Oxford: Oxford University Press.

Garland, D. (2002) 'Of Crimes and Criminals: The Development of Criminology in Britain', in Maguire, M., R. Morgan and R. Reiner (eds.) *The Oxford Handbook of Criminology*, 3rd edn. Oxford: Oxford University Press.

Garland, D. (2008) 'On the Concept of Moral Panic', *Crime, Media, Culture*, 4(1):9–30.

Garland, D. (2011) 'Criminology's Place in the Academic Field', in Bosworth, M. and C. Hoyle (eds.) *What Is Criminology?*, Oxford: Oxford University Press.

Garland, D. (2014) 'The Welfare State: A Fundamental Dimension of Modern Government', *European Journal of Sociology*, 55(3):327–364.

Garland, D. (2016) *The Welfare State: A Very Short Introduction*, Oxford: Oxford University Press.

Garland, D. and R. Sparks (2000) 'Criminology, Social Theory and the Challenge of Our Times', in Garland, D. and R. Sparks (eds.) *Criminology and Social Theory*, Oxford: Oxford University Press.

Garland, D. and P. Young (eds.) (1983) *The Power to Punish*, Aldershot: Ashgate.

Gatrell, V. (1994) *The Hanging Tree: Execution and the English People, 1770–1868*. Oxford: Oxford University Press.

Gefter, P. (2009) *Photography After Frank*, London: Aperture.

Geis, G. (1974) 'Avocational Crime', in Glaser, D. (ed.) *Handbook of Criminology*, Chicago, IL: Rand McNally.

Gelder, K. (2007) *Subcultures*, London: Routledge.

Giddens, A. (1984) *The Constitution of Society*, Cambridge: Polity Press.

Giddens, A. (1990) *The Consequences of Modernity*, Cambridge: Polity Press.

Gill, R. (2010) 'Supersexualise Me! Advertising and the "Midriffs"', in Attwood, F. (ed.) *Mainstreaming Sex*, London: I.B. Taurus, pp. 93–109.

Gilligan, C. (1982) *In a Different Voice*, Cambridge, MA: Harvard University Press.

Gilmore, R. (2007) *Golden Gulag: Prisons, Surplus, and Opposition in Globalizing California*, Berkeley, CA: University of California Press.

Gilroy, P. (1987a) 'The Myth of Black Criminality', in Scraton, P. (ed.) *Law, Order and the Authoritarian State: Readings in Critical Criminology*, Milton Keynes: Open University Press.

Gilroy, P. (1987b) *There Ain't No Black in the Union Jack: The Cultural Politics of Nation and Race*, London: Unwin Hyman.

Gilroy, P. (1993) *The Black Atlantic: Modernity and Double Consciousness*, London: Verso.

Gilroy, P. (2000) *Between Camps: Nations, Cultures and the Allure of Race*, London: Penguin.

Gilroy, P. (2004) *After Empire: Melancholia or Convivial Culture*, London: Routledge.

Girouard, M. (1986) *Cities and People: A Social and Architectural History*, New Haven, CT: Yale University Press.

Gitlin, T. (2007) 'C. Wright Mills, Free Radical', from http://www.uni-muenster.de/PeaCon/dgs-mills/mills-texte/GitlinMills.htm, Retrieved 23 October 2013

Goffman, A. (2014) *On the Run: Fugitive Life in an American City*, Chicago: University of Chicago Press.

Goffman, E. (1962) *Asylums: Essays on the Social Situation of Mental Patients and Other Inmates*, Harmondsworth: Penguin.

Goffman, E. (1979) *Gender Advertisements*, London: Macmillan.

Goode, E. (2008) 'From the Western to the Murder Mystery: The Sociological Imagination of C. Wright Mills', *Sociological Spectrum*, 28:237–253.

Goode, E. and N. Ben-Yehuda (1994) *Moral Panics: The Social Construction of Deviance*, Oxford: Blackwell.

Goring, C. (1913) *The English Convict: A Statistical Study*, London.

Gottfredson, M. and T. Hirschi (1990) *A General Theory of Crime*, Stanford: Stanford University Press.

Gottschalk, M. (2006) *The Prison and the Gallows: The Politics of Mass Incarceration in America*, Cambridge: Cambridge University Press.

Gouldner, A. (1968/1973) 'The Sociologist as Partisan: Sociology and the Welfare State', in *For Sociology*, London: Allen Lane.

Green, P. and T. Ward (2000) 'State Crime, Human Rights and the Limits of Criminology', *Social Justice*, 27(1):101–115.

Greenberg, A. (2016) 'The Silk Road's Dark-Web Dream Is Dead', in http://www.wired.com/2016/01/the-silk-roads-dark-web-dream-is-dead/, Accessed 27 Feb 2016.

Greenfield, L. (2002) *Girl Culture*, San Francisco: Chronicle Books

Greer, C., and E. McLaughlin (2011) 'Trial by Media: Policing, the News 24-7 News Mediasphere, and the Politics of Outrage', *Theoretical Criminology*, 15(1):23–46.

Greer, C., and E. McLaughlin (2012a). 'Media Justice: Madeleine McCann, Intermediatization and 'Trial by Media' in the British Press', *Theoretical Criminology*, 16(4):395–416. doi:10.1177/1362480612454559

Greer, C., and E. McLaughlin (2012b). '"This Is Not Justice": Ian Tomlinson, Institutional Failure and the Press Politics of Outrage', *British Journal of Criminology*, 52(2):274–293. doi:10.1093/bjc/azr086

Greer, C., and E. McLaughlin (2013) 'The Sir Jimmy Savile Scandal: Child Sexual Abuse and Institutional Denial at the BBC', *Crime, Media, Culture*, 9(3):243–263. doi:10.1177/1741659013513782

Greer, C., and E. McLaughlin (2015) 'The Return of the Repressed: Secrets, Lies, Denial and 'Historical' Institutional Child Sexual Abuse Scandals' in Whyte, D. (ed.) *How Corrupt Is Britain?*, London: Pluto.

Greer, C. and E. McLaughlin (2016) 'Theorising Institutional Scandal and the Regulatory State', *Theoretical Criminology* 16(4).

Grierson, J. (1966) 'The First Principles of Documentary', in Hardy, F. (ed.) *Grierson on Documentary*, London: Faber & Faber, pp. 35–46.

Guerry, A. (1833) *Essai sur la statistique morale de la France*, Paris: Crochard.

Gusfield, J. (1963) *Symbolic Crusade: Status Politics and the American Temperance Movement*, Urbana: University of Illinois Press.

Habermas, J. (1962/1989) *The Structural Transformation of the Public Sphere*, Cambridge: Polity Press.

Habermas, J. (1987) *Philosophical Discourse of Modernity*, Cambridge: Polity Press.

Hagan, J. (1977) *The Disreputable Pleasures*, Toronto: McGraw-Hill Ryerson.

Hagan, J. (1985) *Modern Criminology: Crime, Criminal Behavior and its Control*, New York: McGraw-Hill.

Hagan, J. (2010) *Who are the Criminals?*, Princeton: Princeton University Press.

Haggerty, K. and R. Ericson (2000) 'The Surveillant Assemblage', *British Journal of Sociology*, 51(4):605–622.

Halford, S. and T. Strangleman (2009) 'In Search of the Sociology of Work: Past, Present and Future', *Sociology*, 43(5):811–828.

Hall, P. (1999) *Cities in Civilization*, London: Orion.

Hall, S. (1980) 'Cultural Studies: Two Paradigms', *Media, Culture and Society*, 2:57–72.

Hall, S. (1996) 'New Ethnicities', in Morley, D. and K-H. Chen (eds.) *Stuart Hall: Critical Dialogues in Cultural Studies*, London: Routledge.

Hall, S., C. Critcher, T. Jefferson, J. Clarke and B. Roberts (1978) *Policing the Crisis: Mugging, the State and Law and Order*, London: Macmillan.

Hall, S. and T. Jefferson (eds.) (1975) *Resistance Through Rituals*, London: Hutchinson.

Hall, S. and T. Jefferson (2006) 'Once More Around Resistance Through Rituals', in Hall, S. and T. Jefferson (eds.) *Resistance Through Rituals: Youth Subcultures in Post-War Britain*, 2nd edn. London: Routledge.

Hall, S. and S. Winlow (2012) 'Introduction: The Need for New Directions in Criminological Theory', in Hall, S. and S. Winlow (eds.) *New Directions in Criminology*, London: Sage, pp. 1–13.

Hall, S. and S. Winlow (2015) *Revitalizing Criminological Theory: Towards A New Ultra-Realism*, London: Routledge.

Haller, M. (1976) 'Bootleggers and American Gambling, 1920–1950', in Commission on the Review of National Policy toward Gambling (ed.) *Gambling in America*, Commission on Review of National Policy Toward Gambling, 102–143, Washington, DC: US Government Printing Office.

Haller, M. (1990) 'Illegal Enterprise: A Theoretical and Historical Interpretation', *Criminology*, 28(2):207–235.

Hallsworth, S. (2008) 'Street Crime: Interpretation and Legacy in *Policing the Crisis*', *Crime, Media, Culture*, 4(1):137–143.

Hallsworth, S. (2013) *The Gang and Beyond: Interpreting Violent Street Worlds*, London: Palgrave.

Hallsworth, S. and D. James (2014) 'Growing Sanguine About the Weeds: Gardening and Security', in Schuilenburg, M., R. van Steden and B. Oude Breuil (eds.) *Positive Criminology: Reflections on Care, Belonging and Security*, The Hague: Eleven International Publishing, pp. 57–70.

Halsey, A. H. (1985) 'Provincials and Professionals: The British Post-War Sociologists', in Bulmer, M. (ed.) *Essays on the History of British Sociological Research*, Cambridge: Cambridge University Press.

Halsey, A. H. (2004) *A History of Sociology in Britain*, Oxford: Oxford University Press.

Halsey, M. and A. Young (2006) '"Our Desires are Ungovernable": Writing Graffiti in Urban Space', *Theoretical Criminology*, 10(3):275–306.

Hancock, L. and G. Mooney (2013) '"Welfare Ghettos" and the "Broken Society": Territorial Stigmatization in the Contemporary UK', *Housing, Theory and Society*, 30(1):46–64.

Hand, M. (2012) *Ubiquitous Photography*, Cambridge: Polity Press.

Hannah-Moffat, K. (2011) 'Criminological Cliques: Narrowing Dialogues, Institutional Protectionism, and the Next Generation', in Bosworth, M. and C. Hoyle (eds.) *What Is Criminology?*, Oxford: Oxford University Press.

Harcourt, B. (2010) 'Neoliberal Penality: A Brief Genealogy', *Theoretical Criminology*, 14(1):74–92.

Harper, D. (2012) *Visual Sociology*, Oxon: Routledge.

Harvey, D. (1973) *Social Justice and the City*, London: Hodder & Stoughton.

Harvey, D. (2003) *The New Imperialism*, Oxford: Oxford University Press.

Hawthorn, G. (1987) *Enlightenment and Despair: A History of Social Theory*, Cambridge: Cambridge University Press.

Hay, D. (1975) 'Property, Authority, and the Criminal Law', in Hay, D., P. Linebaugh and E. P. Thompson (eds.) *Albions Fatal Tree: Crime and Society in Eighteenth Century England*. Harmondsworth: Penguin.

Hayden, T. (2006) *Radical Nomad: C. Wright Mills and His Times*, Boulder, CO: Paradigm.

Hayward, K. (2002) 'The Vilification and Pleasures of Youthful Transgression', in Muncie, J., G. Hughes and E. McLaughlin (eds.) *Youth Justice: Critical Readings*, London: Sage.

Hayward, K. (2010) 'Opening the Lens: Cultural Criminology and the Image', in Hayward, K. and M. Presdee (eds.) *Framing Crime: Cultural Criminology and the Image*, London: Routledge.

Hayward, K. and M. Yar (2006) 'The "Chav" Phenomenon: Consumption, Media and the Construction of a New Underclass', *Crime, Media, Culture*, 2(1):9–28.

Hearn, F. (1985) *Reason and Freedom in Sociological Thought*, London: Allen and Unwin.

Hebdige, D. (1979) *Subculture: The Meaning of Style*, London: Routledge.

Hebdige, D. (1988) *Hiding in the Light*, Routledge.

Heidensohn, F. (1985) *Women and Crime*, London: Macmillan.

Heidensohn, F. (1986) 'Models of Justice: Portia or Persephone? Some Thoughts on Equality, Fairness and Gender in the Field of Criminal Justice', *International Journal of the Sociology of Law*, 14:287–298.

Heidensohn, F. and M. Silvestri (2012) 'Gender and Crime', in Maguire, M., R. Morgan and R. Reiner (eds.) *The Oxford Handbook of Criminology*, 5th edn. Oxford: Clarendon Press.

Heilbron, J. (1995) *The Rise of Social Theory*, Cambridge: Polity Press.

Henne, K. and E. Troshynski (2013) 'Mapping the Margins of Intersectionality: Criminological Possibilities in a Transnational World', *Theoretical Criminology*, 17(4):455–473.

Hesmondhalgh, D. (2008) 'Neoliberalism, Imperialism and the Media', in Hesmondhalgh, D. and J. Toynbee (eds.) *The Media and Social Theory*, London: Routledge.

Hier, S. (2002) 'Conceptualizing Moral Panic Through a Moral Economy of Harm', *Critical Sociology*, 28(3):311–344.

Hier, S. (2008) 'Thinking Beyond Moral Panic: Risk, Responsibility, and the Politics of Moralization', *Theoretical Criminology*, 12(2):173–190.

Hillyard, P., C. Pantazis, S. Tombs and D. Gordon (eds.) (2004) *Beyond Criminology: Taking Harm Seriously*, London: Pluto Press.

Hirst, P. (1975) 'Marx and Engels on Law, Crime and Morality', in I. Taylor, P. Walton and J. Young (ed.), *Critical Criminology*. London: Routledge and Kegan Paul.

Hobbes, T. (1651/2008) *Leviathan*, Oxford: Oxford University Press.

Hobbs, D. (1988) *Doing the Business*, Oxford: Oxford University Press.

Hobbs, D. (1997) 'Professional Crime: Change, Continuity and the Enduring Myth of the Underworld', *Sociology*, 31(1):57–72.

Hobbs, D. (1998) 'Going Down the Glocal: The Local Context of Organised Crime', *The Howard Journal*, 37(4):407–422.

Hobbs, D. (2001) 'The Firm: Organizational Logic and Criminal Culture on a Shifting Terrain', *British Journal of Criminology*, 41(4):549–560.

Hobbs, D. (2012) '"It Was Never About the Money": Market Society, Organised Crime and UK Criminology', in Hall, S. and S. Winlow (eds.) *New Directions in Criminological Theory*, London: Routledge.

Hobbs, D. (2013) *Lush Life: Constructing Organized Crime in the UK*, Oxford: University of Oxford.

Hobsbawm, E. (1973) *The Age of Revolution*, London: Cardinal.

Hodkinson, P. (2012) 'Beyond Spectacular Specifics in the Study of Youth (Sub)cultures', *Journal of Youth Studies*, 15(5):557–572.

Hohendahl, P. (1982) *The Institution of Criticism*, Ithaca, NY: Cornell University Press.

Holland, P. (2006) *Picturing Childhood: The Myth of the Child in Popular Imagery*, London: I.B.Tauris.

Holmwood, J. (2010) 'Sociology's Misfortune: Disciplines, Interdisciplinarity and the Impact of Audit Culture', *The British Journal of Sociology*, 61(4):639–658.

Homans, G. (1960) 'Book Review of *The Sociological Imagination*', *American Journal of Sociology*, 65(5):517–518.

Hood, R. (2004) 'Hermann Mannheim and Max Grünhut: Criminological Pioneers in London and Oxford', *British Journal of Criminology*, 44(4):469–495.

Hooker, E. (1963) 'Male Homosexuality', in Farberow, N. (ed.) *Taboo Topics*, New York: Prentice Hall.

Howard, J. (1777) *The State of the Prisons*, Warrington.

Howe, A. (1994) *Punish and Critique: Towards a Feminist Analysis of Penality*, London: Routledge.

Hubbard, P. (2003) 'Fear and Loathing at the Multiplex: Everyday Anxiety in the Post-Industrial City', *Capital and Class*, 80:51–75.

Hudson, B. (1993) *Penal Policy and Social Justice*, Basingstoke: Macmillan.

Hudson, B. (1997) *Understanding Justice*, Milton Keynes: Open University Press.

Hudson, B. (2003) *Understanding Justice*, 2nd edn, London: Sage.

Hughes, B., L. McKie, D. Hopkins and N. Watson (2005) 'Love's Labour Lost? Feminism, the Disabled People's Movement and an Ethic of Care', *Sociology*, 39(2):259–275.

Hunnicutt, G. (2009) 'Varieties of Patriarchy and Violence against Women: Resurrecting "Patriarchy" as a Theoretical Tool', *Violence Against Women*, 15(5):553–573.

Hunt, T. (2005) *Building Jerusalem: The Rise and Fall of the Victorian City*, London: Orion.

Iadicola, P. (2010) 'The Centrality of Empire in the Study of State Crime and Violence', in Chambliss, W., R. Michalowski and R. Kramer (eds.) *State Crime in the Global Age*, Cullompton: Willan.

Ignatieff, M. (1999) *The Warrior's Honor: Ethnic War and the Modern Conscience*, London: Vintage.

Ilan, J. (2015) *Understanding Street Culture: Poverty, Crime, Youth and Cool*, London: Palgrave.

Irigaray, L. (1985) *Speculum of the Other Woman*, Ithaca, NY: Cornell University Press.

Irwin, J. (1990) *The Jail: Managing the Underclass in American Society*, Berkeley, CA: University of California Press.

Jackson, B. (1969) *A Thief's Primer*, London: Macmillan.

Jackson, B. (1977) *Killing Time*, Ithaca, NY: Cornell University Press.

Jackson, B. (2009) *Pictures from a Drawer: Prison and the Art of Portraiture*, Philadelphia: Temple University Press.

Jackson, B. and D. Christian (2012) *In This Timeless Time: Living and Dying on Death Row in America*, The University of North Carolina Press.

Jacobs, J. (2000) *Race, Media, and the Crisis of Civil Society*, Cambridge: Cambridge University Press.

Jacobs, J. B. (1977) *Stateville: The Penitentiary in Mass Society*, Chicago: University of Chicago Press.

Jacobs, J. B., J. Worthington and C. Panarella (1994) *Busting the Mob*, New York: New York University Press.

Jacoby, R. (2000) 'False Indignation', *New Left Review*, 2:154–159.

Jaffe, R. (2012) 'Talkin' 'bout the Ghetto: Popular Culture and Urban Imaginaries of Immobility', *International Journal of Urban and Regional Research*, 36(4):674–688.

Jay, M. (1993) *Downcast Eyes: The Denigration of Vision in Twentieth-century French Thought*, Berkeley, CA: California University Press.

Jefferson, T. (1997) 'Masculinities and Crimes', in Maguire, M., R. Morgan and R. Reiner (eds.) *The Oxford Handbook of Criminology*, 2nd edn. Oxford: Clarendon Press.

Jefferson, T. (2002) 'Subordinating Hegemonic Masculinity', *Theoretical Criminology*, 6(1):63–88.

Jenkins, P. (1992) *Intimate Enemies: Moral Panics in Contemporary Britain*, New York: Aldine de Gruyter.

Jenks, C. (2003) *Transgression*, London: Routledge.

Jervis, J. (1998) *Exploring the Modern*, Oxford: Blackwell.

Jervis, J. (1999) *Transgressing the Modern: Explorations in the Western Experience of Otherness*, Oxford: Blackwell.

Jewkes, Y. (2003) 'Policing the Net: Crime, Regulation and Surveillance in Cyberspace', in Jewkes, Y. (ed.) *Dot.cons: Crime, Deviance and Identity on the Internet*, Devon: Willan.

Johnston, C. and G. Mooney (2007) '"Problem" People, "Problem" Places? New Labour and Council Estates', in Atkinson, R. and G. Helms (eds.) *Securing an Urban Renaissance: Crime, Community, and British Urban Policy*, Bristol: Policy Press.

Johnston, L. (2000) *Policing Britain: Risk, Security and Governance*, Harlow: Longman.

Jones, R. (2000) 'Digital Rule: Punishment, Control and Technology', *Punishment & Society*, 2(1):5–22.

Katz, J. (1988) *The Seductions of Crime*, New York: Basic Books.

Kerr, K. (2009) *Postmodern Cowboy: C. Wright Mills and a New 21st Century Sociology*, Boulder, CO: Paradigm.

King, A. (2003) 'Postcolonialism, Representation and the City', in Bridge, G. and S. Watson (eds.) *A Companion to the City*, Oxford: Blackwell.

King, A. (2006) 'Serial Killing and the Postmodern Self', *History of the Human Sciences*, 19(3):109–125.

King, R. (2007) 'Imprisonment: Some International Comparisons and the Need to Revisit Panopticism', in Jewkes, Y. (ed.) *Handbook on Prisons*, Devon: Willan.

Kolb, W. (1960) 'Book Review of *The Sociological Imagination*', *American Sociological Review*, 29(5):966–969.

Koselleck, R. (2004) *Futures Past: On the Semantics of Historical Time*, New York: Columbia University Press.

Ku, A. (1999) *Narrative, Politics, and the Public Sphere*, Aldershot: Ashgate.

Lampe, K. von (2002) 'Afterword: Organized Crime Research in Perspective', in Duyne, P. von, K. von Lampe and N. Passas (eds.) *Upperworld and Underworld in Cross-Border Crime*, Nijmegen: Wolf Legal Publishers.

Landesco, J. (1929/1968) *Organized Crime in Chicago. Part III of the Illinois Crime Survey*, Chicago, IL and London: The University of Chicago Press.

Lasch, C. (1978) *Culture of Narcissism*, New York: Norton.

Laub, J. and R. Sampson (2003) *Shared Beginnings, Divergent Lives*, Cambridge, MA: Harvard University Press.

Lea, J. and J. Young (1984) *What Is To Be Done About Law and Order?* London: Pluto Press.

Lee, A. and R. Meyer (2008) *Weegee and the Naked City*, California: University of California Press.

Lees, S. (1989) 'Learning to Love: Sexual Reputation, Morality and the Social Control of Girls', in Cain, M. (ed.) *Growing Up Good: Policing the Behaviour of Girls in Europe*, London: Sage, pp. 19–37.

Lemert, E. (1951) *Social Pathology*, New York: McGraw-Hill.

Lemert, E. (1967) *Human Deviance, Social Problems and Social Control*, Englewood Cliffs, NJ: Prentice Hall.

Levi, M. (1998) 'Perspectives on "Organised Crime": An Overview', *The Howard Journal*, 37(4):335–345.

Levi, M. (2012) 'The Organization of Serious Crimes for Gain', in Maguire, M., R. Morgan and R. Reiner (eds.) *The Oxford Handbook of Criminology*, Oxford: Oxford University Press.

Levi, M. (2014) 'Thinking About Organized Crime: Structure and Threat', *RUSI Journal*, 159(1):6–14.

Lewis-Kraus, G. (2016) 'The Trials of Alice Goffman', *The New York Times Magazine*, 12 January 2016. Available at http://www.nytimes.com/2016/01/17/magazine/the-trials-of-alice-goffman.html?smid=tw-nytimes&smtyp=cur&_r=2

Liazos, A. (1972) 'The Poverty of the Sociology of Deviance: Nuts, Sluts and Preverts', *Social Problems*, 20(1):103–120.

Lin, J. (2005) 'Community, Ethnicity, and Urban Sociology', in Kleniewski, N. (ed.) *Cities and Society*, Oxford: Blackwell.

Loader, I. and R. Sparks (2012) 'Situating Criminology: On the Production and Consumption of Knowledge About Crime and Justice', in Maguire, M., R. Morgan and R. Reiner (eds.) *The Oxford Handbook of Criminology*, 5th edn. Oxford: Clarendon Press.

Locke, J. (1661/2003) *Two Treatises of Civil Government*, New Haven, CT: Yale University Press.

Logan, J. and H. Molotch (1987) *Urban Fortunes*, Berkeley, CA: University of California Press.

Lombroso, C. (1876) *L'uomo delinquent*, Turin: Boca.

Lowe, P. (2014) 'The Forensic Turn: Bearing Witness and the "Thingness" of the Photograph', in Kennedy, L. and C. Patrick (eds.) *The Violence of the Image: Photography and International Conflict*, London: I.B.Tauris.

Lowman, J., R. Menzies and T. Palys (eds.) (1987) *Transcarceration: Essays in the Sociology of Social Control*, Aldershot: Gower.

Ludvig, A. (2006) 'Differences Between Women? Intersecting Voices in a Female Narrative', *European Journal of Women's Studies*, 13(3):245–258.

Lynch, M. (2009) *Sunbelt Justice: Arizona and the Transformation of American Punishment*, Stanford, CA: Stanford University Press.

Lynch, M. (2012) 'Theorizing the Role of the "War on Drugs" in US Punishment', *Theoretical Criminology*, 16(2):175–199.

Lyng, S. (1990) 'Edgework', *American Journal of Sociology*, 94(5):851–886.

Lyon, D. (2001) *Surveillance Society: Monitoring Everyday Life*, Buckingham: Open University Press.

Lyon, D. (2003a) *Surveillance After September 11*, Cambridge: Polity Press.

Lyon, D. (2003b) 'Surveillance as Social Sorting', in Lyon, D. (ed.) *Surveillance as Social Sorting: Privacy, Risk and Digital Discrimination*, London: Routledge, pp. 13–30.

McGuigan, J. (2005) 'The Cultural Public Sphere', *European Journal of Cultural Studies*, 8(4):427–443.

McIntosh, M. (1971) 'Changes in the Organization of Thieving', in Cohen, S. (ed.) *Images of Deviance*, Middlesex: Penguin Books.

McIntosh, M. (1977) 'Review Symposium on *Women, Crime and Criminology*, Smart, C.', *British Journal of Criminology*, 17(4):395–397.

McKenzie, L. (2014) *Getting By: Estates, Class and Culture in Austerity Britain*, Bristol: Policy Press.

MacKinnon, C. (1987) *Feminism Unmodified: Discourses on Life and Law*, Cambridge, MA: Harvard University Press.

McLennan, G. (2005) 'The "New American Cultural Sociology": An Appraisal', *Theory, Culture & Society*, 22(6):1–18.

McLennan, G. (2013) 'Postcolonial Critique: The Necessity of Sociology', *Political Power and Social Theory*, 24:119–144.

McLuhan, M. (1964/1994) *Understanding Media: The Extensions of Man*, London: Routledge.

McMullan, J. (1984) *The Canting Crew: London's Criminal Underworld, 1550–1700*, New Brunswick, NJ: Rutgers University Press.

McNair, B. (2002) *Striptease Culture: Sex, Media and the Democratisation of Desire*, London: Routledge.

McNay, L. (1994) *Foucault: A Critical Introduction*, Cambridge: Polity Press.

McRobbie, A. (1981) 'Settling the Accounts with Subcultures: A Feminist Critique' in *Screen Education*, 34:37–49.

McRobbie, A. (2009) *The Aftermath of Feminism: Gender, Culture, and Social Change*, London: Sage.

McRobbie, A. and S. Thornton (1995) 'Rethinking "Moral Panic" for Multi-mediated Social Worlds', *British Journal of Sociology*, 46(4):559–574.

Maffesoli, M. (1996) *The Time of the Tribes*, London: Sage.

Maher, L. (1997) *Sexed Work: Gender, Race and Resistance in a Brooklyn Drug Market*, Oxford: Clarendon Press.

Maidment, M. (2006) 'Transgressing Boundaries: Feminist Perspectives in Criminology', in DeKeseredy, W. and B. Perry (eds.) *Advancing Critical Criminology: Theory and Application*, Landham, MD: Lexington.

Marcuse, P. (1989) 'Dual City: A Muddy Metaphor for a Quartered City', *International Journal of Urban and Regional Research*, 13(4):697–708.

Marcuse, P. (1995) 'Not Chaos but Walls: Postmodernism and the Partitioned City', in Watson, S. and K. Gibson (eds.) *Postmodern Cities and Spaces*, Oxford: Blackwell.

Marcuse, P. (2000) 'Cities in Quarters', in Bridges, G. and S. Watson (eds.) *Companion to the City*, Oxford: Blackwell.

Marien, M. (2010) *Photography: A Cultural History*, London: Laurence King.

Martin, J. (1988) 'The Development of Criminology in Britain: 1948–1960', in Rock, P. (ed.) *A History of British Criminology*, Oxford: Clarendon Press.

Matthews, R. (1999) *Doing Time*, Basingstoke: Macmillan.

Matthews, R. (2002) *Armed Robbery*, Cullompton: Willan.

Matthews, R. (2009) 'Beyond "So What" Criminology: Rediscovering Realism', *Theoretical Criminology*, 13:341–362.

Matthews, R. (2014) 'Cultural Realism?', *Crime, Media, Culture*, 10(3):203–214.

Matza, D. (1964) *Delinquency and Drift*, New York: Wiley.

Matza, D. (1969) *Becoming Deviant*, Englewood Cliffs, NJ: Prentice Hall.

Mauer, M. (1997) *Intended and Unintended Consequences: State Racial Disparities in Imprisonment*, Washington, DC: The Sentencing Project.

Mayhew, H. (1861–62) *London Labour and the London Poor*, London: Griffin, Bohn and Company.

Mayhew, H. and J. Binny (1862) *The Criminal Prisons of London and Scenes of Prison Life*. London: Griffin, Bohn and Company.

Melbin, M. (1978) 'Night as Frontier', *American Sociological Review*, 43(1):3–22.

Melossi, D. (1979) 'Institutions of Social Control and the Capitalist Organization of Work', in Fine, B. et al. (eds.) *Capitalism and the Rule of Law*, London: Hutchinson.

Melossi, D. (2008) *Controlling Crime, Controlling Society: Thinking About Crime in Europe and America*, Cambridge: Polity Press.

Melossi, D. and M. Pavarini (1978) *The Prison and the Factory*, London: Macmillan.

Merrin, W. (2005) *Baudrillard and the Media*, Cambridge: Polity Press.

Merton, R. K. (1938) 'Social Structure and Anomie', *American Sociological Review*, 3(5):672–682.

Merton, R. K. (1957) *Social Theory and Social Structure*, 2nd edn. Glencoe, IL: Free Press.

Messerschmidt, J. (1993) *Masculinities and Crime: Critique and Reconceptualisation of Theory*, Lanham, MD: Rowman and Littlefield.

Messerschmidt, J. (1997) *Crime as Structured Action: Gender, Race, Class, and Crime in the Making*, London: Sage.

Messerschmidt, J. (2005) 'Masculinities and Crime: Beyond a Dualist Criminology', in Renzetti, C., L. Goodstein and S. Miller (eds.) *Gender, Crime and Criminal Justice: Original Feminist Readings*, Los Angeles, CA: Roxbury.

Messerschmidt, J. (2014) *Crime as Structured Action: Doing Masculinities, Race, Class, Sexuality and Crime*, Lanham, MD: Rowman & Littlefield.

Miller, D. and J. Kitzinger (1998) 'AIDS, the Policy Process and Moral Panics', in Miller, D., Kitzinger, J., K. Williams and P. Beharrell (eds.) *The Circuit of Mass Communication*, London: Sage.

Miller, E. (1991) 'Assessing the Risk of Inattention to Class, Race, Ethnicity and Gender: Comment on Lyng', *American Journal of Sociology*, 96:1530–1534.

Miller, J. (1998) 'Up it Up: Gender and the Accomplishment of Street Robbery', *Criminology*, 36(1):37–66.

Miller, J. (2001) *One of the Guys: Girls, Gangs and Gender*, Oxford: Clarendon.

Miller, J. (2002) 'The Strengths and Limits of "Doing Gender" for Understanding Street Crime', *Theoretical Criminology*, 6(4):433–460.

Mills, C. W. (1959) *The Sociological Imagination*, Oxford: Oxford University Press.

Molotch, H. (1976) 'The City as a Growth Machine: Toward a Political Economy of Place', *American Journal of Sociology*, 82(2):309–332.

Molotch, H. (2014) *Against Security*, Princeton, NJ: Princeton University Press.

Morris, T. (1957) *The Criminal Area*, London: Routledge and Kegan Paul.

Morris, T. (1988) 'British Criminology: 1935–1948', in Rock, P. (ed.) *A History of British Criminology*, Oxford: Clarendon Press.

Morris, T. and P. Morris (1963) *Pentonville: A Sociological Study of an English Prison*, London: Routledge and Kegan Paul.

Mosendz, P. (2014) 'Beheadings as Terror Marketing', in http://www.theatlantic.com/international/archive/2014/10/beheadings-as-terror-marketing/381049/, Accessed 22 March 2016.

Muggleton, D. (1997) 'The Post-Subculturalists', in Redhead, S. (ed.) *The Club Culture Reader*, Oxford: Blackwell.

Muggleton, D. (2000) *Inside Subcultures: The Postmodern Meaning of Style*, London: Berg.

Mungham, G. (1980) 'The Career of a Confusion: Radical Criminology in Britain', in Inciardi, J. (ed.) *Radical Criminology: The Coming Crisis*, Beverley Hills, CA: Sage.

Murray, S. (2008) 'Digital Images, Photo-Sharing, and Our Shifting Notions of Everyday Aesthetics', *Journal of Visual Culture*, 7(2):147–163.

Naffine, N. (1990) *Law and the Sexes*, London: Allen and Unwin.

Naffine, N. (1997) *Feminism and Criminology*, Cambridge: Polity Press.

Naylor, R. (1994) 'Loose Cannons: Covert Commerce and Underground Finance in the Modern Arms Black Market', *Crime, Law and Social Change*, 22(1):1–57.

Naylor, R. (1996) 'From Underworld to Underground', *Crime, Law and Social Change*, 24(2):79–150.

Nead, L. (2005) *Victorian Babylon: People, Streets and Images in Nineteenth-Century London*, New Haven, CT: Yale University Press.

Negri, A. and M. Hardt (2000) *Empire*, Cambridge, MA: Harvard University Press.

Nelken, D. (1989) 'Discipline and Punish: Some Notes on the Margins', *Howard Journal of Criminal Justice*, 28(4):245–254.

Nelken, D. (2012) 'White-Collar and Corporate Crime', in Maguire, M., R. Morgan and R. Reiner (eds.) *The Oxford Handbook of Criminology*, Oxford: Oxford University Press.

Newburn, T. (2007) '"Tough on Crime": Penal Policy in England and Wales', *Crime and Justice*, 36:425–470.

Newburn, T. (2011) 'Criminology and Government: Some Reflections on Recent Developments in England', in Bosworth, M. and C. Hoyle (eds.) *What Is Criminology?*, Oxford: Oxford University Press.

Newman, K. (1999) *No Shame in My Game: The Working Poor in the Inner City*, New York: Vintage.

Norfolk, S. (2005) *Bleed*, Stockport: Dewi Lewis.

Oakes, G. and A. Vidich (1999) *Collaboration, Reputation and Ethics in American Academic Life: Hans H. Gerth and C. Wright Mills*, University of Illinois: Urbana.

O'Donovan, K. (1993) 'Law's Knowledge: The Judge, the Expert, the Battered Woman, and Her Syndrome', *Journal of Law and Society*, 20(4):427–437.

Olmos, A. (2013) *Landscape of Murder*, Stockport: Dewi Lewis.

O'Malley, P. (1992) 'Risk, Power and Crime Prevention', *Economy and Society*, 21(3):242–275.

O'Malley, P. (2010) *Crime and Risk*, London: Sage.

O'Malley, P. and S. Mugford (1994) 'Crime, Excitement and Modernity', in Barak, G. (ed.) *Varieties of Criminology*, Westport, CN: Praeger.

Outhwaite, W. (2000) 'Classical and Modern Social Theory', in Anderson, H. and L. Bo Kasperson (eds.) *Classical and Modern Social Theory*, Oxford: Blackwell.

Outhwaite, W. (2015) *Social Theory*, London: Profile.

Panofsky, E. (1951) *Gothic Architecture and Scholasticism*, London: Meridian.

Park, R. (1915) 'The City: Suggestions for the Investigation of Human Behaviour in the City Environment', *American Journal of Sociology*, 36(3):577–612.

Park, R. (1925) 'Community Organization and Juvenile Delinquency', in Park, R. and E. Burgess (eds.) *The City*, Chicago, IL: University of Chicago Press.

Park, R. (1926) 'The Urban Community as a Spatial Pattern and Moral Order', in Burgess, E. (ed.) *The Urban Community*, Chicago: University of Chicago Press.

Pearce, F. (1976) *Crimes of the Powerful: Marxism, Crime and Deviance*, London: Pluto.

Pearce, F. (1989) *The Radical Durkheim*, London: Unwin Hyman.

Pearson, G. (1975) *The Deviant Imagination*, London: Macmillan.

Pearson, G. (1983) *Hooligan: A History of Respectable Fears*, London: Macmillan.

Pearson, G. and R. Hobbs (2003) 'King Pin? A Case Study of a Middle Market Drug Broker', *The Howard Journal of Criminal Justice*, 42(4):335–347.

Peters, T. (2006) 'The Academic Status of Criminology', *International Annals of Criminology*, 44(1):53–63.

Phoenix, A. and P. Pattynama (2006) 'Intersectionality', *European Journal of Women's Studies*, 13(3):187–192.

Pink, S. (2013) *Doing Visual Ethnography*, 3rd edn. London: Sage.

Pirenne, H. (1925) *Medieval Cities*, Princeton, NJ: Princeton University Press.

Piven, F. (2010) 'A Response to Wacquant', *Theoretical Criminology*, 14(1):111–116.

Plummer, K. (ed.) (1997) *The Chicago School: Critical Assessments*, London: Unwin.

Polsky, N. (1967/1998) *Hustlers, Beats and Others*, New York: Lyons Press.

Pontell, H., W. Black and G. Geis (2014) 'Too Big to Fail, Too Powerful to Jail? In the Absence of Criminal Prosecutions after the 2008 Financial Meltdown', *Crime, Law and Social Change*, 61:1–13.

Pratt, J. (2000) 'Civilization and Punishment', *The Australian and New Zealand Journal of Criminology*, 33(2):183–201.

Pratt, J. (2002) *Punishment and Civilization: Penal Tolerance and Intolerance in Modern Society*, London: Routledge.

Pratt, J. (2008) 'Scandinavian Exceptionalism in an Era of Penal Excess', *British Journal of Criminology*, 48(2):119–137.

Pratt, J. (2013) 'Punishment and the Civilizing Process', in Simon, J. and R. Sparks (eds.) *The SAGE Handbook of Punishment and Society*, London: Sage, pp. 90–113.

Presdee, M. (2000) *Cultural Criminology and the Carnival of Crime*, London: Routledge.

Price, D. (2009) 'Surveyors and Surveyed: Photography Out and About', in Wells, L. (ed.) *Photography: A Critical Introduction*, London: Routledge, pp. 65–115.

Quételet, A. (1835) *Sur l'homme et le développement de ses faculties*, Paris: Bachlier.

Quinney, R. (1977) *Class, State and Crime*, New York: David McKay.

Radzinowicz, L. (1961) *In Search of Criminology*, London: Heinemann.

Radzinowicz, L. and R. King (1979) *The Growth of Crime: The International Experience*, Harmondsworth: Penguin.

Rafter, N. H. (ed.) (2009) *Origins of Criminology: Readings from the Nineteenth Century*, London: Routledge.

Rafter, N. H. (2016) *The Crime of all Crimes: Toward a Criminology of Genocide*, New York: New York University Press.

Rancière, J. (2011) *The Emancipated Spectator*, London: Verso.

Ranulf, S. (1938) *Moral Indignation and Middle Class Psychology: A Sociological Study*, Copenhagen: Levin & Munksgaard.

Rawlinson, P. (2010) *From Fear to Fraternity: A Russian Tale of Crime, Economy and Modernity*, London: Pluto Press.

Reckless, W. (1971) 'The Distribution of Vice in the City', in Short, J. (ed.) *The Social Fabric of the Metropolis: Contributions of the Chicago School of Urban Sociology*, Chicago: University of Chicago Press.

Redhead, S. (1997) *Subculture to Clubcultures*, Oxford: Blackwell.

Reiner, R. (1988) 'British Criminology and the State', in Rock, P. (ed.) *A History of British Criminology*, Oxford: Clarendon Press, pp. 138–158.

Reiner, R. (2012) 'Political Economy and Criminology: The Return of the Repressed', in Hall, S. and S. Winlow (eds.) *New Directions in Criminological Theory*, Abingdon: Routledge, pp. 30–51.

Reinhardt, M. (2007) 'Picturing Violence: Aesthetics and the Anxiety of Critique', in Reinhardt, M., H. Edwards and E. Duganne (eds) *Beautiful Suffering: Photography and the Traffic in Pain*, Williamstown, MA: Williams College Museum of Art, pp. 13–36.

Resnick, J. and D. Curtis (2011) *Representing Justice*, New Haven: Yale University Press.

Reuter, P. (1983) *Disorganised Crime*, Cambridge, MA: MIT Press.

Rex, J. (1983) 'Doctors of the Revolution', *New Society*, (13 January):67–68.

Rios, V. (2011) *Punished: Policing the Lives of Black and Latino Boys*, New York: New York University Press.

Robertson, G. (2000) *Crimes against Humanity: The Struggle for Global Justice*, London: Penguin.

Robertson, R. (1995) 'Glocalisation: Time-Space and Homogeneity-Heterogeneity', in Featherstone, M., S. Lash and R. Robertson (eds.) *Global Modernities*, London: Sage.

Rock, P. (1988) 'The Present State of Criminology in Britain', in Rock, P. (ed.) *A History of British Criminology*, Oxford: Clarendon Press.

Rock, P. (1994) 'Introduction', in Rock, P. (ed.) *A History of Criminology*, Aldershot: Ashgate.

Rock, P. (2011) '"What Have We Done?" Trends in Criminological Theorising', *Acta Criminologica*, 24(1):19–43.

Rock, P. (2012) 'Sociological Theories of Crime', in Maguire, M., R. Morgan and R. Reiner (eds.) *The Oxford Handbook of Criminology*, 5th edn. Oxford: Oxford University Press.

Rose, G. (2004) '"Everyone's Cuddled Up and It Just Looks Really Nice": An Emotional Geography of Some Mums and Their Photos', *Social & Cultural Geography*, 5(4):549–564.

Rose, G. (2012) *Visual Methodologies*, 3rd edn. London: Sage.

Rose, N. (1996) 'Governing "Advanced" Liberal Democracies', in Barry, A., T. Osborne and N. Rose (eds.) *Foucault and Political Reason*, London: University College London Press.

Rothe, D. and D. Friedrichs (2006) 'The State of the Criminology of Crimes of the State', *Social Justice*, 33(1):147–161.

Rothe, D. and D. Friedrichs (2015) *Crimes of Globalization*, London: Routledge.

Rothe, D., C. Mullins and K. Sandstorm (2009) 'The Rwandan Genocide: International Finance Polices and Human Rights', *Social Justice*, 35(3):66–86.

Ruggiero, V. (1995) 'Drug Economics: A Fordist Model of Criminal Capital', in *Capital and Class*, 55:131–150.

Ruggiero, V. (2010) 'War as Corporate Crime', in Chambliss, W., R. Michalowski and R. Kramer (eds.) *State Crime in the Global Age*, Cullompton: Willan.

Ruggiero, V. (2013) 'The Environment and the Crimes of the Economy', in South, N. and A. Brisman (eds.) *Routledge International Handbook of Green Criminology*, Abingdon: Routledge.

Rusche, G. and O. Kirchheimer (1968, orig. pub. 1939) *Punishment and Social Structure*, New York: Russell and Russell.

Said, E. (1988) 'Michel Foucault, 1926–1984', in Arac, J. (ed.) *After Foucault*, New Brunswick: Rutgers University Press.

Salgãdo, G. (1977) The Elizabethan Underworld, London: J. M. Dent & Sons.

Sampson, R. and J. Laub (1993) *Crime in the Making*, Cambridge, MA: Harvard University Press.

Sampson, R., S. Raudenbush and F. Earls (1997) 'Neighbourhoods and Violent Crime: A Multilevel Study of Collective Efficacy', *Science*, 277:918–924.

Santoro, M. and M. Solari (2016) 'Contesting Culture: Bourdieu and the Strong Program in Cultural Sociology', in L. Hanquinet and M. Savage (eds) *The Routledge International Handbook of the Sociology of Art and Culture*, London: Routledge, pp. 49–76.

Santos, B. (2014) *Epistemologies of the South: Justice against Epistemicide*, Boulder, CO: Paradigm.

Savage, M. (2010) 'Unpicking Sociology's Misfortunes', *British Journal of Sociology*, 61(4):659–665.

Savelsberg, J. and R. Sampson (2002) 'Mutual Engagement: Criminology and Sociology?', *Crime, Law and Social Change*, 37(2):99–105.

Scheff, T. (1966) *Being Mentally Ill*, London: Weidenfeld & Nicolson.

Schuilenburg, M. (2015) *The Securitization of Society*, New York: New York University Press.

Schur, E. (1963) *Narcotic Addiction in Britain and America*, London: Tavistock.

Scott, J. (2005) 'Sociology and Its Others: Reflections on Disciplinary Specialization and Fragmentation', *Sociological Research Online*, 10(1), URL (consulted July 2015): http://www.socresonline.org.uk/10/1/scott.html

Scott, J. (2006) *Social Theory: Central Issues in Sociology*, London: Sage.

Scull, A. (1977) *Decarceration: Community Treatment and the Deviant – A Radical View*, Englewood Cliffs, NJ: Prentice-Hall.

Sennett, R. (1990) *The Conscience of the Eye*, London: Faber.

Sharpe, J, (1999) *Crime in Early Modern England, 1550–1750*, London: Longman.

Shaw, C. R. and H. D. McKay (1931) *Social Factors in Juvenile Delinquency, Volume 2. Report on the Causes of Crime*, US Government Printing Office, National Commission on Law Observance and Enforcement, Washington, DC.

Shearing, C. and P. Stenning (1985) 'From the Panopticon to Disney World: The Development of Discipline', in Doob, A. and E. Greenspan (eds.) *Perspectives in Criminal Law*, Ontario: Canada Law Books, pp. 335–349.

Shelley, L. (2006), 'The Globalization of Crime and Terrorism', *EJournal USA*, 11:42–5 (February).

Sherman, L. (2011) 'Criminology as Invention', in Bosworth, M. and C. Hoyle (eds.) *What Is Criminology?*, Oxford: Oxford University Press.

Shields, D. (2015) *War Is Beautiful*, New York: Powerhouse.

Shields, R. (1991) *Places on the Margin*, London: Routledge.

Shils, E. (1960) 'Imaginary Sociology', *Encounter*, 14:77–80 (June).

Shore, H. (2015) *London's Criminal Underworlds, c. 1720 – c. 1930: A Social and Cultural History*, London: Palgrave Macmillan.

Short, F. with Hughes, L. (2007) 'Criminology, Criminologists, and the Sociological Enterprise', in Calhoun, C. (ed.) *Sociology in America: A History*, Chicago, IL: University of Chicago Press.

Short, J. and F. Strodtbeck, (1967) *Group Process and Gang Delinquency*, Chicago: University of Chicago Press.

Sim, J. (2009) *Punishment and Prisons: Power and the Carceral State*, London: Sage.

Sim, J., P. Scraton and P. Gordon (1987) 'Introduction: Crime, the State and Critical Analysis', in Scraton, P. (ed.) *Law, Order and the Authoritarian State: Readings in Critical Criminology*, Milton Keynes: Open University Press.

Simmel, G. (1903/1950) 'The Metropolis and Mental Life', in *The Sociology of Georg Simmel*, New York: Free Press.

Simon, J. (2007) *Governing Through Crime: How the War on Crime Transformed American Democracy and Created a Culture of Fear*, New York: Oxford University Press.

Simon, J. (2013) 'Punishment and the Political Technologies of the Body', in Simon, J. and R. Sparks (eds.) *The SAGE Handbook of Punishment and Society*, London: Sage, pp. 60–89.

Simon, T., P. Neufeld and B. Scheck (2003) *The Innocents*, New York: Umbrage.

Slapper, G. and S. Tombs (1999) *Corporate Crime*, Harlow: Pearson.

Smart, B. (1983) 'On Discipline and Social Regulation', in Garland, D. and P. Young (eds.) *The Power to Punish*, London: Heinemann.

Smart, C. (1976) *Women, Crime and Criminology*, London: Routledge and Kegan Paul.

Smart, C. (1989) *Feminism and the Power of Law*, London: Routledge.

Smart, C. (1995) *Law, Crime and Sexuality: Essays in Feminism*, London: Sage.

Smith, D. (1975) *The Mafia Mystique*, New York: Basic Books.

Smith, D. (1980) 'Paragons, Pariahs, and Pirates: A Spectrum-Based Theory of Enterprise', *Crime & Delinquency*, 26(3):358–386.

Smith, P. (2008) *Punishment and Culture*, Chicago: University of Chicago Press.

Snacken, S. (2010) 'Resisting Punitiveness in Europe?', *Theoretical Criminology*, 14(3):272–292.

Sonnevend, J. (2012) 'Iconic Rituals: Towards a Social Theory of Encountering Images', in Alexander, J. D. Bartmański and B. Giesen (eds.) *Iconic Power: Materiality and Meaning in Social Life*, Basingstoke: Palgrave, pp. 219–232.

Sontag, S. (2003) *Regarding the Pain of Others*, London: Penguin.

South, N. (2015) 'Anticipating the Anthropocene and Greening Criminology', *Criminology & Criminal Justice*, 15(3):270–276.

Sparks, R. (1992)*Television and the Drama of Crime: Moral Tales and the Place of Crime in Public Life*, Buckingham: Open University Press.

Sparks, R. (2000) 'Perspectives on Risk and Penalk Politics', in Hope, T. and R. Sparks (eds.) *Crime, Risk and Insecurity*, London: Routledge.

Spierenburg, P. (1984) *The Spectacle of Suffering*, Cambridge: Cambridge University Press.

Spitzer, S. (1983) 'The Rationalization of Crime Control in Capitalist Society', in Cohen, S. and A. Scull (eds.) *Social Control and the State*, New York: Palgrave MacMillan.

Stallybrass, P. and A. White (1986), *The Politics and Poetics of Transgression*, London: Methuen.

Stanley, L. (2005) 'A Child of Its Time: Hybridic Perspectives on Othering in Sociology', *Sociological Research Online*, 10(3) http://www.socresonline.org.uk/10/3/stanley.html

Sterling, C. (1990) *Octopus: The Long Reach of the International Sicilian Mafia*, New York: Norton.

Sterling, C. (1994) *Crime Without Frontiers*, London: Little, Brown.

Stevenson, D. (2003) *Cities and Urban Cultures*, Maidenhead: Open University Press.

Stott, W. (1973) *Documentary Expression and Thirties America*, Chicago, IL: University of Chicago Press.

Straw, W. (2015) 'After the Event: The Challenges of Crime Photography', in Hill, J. and V. Schwartz (eds.) *Getting the Picture: The Visual Culture of the News*, London: Bloomsbury, pp. 139–144.

Stumpf, J. (2006) 'The Crimmigration Crisis: Immigrants, Crime and Sovereign Power', *American University Law Review*, 56:367.

Sumner, C. (1994) *The Sociology of Deviance: An Obituary*, Milton Keynes: Open University Press.

Sutherland, E. (1924) *Criminology*, Philadelphia, PA: Lippincott.

Sutherland, E. (1940) 'White-Collar Criminality', *American Sociological Review*, 5(1):1–12.

Sutherland, E. (1949) *White-Collar Crime*, New York: Holt, Rinehart and Winston.

Sweetman, P. (2013) 'Structure, Agency, Subculture: The CCCS, *Resistance Through Rituals*, and "Post-Subcultural" Studies', *Sociological Research Online*, 18(4):22 http://www.socresonline.org.uk/18/4/22.html

Sykes, G. (1958) *The Society of Captives*, Princeton, NJ: Princeton University Press.

Sykes, G. and D. Matza (1957) 'Techniques of Neutralization: A Theory of Delinquency', *American Sociological Review*, 22(6):664–670.

Tappan, P. (1947) 'Who Is the Criminal?', *American Sociological Review*, 12:96–102.

Taylor, I. (1999) *Crime in Context*, Cambridge: Polity Press.

Taylor, I., P. Walton and J. Young (1973) *The New Criminology*, London: Routledge and Kegan Paul.

Taylor, L. (1984) *In the Underworld*, Oxford: Blackwell.

Thom, D. (1992) 'Wishes, Anxieties, Play, and Gestures: Child Guidance in Inter-War England', in Cooter, R. (ed.) *In the Name of the Child: Health and Welfare, 1880–1940*, London and New York: Routledge.

Thomas, D. and B. D. Loader (eds.) (2000) *Cybercrime: Law Enforcement, Security and Surveillance in the Information Age*, London, Routledge.

Thompson, E. P. (1977) *Whigs and Hunters: The Origin of the Black Act*, Harmondsworth: Penguin.

Thompson, J. (1870/2009) 'The Psychology of Criminals', in Rafter, N. (ed.) *The Origins of Criminology*, London: Routledge, pp. 95–100.

Thompson, K. (1998) *Moral Panics*, London: Routledge.

Thornton, S. (1995) *Club Cultures*, Cambridge: Polity Press.

Thornton, S. (2007) 'The Social Logic of Subcultural Capital', in Gelder, K. (ed.) *The Subcultures Reader*, London: Routledge.

Thrasher, F. (1927) *The Gang: A Study of 1,313 Gangs in Chicago*, Chicago: University of Chicago Press.

Tombs, S. (2000) 'Official Statistics and Hidden Crime: Researching Safety Crimes', in Jupp, V., P. Davies and P. Francis (eds.) *Doing Criminological Research*, London: Sage.

Tombs, S. (2004) 'Workplace Injury and Death: Social Harm and the Illusion of the Law', in Hillyard, P. C. Pantazis, S. Tombs and D. Gordon (eds.) *Beyond Criminology: Taking Harm Seriously*, London: Pluto Press, pp. 156–177.

Tombs, S. (2015) 'Crisis, What Crisis? Regulation and the Academic Orthodoxy', *Howard Journal of Criminal Justice*, 54(1):57–72.

Tönnies, F. (1887/1957) *Communities and Association*, London: Routledge & Kegan Paul.

Tonry, M. (2011) *Punishing Race: A Continuing American Dilemma*, Oxford: Oxford University Press.

Treviño, A. (2012) *The Social Thought of C. Wright Mills*, London: Sage.

Turner, S. (2009) 'The Future of Social Theory', in Turner, B. (ed.) *The New Blackwell Companion to Social Theory*, Oxford: Wiley-Blackwell.

Turner, S. (2014) *American Sociology: From Pre-Disciplinary to Post-Normal*, Basingstoke: Palgrave.

Turner, V. (1967) *Forest of Symbols*, Ithaca, NY: Cornell University Press.

Turner, V. (1974) *Dramas, Fields and Metaphors: Symbolic Action in Human Society*, Ithaca, NY: Cornel University Press.

Tyler, I. (2013) 'The Riots of the Underclass?: Stigmatisation, Mediation and the Government of Poverty and Disadvantage in Neoliberal Britain', *Sociological Research Online*, 18(4):6.

Urry, J. (1981) 'Sociology as a Parasite: Some Vices and Virtues', in Abrams, P., R. Deem, J. Finch and P. Rock (eds.) *Practice and Progress: British Sociology, 1950–1980*, London: George Allen and Unwin.

Urry, J. (2005) 'Beyond the "Science" of Society', *Sociological Research Online* 10(2), URL (consulted July 2015): http://www.socresonline.org.uk/10/2/urry.html

Valiér, C. (1995) 'Psychoanalysis and Crime in Britain during the Inter-War Years', The British Criminology Conferences: *Selected Proceedings. Volume 1: Emerging Themes in Criminology. Papers from the British Criminology Conference*. Loughborough University, 18–21 July.

Valiér, C. V. (2002) *Theories of Crime and Punishment*, Harlow: Pearson.

Valverde, M. (1996) 'Social Facticity and the Law: A Social Expert's Eyewitness Account of Law', *Social and Legal Studies*, 5(2):201–208.

Valverde, M. (2012) 'Analyzing Punishment: Scope and Scale', *Theoretical Criminology*, 16(2):245–253.

Van Gelder, H. and H. Westgeest (2011) *Photography Theory in Historical Perspective*, Oxford: Blackwell.

Varese, F. (2011) *Mafias on the Move: Now Organized Crime Conquers New Territories*, Princeton, NJ: Princeton University Press.

Varese, F. (2012) 'How Mafias Take Advantage of Globalization: The Russian Mafia in Italy', *British Journal of Criminology*, 52(2):235–253.

Varese, F. (2013) 'The Structure and the Content of Criminal Connections: The Russian Mafia in Italy', *European Sociological Review*, 29(5):899–909.

Veblen, T. (1899/1953) *The Theory of the Leisure Class*, Scarborough, Ontario: Mentor Edition.

Virdee, S. (2014) 'Challenging the Empire', *Ethnic and Racial Studies*, 37(10):1823–1829.

Virilio, P. (1986) *Speed and Politics*, New York: Semiotext(e).

Wacquant, L. (2001) 'Deadly Symbiosis: When Prison and Ghetto Meet and Merge', *Punishment & Society*, 3(1):95–134.

Wacquant, L. (2002) 'Scrutinizing the Street: Poverty, Morality and the Pitfalls of Urban Ethnography', *American Journal of Sociology*, 107(6):1468–1532.

Wacquant, L. (2007) 'Territorial Stigmatization and the Age of Advanced Marginality', *Thesis Eleven*, 91.

Wacquant, L. (2008) *Urban Outcasts: A Comparative Sociology of Advanced Marginality*, Cambridge: Polity Press.

Wacquant, L. (2009) *Punishing the Poor: The Neoliberal Government of Social Insecurity*, Durham, NC: Duke University Press.

Waddington, P. (1986) 'Mugging as a Moral Panic: A Question of Proportion', *British Journal of Sociology*, 32(2):245–259.

Walker, S. (1980) *Popular Justice: A History of American Criminal Justice*, Oxford: Oxford University Press.

Walklate, S. (1997) 'Risk and Criminal Victimization', *British Journal of Criminology*, 37(1):35–45.

Walklate, S. (2001) *Gender, Crime and Criminal Justice*, Devon: Willan.

Wall, D. (2001) 'Cybercrimes on the Internet', in Wall, D. (ed.) *Crime and the Internet*, London: Routledge.

Walmsley, R. (2011) *World Prison Population List*, 9th edn. London: International Centre for Prison Studies.

Ward, T. (2004) 'State Harms', Hillyard, P. C. Pantazis, S. Tombs and D. Gordon (eds.) *Beyond Criminology: Taking Harm Seriously*, London: Pluto Press, pp. 84–100.

Watney, S. (1997) *Policing Desire: Pornography, Aids and the Media*, 3rd edn. London: Cassell.

Webber, F. (2004) 'The War on Migration', in Hillyard, P. C. Pantazis, S. Tombs and D. Gordon (eds.) *Beyond Criminology: Taking Harm Seriously*, London: Pluto Press, pp. 133–155.

Weber, M. (1921/1958) *The City*, New York: Free Press.

Weber, M. (1968a) *Economy and Society: An Outline of Interpretative Sociology, Volume 1*. New York: Bedminster Press.

Weber, M. (1968b) *Economy and Society: An Outline of Interpretative Sociology, Volume 3*. New York: Bedminster Press.

Welch, M. and L. Schuster (2005) 'Detention of Asylum Seekers in the UK and USA: Deciphering Noisy and Quiet Constructions', *Punishment & Society*, 7(4):397–417.

West, C. and S. Fenstermaker (1995) 'Doing Difference', *Gender & Society*, 9(1):8–37.

West, C. and D. Zimmerman (1987) 'Doing Gender', *Gender & Society*, 1(2):125–151.

Western, B. (2006) *Punishment and Inequality in America*, New York: Russell Sage Foundation.

Wilkins, L. (1964) *Social Deviance: Social Policy, Action and Research*, London: Tavistock.

Wilkinson, I. (2013) 'The Provocation of the Humanitarian Social Imaginary', *Visual Communication*, 12(3):261–276.

Williams, P. (2001) 'Transnational Criminal Networks', in Arquilla, J. & D. F. Ronfeldt (eds.), *Networks and Netwars: The Future of Terror, Crime, and Militancy*, Washington, DC: Rand Corporation. pp. 61–97.

Williams, R. (1975) *The Country and the City*, London: Paladin.

Willis, P. (1977) *Learning to Labour*, London: Saxon House.

Winlow, S. and R. Atkinson (2013) 'Introduction', in Winlow, S. and R. Atkinson (eds.) *New Directions in Crime and Deviancy*, London: Routledge.

Wirth, L. (1938) 'Urbanism as a Way of Life', *American Journal of Sociology*, 44(1): 1–24.

Wootton, B. (1959) *Social Science and Social Pathology*, London: Allen and Unwin.

Wright, R. and S. Decker (1997) *Armed Robbers in Action*, Boston, MA: Northeastern University Press.

Young, A. (2005) *Judging the Image*, Oxon: Routledge.

Young, J. (1971) *The Drugtakers*, London: Paladin.

Young, J. (1983) 'Striking Back Against the Empire', *Critical Social Policy*, 8:130–140.

Young, J. (1998) 'Breaking Windows: Situating the New Criminology', in Walton, P. and J. Young (eds.) *The New Criminology Revisited*, London: Macmillan.

Young, J. (1999) *The Exclusive Society*, London: Sage.

Young, J. (2007) *The Vertigo of Late Modernity*, London: Sage.

Young, J. (2009) 'Moral Panic: Its Origins in Resistance, Ressentiment and the Translation of Fantasy in to Reality', *The British Journal of Criminology*, 49(1): 4–16.

Young, J. (2011) *The Criminological Imagination*, Cambridge: Polity Press.

Young, J. (2013) 'Introduction to 40th Anniversary Edition', in Taylor, I., P. Walton and J. Young (eds.) (1973/2013) *The New Criminology*, Oxon: Routledge.

Yuval-Davis, N. (2006) 'Intersectionality and Feminist Politics', *European Journal of Women's Studies*, 13(3):193–209.

Zedner, L. (1991) 'Women, Crime, and Penal Responses: A Historical Account', in Tonry, M. (ed.) *Crime and Justice: A Review of Research*, *Volume 14*. Chicago: University of Chicago Press, pp. 307–362.

Zedner, L. (2009) *Security*, London: Routledge.

Index

Index

Printed by Printforce, the Netherlands